**REFERENCE
DOES NOT CIRCULATE**

R 821.8 Kipli.R Duran.R
Durand, Ralph,
A handbook to the poetry of
Rudyard Kipling.

A HANDBOOK TO THE POETRY
OF RUDYARD KIPLING

A HANDBOOK TO THE POETRY OF RUDYARD KIPLING

BY
RALPH DURAND

GARDEN CITY   NEW YORK
DOUBLEDAY, PAGE & COMPANY
1914

Copyright, 1914, by
DOUBLEDAY, PAGE & COMPANY
All rights reserved, including that of translation into foreign languages, including the Scandinavian

DEDICATION

TO

HENRY JOHN STALLEY ('UNCLE JOHN')

FOR MANY YEARS ASSISTANT MASTER OF THE RELIGIOUS, ROYAL AND ANCIENT FOUNDATION OF CHRIST'S HOSPITAL

It used to be the custom in the East when a man had committed a capital offence to execute not only the criminal but also the man who had been entrusted with the criminal's education. We in the West are not so logical. We do not punish the tutor for the pupil's misdeeds, and, on the other hand, those of us who escape the gallows are apt to forget to what extent our escape is due to the men who educated us. I wonder how many of the thousands of 'Old Blues' who have passed through your class-room realise how great is the debt they owe you. Most of us knew you first as the dread Pluto of the Detention School. Without the care that in that capacity you lavished on us we should probably all be worse men than we are. That point of view, however, did not occur to us at the time, and it was not until in fear and dread we entered your class-room that we began to learn to love you. When we first came to you, not as defaulters but as pupils, we believed that the science of Geography consisted of nothing more than an endless string of meaningless and unpronounceable names. You taught us that the world was a very wonderful and fascinating place, and made us yearn for the time when we should be able to go forth and have a look at it for ourselves. We came

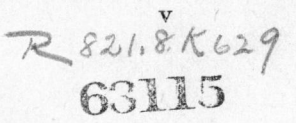

DEDICATION

to you holding the belief that the science of History was nothing more than 'William-the-Conquerer-ten-sixty-six-William-the-Second-ten-eighty-seven,' multiplied by dreariness to an indefinite degree. Under the magic of your wand we saw Norman knight and Saxon footman fight to the death on Senlac Hill; we heard the thunder of Spanish guns echo along the Sussex shore; we mingled with the crowd in Whitehall, and, with a clearer focus than our forefathers could have used, saw how much there was of good and how much of base both in the king who died there and in the men who killed him. You taught us directly the measure of the privileges and responsibilities bequeathed to us by those who lived and fought and died for England. Indirectly you taught us that knowledge has a value more precious than its power to win marks in school and money in after life. Soon after I began work on this book, I re-read the lines, addressed by Rudyard Kipling to one of his former masters:

> '*Let us now praise famous men*'—
> *Men of little showing—*
> *For their work continueth,*
> *And their work continueth,*
> *Broad and deep continueth,*
> *Greater than their knowing!*

The words immediately called you to my mind. For that reason I dedicate this book to you, not in payment of the debt I owe you—I have not wealth enough for that—but in acknowledgment of it.

RALPH DURAND.

INTRODUCTION

THIS book is offered to the public in the hope that it will prove of service to those to whom Mr. Rudyard Kipling's poems are a constant source of delight. Rudyard Kipling has made

> Extended observation of the ways and works of man,
> From the Four-mile Radius roughly to the plains of Hindustan,

with excursions into prehistoric times, ships' engine-rooms, Freemasonry, and other subjects. His poems consequently abound in precise technicalities, archaic words, and slang expressions enough to justify a glossary of the terms that he uses. An engineer does not need to refer to a dictionary for a definition of the word *slip;* a soldier perhaps understands what exactly are *slingers;* a Biblical student may know all that is now guessed as to the whereabouts of *Javan*, and a classical scholar needs no information as to the difference between a *thranite* and a *thalamite*. But the general reader who wishes to understand these terms must search for them in dictionaries and other works of reference, and may possibly find his search fruitless. When doubt arose as to whether expressions were too well known to need explanation, it was de-

INTRODUCTION

cided, for the benefit of the foreign reader, to err on the side of giving too much rather than too little information.

A mere glossary of the obscure expressions which he uses would, however, leave the student of Rudyard Kipling's poems but half satisfied. For this reason no apology is needed for embodying in this book short biographical notices, such as those on 'Eddi of Manhood End,' on 'Gholam Hyder, the Red Chief,' and on 'her that fell at Simon's Town in service on our foes,' or for including references to the rite of *johar*, the myth concerning 'Upsaras,' or the original propounder of the question 'Is not Calno like Carchemish?' And this book would certainly be incomplete without an explanation of the personal interest that attaches to 'The Rhyme of the Three Captains.'

My notes follow the order of the poems as they appear in the various volumes in which they have been collected, from *Departmental Ditties* to *Songs from Books*. The last pages are devoted to a few poems that appeared originally in Mr. Kipling's prose works but have not yet been collected into volume form. An alphabetical list of titles and a general index will be found at the end of the volume.

RALPH DURAND.

TITLES OF POEMS ANNOTATED

FROM 'DEPARTMENTAL DITTIES AND OTHER VERSES'

	PAGE
ARMY HEADQUARTERS	3
A LEGEND OF THE FOREIGN OFFICE	3
PUBLIC WASTE	4
WHAT HAPPENED	5
THE MAN WHO COULD WRITE	8
MUNICIPAL	8
A CODE OF MORALS	9
THE LAST DEPARTMENT	9
TO THE UNKNOWN GODDESS	10
THE RUPAIYAT OF OMAR KAL'VIN	11
DIVIDED DESTINIES	12
THE MASQUE OF PLENTY	12
THE SONG OF THE WOMEN	14
THE BALLAD OF FISHER'S BOARDING-HOUSE	16
AS THE BELL CLINKS	17
THE GRAVE OF THE HUNDRED HEAD	17
WHAT THE PEOPLE SAID	18
ONE VICEROY RESIGNS	19
A TALE OF TWO CITIES	22
GIFFEN'S DEBT	23

TITLES OF POEMS ANNOTATED

	PAGE
IN SPRING TIME	24
THE GALLEY SLAVE	24

FROM 'BARRACK-ROOM BALLADS AND OTHER VERSES'

BEYOND THE PATH OF THE OUTMOST SUN	26
TO T. A. (THOMAS ATKINS)	26
DANNY DEEVER	27
TOMMY	28
'FUZZY-WUZZY'	29
SCREW-GUNS	31
CELLS	32
GUNGA DIN	34
OONTS	35
LOOT	37
'SNARLEYOW'	38
THE WIDOW AT WINDSOR	40
BELTS	40
THE YOUNG BRITISH SOLDIER	41
MANDALAY	42
TROOPIN'	43
THE WIDOW'S PARTY	43
FORD O' KABUL RIVER	44
GENTLEMEN-RANKERS	44
ROUTE MARCHIN'	45
SHILLIN' A DAY	47
THE BALLAD OF EAST AND WEST	49
THE LAST SUTTEE	52

x

TITLES OF POEMS ANNOTATED

	PAGE
THE BALLAD OF THE KING'S MERCY	53
THE BALLAD OF THE KING'S JEST	57
WITH SCINDIA TO DELHI	59
THE DOVE OF DACCA	64
THE BALLAD OF BOH DA THONE	65
THE LAMENT OF THE BORDER CATTLE THIEF	68
THE RHYME OF THE THREE CAPTAINS	69
THE BALLAD OF THE 'CLAMPHERDOWN'	75
THE BALLAD OF THE 'BOLIVAR'	76
THE SACRIFICE OF ER-HEB	79
THE GIFT OF THE SEA	80
EVARRA AND HIS GODS	81
THE CONUNDRUM OF THE WORKSHOPS	81
THE LEGENDS OF EVIL	82
THE ENGLISH FLAG	82
'CLEARED'	84
AN IMPERIAL RESCRIPT	86
TOMLINSON	87
THE LONG TRAIL	88

FROM 'THE SEVEN SEAS'

TO THE CITY OF BOMBAY	93
THE SONG OF THE ENGLISH	93
THE COASTWISE LIGHTS	93
THE SONG OF THE DEAD	94
THE DEEP-SEA CABLES	96
THE SONG OF THE SONS	97
THE SONG OF THE CITIES	97
ENGLAND'S ANSWER	99

TITLES OF POEMS ANNOTATED

	PAGE
THE FIRST CHANTEY	99
THE LAST CHANTEY	101
THE MERCHANTMEN	103
M'ANDREW'S HYMN	108
THE MIRACLES	119
THE NATIVE-BORN	119
THE KING	122
THE RHYME OF THE THREE SEALERS	124
THE DERELICT	134
THE SONG OF THE BANJO	135
THE LINER SHE'S A LADY	138
MULHOLLAND'S CONTRACT	139
ANCHOR SONG	140
THE LOST LEGION	146
THE SEA-WIFE	152
HYMN BEFORE ACTION	152
TO THE TRUE ROMANCE	152
THE FLOWERS	153
THE LAST RHYME OF TRUE THOMAS	155
IN THE NEOLITHIC AGE	158
THE STORY OF UNG	162
THE THREE-DECKER	164
THE AMERICAN	167
THE 'MARY GLOSTER'	167
SESTINA OF THE TRAMP-ROYAL	171
WHEN 'OMER SMOTE 'IS BLOOMIN' LYRE	171
'BACK TO THE ARMY AGAIN'	172
'BIRDS OF PREY' MARCH	176

TITLES OF POEMS ANNOTATED

	PAGE
'SOLDIER AND SAILOR TOO'	178
SAPPERS	180
THAT DAY	182
'THE MEN THAT FOUGHT AT MINDEN'	182
CHOLERA CAMP	184
THE MOTHER-LODGE	185
'FOLLOW ME 'OME'	188
THE SERGEANT'S WEDDIN'	189
THE JACKET	189
THE 'EATHEN	191
THE SHUT-EYE SENTRY	194

FROM 'THE FIVE NATIONS'

BEFORE A MIDNIGHT BREAKS IN STORM	196
THE SEA AND THE HILLS	196
THE BELL-BUOY	198
CRUISERS	199
DESTROYERS	200
WHITE HORSES	202
THE SECOND VOYAGE	203
THE DYKES	204
THE SONG OF DIEGO VALDEZ	205
THE BROKEN MEN	206
THE FEET OF THE YOUNG MEN	207
THE TRUCE OF THE BEAR	208
THE OLD MEN	209
THE EXPLORER	209

TITLES OF POEMS ANNOTATED

	PAGE
THE BURIAL	213
GENERAL JOUBERT	215
THE PALACE	215
SUSSEX	216
SONG OF THE WISE CHILDREN	221
BUDDHA AT KAMAKURA	222
THE WHITE MAN'S BURDEN	229
PHARAOH AND THE SERGEANT	230
OUR LADY OF THE SNOWS	231
ET DONA FERENTES	232
KITCHENER'S SCHOOL	233
THE YOUNG QUEEN	235
RIMMON	236
THE OLD ISSUE	237
BRIDGE-GUARD IN THE KARROO	239
THE LESSON	240
THE FILES	241
THE REFORMERS	244
DIRGE OF DEAD SISTERS	244
THE ISLANDERS	245
THE PEACE OF DIVES	248
THE SETTLER	250
CHANT PAGAN	251
M. I.	253
COLUMNS	257
THE PARTING OF THE COLUMNS	259
TWO KOPJES	260
BOOTS	262

TITLES OF POEMS ANNOTATED

	PAGE
THE MARRIED MAN	262
LICHTENBERG	263
STELLENBOSH	264
HALF-BALLAD OF WATERVAL	265
PIET	266
'WILFUL-MISSING'	270
UBIQUE	270
RECESSIONAL	272

FROM 'SONGS FROM BOOKS'

PUCK'S SONG	274
A THREE-PART SONG	277
THE RUN OF THE DOWNS	277
BROOKLAND ROAD	278
SIR RICHARD'S SONG	279
A TREE SONG	279
A CHARM	280
CHAPTER HEADINGS: *PLAIN TALES FROM THE HILLS*	
Heading to *In the House of Suddhoo*—	
'A STONE'S THROW OUT ON EITHER HAND'	281
Heading to *Cupid's Arrows*—	
'PIT WHERE THE BUFFALO COOLED HIS HIDE'	281
COLD IRON	282
A SONG OF KABIR	282
'MY NEW-CUT ASHLAR'	284
EDDI'S SERVICE	284
SHIV AND THE GRASSHOPPER	284
THE FAIRIES' SIEGE	285
A SONG TO MITHRAS	285

TITLES OF POEMS ANNOTATED

	PAGE
THE NEW KNIGHTHOOD	286
OUTSONG IN THE JUNGLE	287
A ST. HELENA LULLABY	287
CHIL'S SONG	288
THE CAPTIVE	288
HADRAMAUTI	290
CHAPTER HEADINGS: *THE NAULAHKA*	
'BEAT OFF IN OUR LAST FIGHT WERE WE?'	292
'WE BE GODS OF THE EAST'	292
CHAPTER HEADINGS: *THE LIGHT THAT FAILED*	
'THE LARK WILL MAKE HER HYMN TO GOD'	293
'YET AT THE LAST, ERE OUR SPEARMEN HAD FOUND HIM'	293
GALLIO'S SONG	293
THE BEES AND THE FLIES	295
ROAD-SONG OF THE BANDAR-LOG	296
A BRITISH ROMAN SONG	296
A PICT SONG	296
RIMINI	297
'POOR HONEST MEN'	298
PROPHETS AT HOME	300
JUBAL AND TUBAL-CAIN	300
THE VOORTREKKER	301
A SCHOOL SONG	302
'OUR FATHERS OF OLD'	304
CHAPTER HEADINGS: *BEAST AND MAN IN INDIA*	
'DARK CHILDREN OF THE MERE AND MARSH'	306
SONG OF THE FIFTH RIVER	307
PARADE SONG OF THE CAMP ANIMALS	308
THE TWO-SIDED MAN	309
'LUKANNON'	311

TITLES OF POEMS ANNOTATED

	PAGE
AN ASTROLOGER'S SONG	312
THE BEE BOY'S SONG	312
MERROW DOWN	313
OLD MOTHER LAIDINWOOL	316
CHAPTER HEADINGS: *JUST-SO STORIES*	
'WHEN THE CABIN PORT-HOLES ARE DARK AND GREEN'	318
'THIS IS THE MOUTH-FILLING SONG'	318
'CHINA-GOING P. AND O.'S'	319
'THERE WAS NEVER A QUEEN LIKE BALKIS'	321
THE QUEEN'S MEN	322
GOW'S WATCH	322
SONG OF THE RED WAR BOAT	323
A RIPPLE SONG	324
BUTTERFLIES	325
THE NURSING SISTER	325
THE ONLY SON	325
MOWGLI'S SONG AGAINST PEOPLE	326
CHAPTER HEADINGS: *THE JUNGLE BOOKS*	
'AT THE HOLE WHERE HE WENT IN'	327
THE EGG-SHELL	328
THE KING'S TASK	328
POSEIDON'S LAW	332
A TRUTHFUL SONG	334
A SMUGGLER'S SONG	335
KING HENRY VII. AND THE SHIPWRIGHTS	336
THE WET LITANY	337
THE BALLAD OF MINEPIT SHAW	338
HERIOT'S FORD	339
FRANKIE'S TRADE	340

TITLES OF POEMS ANNOTATED

	PAGE
THORKILD'S SONG	341
ANGUTIVAUN TAINA	341
THE SONG OF THE MEN'S SIDE	341
DARZEE'S CHAUNT	344
THE PRAYER	345

FROM 'A SCHOOL HISTORY OF ENGLAND'

THE ROMAN CENTURION	346
THE PIRATES IN ENGLAND	347
THE SAXON FOUNDATIONS OF ENGLAND	347
WILLIAM THE CONQUEROR'S WORK	348
NORMAN AND SAXON	348
THE REEDS OF RUNNYMEDE	349
WITH DRAKE IN THE TROPICS	350
BEFORE EDGEHILL FIGHT	351
THE DUTCH IN THE MEDWAY	352
'BROWN BESS'	352
AFTER THE WAR	352
THE BELLS AND THE QUEEN	353
THE SECRET OF THE MACHINES	353

FROM OTHER POEMS

CHAPTER HEADING: *PLAIN TALES FROM THE HILLS*
    Heading to *Consequences*—
        'ROSICRUCIAN SUBTLETIES' 354
CHAPTER HEADING: *THE NAULAHKA*
    'IN THE STATE OF KOT-KUMHARSEN' 355
CHAPTER HEADING: *BEAST AND MAN IN INDIA*

TITLES OF POEMS ANNOTATED

Heading to *The Seven Nights of Creation*—   PAGE
    'O HASSAN! SAVING ALLAH, THERE IS NONE' . . . 356
CHAPTER HEADING: *KIM*
    'YEA, VOICE OF EVERY SOUL THAT CLUNG' 357
THE RUNNERS (*Traffics and Discoveries*) . . 358
THE RUNES ON WELAND'S SWORD (*Puck of Pook's Hill*) 358
PHILADELPHIA (*Rewards and Fairies*) . . 361
    ALPHABETICAL LIST OF POEMS ANNOTATED 363
    GENERAL INDEX 367

A HANDBOOK TO THE POETRY
OF RUDYARD KIPLING

Departmental Ditties and Other Verses
ARMY HEADQUARTERS

Stanza 2. *He clubbed his wretched company a dozen times a day.* *I. e.* he drilled his company so badly that it became entangled and could not be put straight by any recognised word of command. To restore order the men would have to 'fall out' or scatter and re-form again.

Stanza 3. *Simla* is a cool, healthy, and beautiful town, built on a spur of the lower Himalayas, between 6,000 and 8,000 feet above sea-level. During the summer months it is the Viceroy's headquarters and the seat of the Supreme Government of India as well as of the Punjab Government. It is, naturally, the centre of Indian society during the summer.

A LEGEND OF THE FOREIGN OFFICE

The Native States in India are governed by their respective princes, each of whom has the help and advice of a political officer appointed by the supreme Indian Government. Negotiations between an Indian State and the Supreme Government are conducted through the Indian Foreign Office. The native princes are allowed to manage the internal

DEPARTMENTAL DITTIES

affairs of their states so long as they do so without injustice or oppression. The progress that some states have made under enlightened rajahs is evident from the very vivid accounts which Rudyard Kipling has given in 'Letters of Marque' (*From Sea to Sea*) of the cities of Jeypore, Udaipur, Chitor, Jodhpur, and Boondi in Rajputana. *The Naulahka*, by Rudyard Kipling and Wolcott Balestier, also depicts life in a Native State.

Stanza 1. *Lusted for a C. S. I.—so began to sanitate.* Many Indian princes do not wholly understand or approve the Supreme Government's love for sanitation, but to humour it on this point is recognised as advisable by those who wish to stand well with the Viceroy. There is an old story to the effect that a native prince, knowing that the Viceroy intended to inspect some interesting old carvings in his dominions, prepared for his visit by having the carvings whitewashed. The Order C. S. I. (Companion of the Star of India) is an honour conferred, on such occasions as the King's birthday, on native princes and other notables who deserve recognition.

Stanza 5. *Nothing more than C. I. E.* The Order Companion of the Indian Empire is lower and consequently less valued than the C. S. I.

PUBLIC WASTE

The Little Tin Gods on the Mountain Side. A disrespectful reference to the Viceroy of India and his

AND OTHER VERSES

Executive Council, who during the summer months have their headquarters in the hills at Simla.

Stanza 1. *Chatham.* A garrison town at which officers of the Royal Engineers attend the School of Military Engineering.

Stanza 3. *Vauban,* a marshal of France of the seventeenth century, was a celebrated military engineer. His work had a profound influence on the arts of fortification and siegecraft.

The 'College.' The Staff College at Camberley, at which officers who wish to qualify for staff appointments are trained.

Stanza 6. *Exempt from the Law of the Fifty and Five.* Exempt from the regulation which requires a man to retire at the age of fifty-five.

Stanza 7. *Four thousand a month.* Four thousand rupees, equivalent to about £260.

WHAT HAPPENED

Hurree Chunder Mookerjee in this poem typifies the Bengali 'babu,' the semi-literate representative of a race of which Macaulay wrote, 'There never, perhaps, existed a people so thoroughly fitted by nature and by habit for a foreign yoke.' Prior to British rule in India the Bengalis were the constant prey of bolder and hardier races, and it is probable that, as this poem forecasts, their lot would not be a happy one if British protection were withdrawn from them. Mentally the Bengalis are exceedingly acute, and

DEPARTMENTAL DITTIES

they succeed admirably in any profession where mechanical intelligence is needed but bravery and initiative are not. No sweeping condemnation of the Bengalis would, however, be just. Though they have an excessive fear of physical pain they have none of death. Either in an aeroplane or on the scaffold a Bengali will be calm and collected. Rudyard Kipling gives the more commendable side of the Bengali character in *Kim*. In that book the Babu, also called Hurree Chunder Mookerjee, admits that he is 'a very fearful man' and turns pale at the sound of the click of a rifle-breech, yet he shows a degree of moral courage that astonishes both the Irish lad and the reckless Afghan, Mahbub Ali.

Each of the other characters in this poem represents one of the warlike races of India. Yar Mahommed Yusufzai represents the Pathans of the N. W. Frontier Province, such as are depicted in 'Wee Willie Winkie,' 'The Drums of the Fore and Aft,' 'The Head of the District' (*Life's Handicap*), 'The Lost Legion' (*Many Inventions*), and other stories. Chimbu Singh represents the Rajpoots. The Bhils are an aboriginal tribe formerly much given to plundering. They appear in 'The Tomb of his Ancestors' (*The Day's Work*). The Marris are a brave and lawless tribe of Baluchistan. The Sikhs provide some of the best soldiers in the Indian army, but, unlike the Marris, they are notable for their loyalty to the British Empire. The tale, 'A Sahib's War' (*Traffics and Discoveries*), is told

AND OTHER VERSES

by a native officer in a Sikh regiment. The Jats of the Punjab, who are agriculturists, also make excellent soldiers. The Wahabis are a fanatical Mohammedan sect who preach the holiness of war against unbelievers. Boh Hla-oo represents the Burmese dacoits, who, when safe opportunity offers, make up in bloodthirstiness what they lack in actual courage. Their methods of warfare are described in 'A Conference of the Powers' (*Many Inventions*), 'The Taking of Lungtungpen' (*Plain Tales from the Hills*), 'The Ballad of Boh da Thone' (*Barrack-Room Ballads*), and 'The Grave of the Hundred Head' (*Departmental Ditties*).

Stanza 7. The *Grand Trunk Road* leads right across northern India from Calcutta to Peshawur (see note, 'Route Marchin',' stanza 1, p. 45).

Stanza 9. The *quoit* is the ancient weapon of the Sikhs. It is sharp on the outside edge, and when thrown will cut through a plantain stalk at a distance of 80 yards.

Stanza 11. *Pubbi* is a village near Peshawur on the N. W. Frontier border.

Stanza 12. *Siva's sacred bull.* Hindoos regard the bull as sacred because Siva, the third god of the Hindoo Trinity, rode on one. The streets of every Indian town are infested with sacred bulls, who feed at will on the grain, etc., exposed for sale in the bazaars.

The Indian Congress men. (See note, 'One Viceroy resigns,' line 128, p. 21.)

DEPARTMENTAL DITTIES

THE MAN WHO COULD WRITE

Stanza 2. *Wicked wit of C-lv-n, irony of L——l.* Sir Auckland Colvin was Financial Member of the Viceroy's Council, 1883-1887. Sir Alfred Comyn Lyall was Lieutenant-Governor of Bengal, 1882-1887.

Stanza 7. *Posed as young Ithuriel, resolute and grim.* Ithuriel is an angel, the touch of whose spear exposes deceit. When Satan contrived to get into Paradise, Gabriel sent Ithuriel to find where he had hidden himself. Satan was disguised, but the touch of Ithuriel's spear compelled him to reveal himself.

MUNICIPAL

Stanza 2. *That Commissariat elephant had suddenly gone musth.* Musth is a state of excitement to which elephants are periodically liable. Their keepers understand and provide for it. Mere bad temper is quite different. In 'My Lord the Elephant' (*Many Inventions*) a mahout says that when an elephant is angry he will kill any one except his keeper, but when he is *musth* he will kill his keeper first. In the same story an elephant loses his temper, creates a panic, and chases 'a gunner orf'cer in full rig'mentals down the road, hell-for-leather, wid his mouth open' till the officer 'dived like a rabbut into a dhrain by the side av the road.'

AND OTHER VERSES

A CODE OF MORALS

Stanza 1. *Heliograph.* The heliograph is an instrument used to signal messages over distances too great to be covered by signalling with flags. Sunlight is caught on a mirror and flashed to those who wait to receive the message. The message, which is sent in the Morse code, is spelt out in a series of long and short flashes, long flashes to represent 'dashes' and short to represent 'dots.' Thus a long flash followed by two short ones—dash, dot, dot (see stanza 5)—spells D; a short flash—dot—spells E; a short followed by a long flash—dot, dash—is A; and dot, dash, dot, is R. One operator wishing to call up and get into conversation with another will make the signal which means 'are you there' again and again until he sees the flash of a reply. Only those almost directly in the line of the flash can see it.

THE LAST DEPARTMENT

Stanza 3. *When idleness of all Eternity*
Becomes our furlough, and the marigold
Our thriftless, bullion-minting Treasury.

In most parts of India it is practically impossible to grow turf. Graves are, therefore, often planted with marigolds.

Stanza 6. *Mallie.* Gardener.

Stanza 7. *Sheristadar.* Clerk of the court, who reads depositions, etc.

DEPARTMENTAL DITTIES

TO THE UNKNOWN GODDESS

Stanza 4. *Will you stay in the plains till September.* Most English women, and all men who can get away, leave the Indian plains in the summer and go to Simla or some other cool hill station. September is the month in which the agony of the long summer culminates. In the poem, 'Pagett, M. P.,' the globe-trotter who regarded the heat of India as a solar myth promises to stay till September to prove his contention. In July, however, he could stand no more of it and fled. A woman who would voluntarily stay in the plains throughout the summer would be commendably faithful, though perhaps foolish.

Thermantidote, an enclosed paddle-wheel, actuated by hand, for driving air through screens of wet scented grass (kus-kus) with the idea of lowering the temperature of rooms in hot weather. The throb of the paddles and the drip of the water is a characteristic hot-weather sound.

Stanza 5. 'Thirteen-two'—a polo pony 13 hands 2 inches in height. The standard size is now 14·2.

Stanza 6. *The Delight of Wild Asses.* Cf. Jeremiah ii. 24: 'A wild ass used to the wilderness, that snuffeth up the wind at her pleasure.'

Stanza 8.
> *As of old on Mars Hill when they raised*
> *To the God that they knew not an altar.*

Cf. Acts xvii. 22, 23: 'Then Paul stood in the midst

AND OTHER VERSES

of Mars hill, and said, Ye men of Athens . . . as I passed by . . . I found an altar with this inscription, "To the unknown God."'

THE RUPAIYAT OF OMAR KAL'VIN

This poem is a parody of Fitzgerald's now famous translation of 'The Rubaiyat of Omar Khayyam.' A 'Rubaiyat' is a poem, and a 'rupiya' is a rupee, the standard coin in India. Sir Auckland Colvin (Omar Kal'vin), when Financial Member of the Viceroy's Council, imposed an Income Tax, the burden of which fell almost entirely on Anglo-Indians.

Stanza 1. *With begging Dish.* Religious mendicants in India carry bowls in which they receive alms, usually in the shape of food, from the charitable. When *Kim* accompanied the Teshoo Lama on his pilgrimage it was his duty to beg with the Lama's bowl.

Stanza 2. *Salt a Lever that I dare not use.* The great majority of the population in India consists of agriculturists, who subsist almost entirely on what they themselves grow, and who use currency very little. It is therefore a difficult problem to find a means of taxing these. Salt, therefore, has been made a government monopoly, and is sold for very much more than it costs to produce and distribute. To raise the price still further, therefore, would cause discontent.

DEPARTMENTAL DITTIES

DIVIDED DESTINIES

Stanza 2. Nor am I plagued with little cards for little drinks at Mess. It is the custom at regimental messes and at most clubs in the East for a man to pay for refreshments by signing a card or 'chit' for the amount due, and paying cash to redeem his chits at the end of the month.

Stanza 3. Peliti's. A restaurant, and a general afternoon rendezvous of Simla society.

THE MASQUE OF PLENTY

CHORUS OF THE CRYSTALLISED FACTS

Strachey. Sir John Strachey entered the Bengal Civil Service in 1842. Among other offices he was member of Legislative Council, member of the Governor-General's Council, acting Viceroy and Financial Minister. His reform of the salt-tax resulted in increased revenue and cheaper salt. He instituted a scheme of government insurance against famine.

Muir. Sir William Muir entered the Bengal Civil Service in 1837. He held the offices of Foreign Secretary to the Indian Government, Lieutenant-Governor of the North-West Provinces, and Financial Member of the Council.

Lytton. Lord Lytton became Governor-General of India in 1875. His title was changed to that of

Viceroy in 1877, when Queen Victoria assumed the title of Empress of India. During his Viceroyalty the Afghan War (1879-1880) was fought. A serious famine in 1876-1878 caused the appointment of a Famine Commission, which recommended increased irrigation, development of communications, the reform of the salt-tax, and famine insurance.

Ripon. Lord Ripon succeeded Lord Lytton as Viceroy of India in 1880. He reversed his predecessor's Afghan policy, extended the rights of the natives and curtailed those of the Europeans in India, a policy which made him very popular with the former and unpopular with the latter.

Temple. Sir Richard Temple in 1868 became a member of the Supreme Government in India, first as Foreign Secretary and then as Finance Minister. He was made Lieutenant-Governor of Bengal in 1874, and did good work during the famine of that year. In 1877 he became Governor of Bombay. He was famed for endurance in the saddle, to the discomfort of his A. D. C.s.

At his heart is his daughter's wedding. Rigid custom demands that an Indian peasant must lavish large sums of money on festivities for his daughter's wedding. To obtain the necessary money he usually borrows at high rates of interest from a money-lender, to whom he mortgages everything he possesses. The debt thus contracted often cripples himself and his son after him.

DEPARTMENTAL DITTIES

THE SONG OF THE WOMEN

When Abdur Rahman, late Amir of Afghanistan, attended the Viceroy's Durbar at Rawalpindi in 1885, he made the acquaintance of Lady Dufferin. Later, when he wrote his autobiography, a work that was not written with the intention of currying favour with any one, he said, 'It was a great delight to me to meet Lady Dufferin, who was the cleverest woman I had ever seen. The people had never seen such a wise statesman as their Viceroy, and Lady Dufferin's residence in India was of hardly less importance than that of her husband.' This tribute is interesting as coming from one who had nothing to gain by flattery; had it come from an Indian prince anxious to curry favour its genuineness might be open to suspicion. It is valuable, too, because it comes from an Asiatic, and the Asiatic point of view on such movements as that initiated by Lady Dufferin seldom coincides with European opinion. Lady Dufferin was no mere aristocratic figure-head lending her name and patronage to a charity conceived and organised by some one else. Her fund for providing female doctors, nurses, and midwives for the Indian women was almost entirely her own idea. Queen Victoria had suggested that she should try and find some way of bettering the lot of Indian women, and Lady Dufferin was helped by the experience and the money of many, English and native, in India; the scheme, nevertheless, was truly hers. She initiated it, and did more than any one else to further its success. How near the work was to her heart can be realised by any one who reads her book, *The Story of our Vice-regal Life in India.*

It is interesting to note that this poem has been inscribed on the wall of a room at Clandeboye, Lord Dufferin's home.

Stanza 1. *The Walls are high.* The great majority of better-class women in India have to spend their whole lives from childhood onwards 'behind the curtain.' The 'harem' or 'zenana' in which a woman is confined may be a luxuriously gilded prison, or it may be a squalid, insanitary, airless garret, according to the means of the husband. In either case, no man except the woman's husband and nearest relations are allowed to visit her. She is therefore beyond the reach of skilled *male* medical aid, except in exceptional circumstances in which a doctor is allowed to feel the pulse of her hand thrust through a curtain. No other arrangement would be allowed whatever the ailment. The women's need for skilled medical aid is the more urgent because many Indian girl-wives become mothers at the age of twelve. It was for these reasons that Lady Dufferin's Fund was instituted, to 'train up and otherwise provide *female* doctors, nurses, and midwives' for Indian women.

The Naulahka, by Rudyard Kipling and Wolcott

DEPARTMENTAL DITTIES

Balestier, deals with an American girl who took charge of a hospital in a Native State.

THE BALLAD OF FISHER'S BOARDING-HOUSE

A seamen's boarding-house is an institution very different from the kind of boarding-house known to most people. The proprietor of a seamen's boarding-house usually obtains his guests in the first place by meeting them as soon as they come off their ships, and winning their regard by advancing them money to spend before their wages are paid them. He will take charge of the money when it is paid, and deduct therefrom charges for board and lodging, for drinks which he supplies, and for articles of kit—oilskins, sea-boots, etc.—all supplied at grossly exorbitant rates. When the time comes for the seaman to go to sea again, the boarding-house master will cash the advance-note which the man receives on account of the wages that he will earn, charging a discount of perhaps fifty per cent. for his trouble. Many boarding-house masters add to their incomes by shanghaiing seamen, that is, drugging them and handing them over at so much per head to any shipmaster who wants them. As a sailor finds it very difficult to recover the money that he has entrusted to the boarding-house master, and as it is to the latter's interest to make him drunk as quickly as possible in order to get rid of him the sooner, seamen's board-

AND OTHER VERSES

ing-houses are seldom models of quiet and respectability.

Collinga and *Jaun Bazar*, the haunts of 'Anne of Austria,' are two of the most disreputable quarters in Calcutta.

AS THE BELL CLINKS

Note here the characteristic noise of curricle-bar on the ponies' saddles. Tongas are now obsolete on the Umballa-Simla route.

THE GRAVE OF THE HUNDRED HEAD

Very little has been written about the Burmese War in a form accessible to the average reader. If the subject-index of a good library be consulted, it will probably be found that the general public must go to Rudyard Kipling more than to any other author for information on the subject. He has dealt with it in 'The Taking of Lungtungpen' (*Plain Tales from the Hills*), 'A Conference of the Powers' (*Many Inventions*), and 'The Ballad of Boh da Thone' (*Barrack-Room Ballads*).

Stanza 4. *Samādh*. Commemoration or memorial service over a grave.

Stanza 6. *A jingal covered the clearing, Calthrops hampered the way.*
A jingal is a small muzzle-loading light cannon almost like the swivel or 'murthering-piece' of the Armada. Cf. 'Taking of Lungtungpen' (*Plain Tales from the*

DEPARTMENTAL DITTIES

Hills). Calthrops, in this case, are sharp pieces of bamboo scientifically placed in narrow jungle tracks to maim the unwary.

Stanza 14. *Kullah*. A foreigner.

WHAT THE PEOPLE SAID

June 21st, 1887, the date attached to the poem, was that on which Queen Victoria celebrated her first jubilee.

Stanza 3. *Mahratta spear*. The Mahrattas rose to power towards the end of the seventeenth century, and by the end of the eighteenth ruled almost the whole of India. Their power was broken by the Afghans at the battle of Paniput in 1761 (see 'With Scindia to Delhi,' stanza 1, p. 59).

Mlech, a term applied by Hindoos to all who are not Hindoos. In this case it refers to the Mohammedan Afghans.

Stanza 4. *Great serpents, blazing, of red and blue*. The people of India are very fond of pyrotechnic displays. They have considerable skill in making fireworks, but less in letting them off. Being blown up in a firework display that went wrong was one of the adventures that befell *Kim* after he evaded his guardians and took to the road.

Stanza 5. *The Bar*. Bar is the name given to each of the sandy tracts, now irrigated by canals, that lie between the different rivers of the Punjab.

Stanza 6. *Mogul*. The Mogul emperors ruled

AND OTHER VERSES

the greater part of India from early in the sixteenth century until the rise of the Mahrattas to power.

ONE VICEROY RESIGNS

Lord Lansdowne succeeded Lord Dufferin as Viceroy of India in 1888. In her book, *Our Vice-regal Life in India*, Lady Dufferin says that on the Sunday following the new Viceroy's arrival, 'D. shut himself up with Lord Lansdowne and talked to him for four hours without stopping.' The conversation was probably on the lines suggested in this poem.

The people whose names are hinted at include the following: Sir Charles Crosthwaite, Chief Commissioner of British Burma, 1883-1884; Sir Theodore Cracroft Hope, Public Works Member of the Governor-General's Council, 1882-1887; Lord Wolseley, Adjutant-General to the Forces in 1888; W. E. Gladstone, Leader of the Opposition in 1888; Lord Cross, Secretary for India, 1886-1892; Lord Reay, Governor of Bombay 1885-1890; Sir Auckland Colvin, Financial Member of the Viceroy's Council, 1883-1887; Sir Alfred Comyn Lyall, Lieutenant-Governor of the North-West Provinces, 1882-1887; Sir Edward Buck, Secretary of Revenue and Agricultural Department, who represented the Government of India at the Indian and Colonial Exhibition of 1886; Sir James Westland, Comptroller-General, Financial Department, 1880-1885; Sir Alexander Wilson, Member of the Legislative Council of India and Chairman of the

DEPARTMENTAL DITTIES

Mercantile Bank of Bengal; and Sir Charles Aitchison, Lieutenant-Governor of the Punjab, Author of *A Collection of Treaties, Engagements, and Sannuds relating to India and neighbouring Countries.*

Line 14. *It frightened Me in Eighty-Four.* In 1884 Lord Dufferin began his term of office as Viceroy of India.

Line 15. *You shouldn't take a man from Canada.* Lord Dufferin was Governor-General of Canada from 1872 to 1878.

Lines 23-24.   *I go back*
          To Rome and leisure.

Lord Dufferin was made Ambassador at Rome after he left India.

Line 27. *Egypt served my turn.* In 1882 Lord Dufferin was sent to Egypt as British Commissioner to report on a scheme of reorganisation.

Lines 41-42. *I took a country twice the size of France,*
         And shuttered up one doorway in the
         North.

During his term of office Lord Dufferin annexed Burma and checked Russia's advance towards India.

Lines 51-53.   *Have you met*
  A grim lay reader with a taste for coins,
  And faith in Sin most men withhold from God?

This refers to Sir T. C. Hope.

Line 64. *Shall I write letters answering H-nt-r—fawn with R-p-n on the Yorkshire grocers?* Sir William Wilson Hunter, the compiler of the *Imperial Gazetteer*,

AND OTHER VERSES

was in the Indian Civil Service from 1862 to 1887. During the latter part of his service he contributed weekly articles on Indian affairs to the *Times*. Lord Ripon was Lord Dufferin's immediate predecessor in India. His policy of curtailing the privileges of the European in India and enlarging those of the native was more popular in Yorkshire than among the English in India.

Line 76. *Hates cats and knows his business.* Lord Roberts's antipathy to cats is well known. During Lord Dufferin's tenure of office Lord (then Sir Frederick) Roberts became Commander-in-Chief in India.

Line 127. *Lift the salt-tax.* (See note, 'The Rupaiyat of Omar Kal'vin,' stanza 2, p. 11.)

Line 128. The *Congress* was a political league founded by A. O. Hume to give the natives an opportunity of expressing their political views. It had no official position. It first met at Calcutta in the winter of 1886-1887.

Lines 131-132.   *Ask a Lady Doctor* once
    How little Begums see the light.
A Begum is a Hindoo princess or lady of rank (see also note, 'The Song of the Women,' stanza 1, p. 15).

Lines 135-136. *I told the Turk he was a gentleman.*
    I told the Russian that his Tartar veins
    Bled pure Parisian ichor.
Lord Dufferin established a high reputation for

DEPARTMENTAL DITTIES

diplomacy when Ambassador at Petersburg (1879-1881) and Constantinople (1881-1882).

Line 142. *That new land where all the wires are cut.* A British-Indian administrator's idea of heaven on earth is said to be a place where there are no telegraphs, and where consequently he can carry out such legislation as he, being on the spot, knows to be right without interference from less well-informed authority in England.

Line 164. *Palaces—with draughts.* During the first few months of her life in India, Lady Dufferin, in her letters to her mother, published in *Our Vice-regal Life in India*, frequently complained of the cold. Until the hot weather came she found the devices for admitting as free a current of air as possible into every room very trying. She speaks particularly of the agony both she and Lord Dufferin suffered from the punkahs in church.

A TALE OF TWO CITIES

Stanza 1. *Stands a City—Charnock chose it—packed away*
  Near a Bay—
  By the sewage rendered fetid.

Calcutta was founded in 1686 by Job Charnock, a merchant seaman who became an 'agent' in the service of the East India Company. For a vigorous denunciation of Calcutta's sanitary arrangements see the articles entitled 'The City of Dreadful Night'

AND OTHER VERSES

(*From Sea to Sea*), in which the Calcutta smell is described as resembling 'the essence of corruption that has rotted for the second time—the clammy odour of blue slime.'

Stanza 4. "*Because for certain months, we boil and stew, So should you.*"

While the seat of the Supreme Government of India was alternately at Calcutta and at Simla, residents of the former considered that the Viceroy and his staff should remain the whole year in Calcutta instead of going to Simla during the summer months.

St. Lawrence. (See note, 'Et Dona Ferentes,' stanza 3, p. 233.)

Stanza 5. *Darjeeling*, a hill station in the lower Himalayas, 367 miles from Calcutta, is the summer quarters of the Bengal Government.

GIFFEN'S DEBT

Line 5. *Turned three parts Mussalman and one Hindu.* A sketch of an English loafer who adopts native life in India is given in 'To be Filed for Reference' (*Plain Tales from the Hills*).

Line 67. *And may in time become a Solar Myth.* A reference to the theories of those students of mythology who believe that every legend of gods, goddesses, demi-gods, etc., is an allegorical reference to some phenomenon of nature.

DEPARTMENTAL DITTIES

IN SPRING TIME

In *Beast and Man in India* John Lockwood Kipling says that whereas a Western ear finds no more in the song of the köil than a tiresome iteration of one or two clear, high, and resonant notes, the Oriental regards it as the most musical of all birds. Moreover, 'the Englishman in India has a grudge against the köil, listening with modified rapture to notes that warn him to put up his punkah, overhaul his thermantidote, and prepare for the long St. Lawrence penance of an Indian summer.'

THE GALLEY SLAVE

This poem is an allegorical tribute to the men of the Indian Civil Service.

Stanza 2. *Bulkheads.* Partitions dividing the interior of the vessel into compartments.

Stepped. A mast is held in position by a 'step' or socket. A mast is 'stepped' at its butt end and 'stayed' with ropes above.

Sweep-head. The handle of the oar.

Stanza 3. *As we snatched her through the water.* Compare the use of the word snatch here with its use in the 'Anchor Song' (*The Seven Seas*), 'Over, snatch her over.'

Stanza 5. *Yawed and Sheered.* Went off her course, first to one side then to the other.

Stanza 10. *Orlop.* The lower deck, on which cables and other heavy gear are stowed.

AND OTHER VERSES

Stanza 11. *The top-men cleared the raffle.* Crews of ships in Nelson's time were so organised that each man had his special place aloft, thus the 'fore-top,' the 'main-top.' and the 'mizzen-top' would each have their respective crews. When a ship was in action her top-men were usually kept busy in repairing rigging damaged by the shot of the enemy.

Barrack-Room Ballads and other Verses

BEYOND THE PATH OF THE OUTMOST SUN

Stanza 6. *To these . . . my brother's spirit came.* Wolcott Balestier, to whose memory these lines are a tribute, died in December 1891, shortly after completing *The Naulahka*, a novel of Indian life which he wrote in collaboration with Rudyard Kipling. In the following year Rudyard Kipling married Miss Caroline Star Balestier, the sister of Wolcott Balestier.

TO T. A. (THOMAS ATKINS)

Thomas or Tommy Atkins is the conventional nickname for a soldier in the British army. At one time the War Office served out to all soldiers manuals in which each man was to enter his name, age, length of service, wounds, medals, etc. Precise instructions as to how these details should be entered were explained by a specimen entry giving particulars of an imaginary soldier, called for the purpose Thomas Atkins. The hypothetical name selected soon became the recognised nickname for a soldier. It is said that the Duke of Wellington, when commander-in-chief, was asked

AND OTHER VERSES

to suggest a name for the purpose of the specimen entry, and that he chose the name of a private whose bravery in action had greatly impressed him.

When they'll give you all your pay. The minimum pay of a private soldier, not counting deferred pay, was a shilling a day at the time when this poem was written. Deductions might be made from this pay for repairs to clothing, the replacing of lost, stolen, or worn-out kit, laundry, hair-cutting, groceries, etc. The regulations provided that not more than $5\frac{1}{2}$d. a day might be stopped at any one time except when a soldier was in hospital, when, as he had diet more liberal than his ordinary fare, 6d. a day might be stopped. The question of stoppages is a grievance to the soldier, who does not hear until he has enlisted that the whole of the pay promised him will not be at his absolute disposal.

DANNY DEEVER

Stanza 1. *Files on parade.* A file consists of a man in the front rank and the man immediately behind him in the rear rank. Only private soldiers and sometimes corporals stand and march in the ranks. 'Files on parade' is therefore a term applied to the common soldier.

Colour-sergeant. The senior sergeant of an infantry company.

In 'ollow square. The soldiers lining the three sides of a square and facing inwards. This is the forma-

BARRACK-ROOM BALLADS

tion adopted on ceremonial occasions such as divine service in the open, or when the battalion is called out to receive a message from the sovereign or commander-in-chief, or, as in this case, when a man is to be publicly hanged. A soldier who had made himself liable to the death penalty in England would be handed over to the civil power, but in India or on active service would be dealt with by the military authorities.

They've taken of his buttons off and cut his stripes away. When a soldier is formally disgraced in the army he is brought under guard to a parade at which the insignia of his rank as a soldier, such as his regimental badge, the stripes that he may have been entitled to wear on his sleeve, his buttons, etc., are cut off.

Stanza 3. *'Is county and the regiment's disgrace.* Most of the infantry regiments in the British army are recruited from special areas, such as the Lancashire Fusiliers, the Cheshire Regiment, etc.

Stanza 4. *You can 'ear the quickstep play.* Before a military funeral the band plays appropriate slow music, but when it is all over the men are marched away to a lively air.

TOMMY

Tommy (see note on 'Thomas Atkins,' p. 26).
Stanza 3. *Paradin' in full kit.* Drilling in full marching order, carrying rifle, bayonet, knapsack,

AND OTHER VERSES

great-coat, ammunition-pouches, haversack, water-bottle, mess-tin, etc.

Thin Red Line. The phrase was coined by Dr. W. H. Russell, the war correspondent, who applied it to the 93rd Highlanders in his account of the battle of Balaclava.

FUZZY–WUZZY

Stanza 1. *Fuzzy-Wuzzy.* A nickname applied to the Sudanese followers of the Mahdi on account of the way that many of them wore their hair—long, frizzled, and often bleached with lime to a dirty hay colour.

Paythan. The Pathans inhabit the mountains on the Indian North-West Frontier, and include several virile and exceedingly warlike tribes.

Suakim. A seaport of the Anglo-Egyptian Sudan on the Red Sea. It was the headquarters of the British and Egyptian troops operating in the eastern Sudan against the dervishes under Osman Digna in 1884.

Cat an' banjo. The sort of phrase that a 'Tommy' who happens to be a wag coins on the spur of the moment. It is possibly suggested by 'Cat and Fiddle,' which is sometimes met with in England as a public-house sign.

Stanza 2. *Kyber 'ills.* The home of the Pathans referred to above, and the scene of much fighting during the nineteenth century.

The Boers knocked us silly. At the battle of Majuba

BARRACK-ROOM BALLADS

(1881) the excellence of the Boer marksmanship resulted in a severe defeat for the British forces.

Irriwaddy chills. The Burman cannot be regarded as an heroic enemy, but the Burmese campaign was made arduous by the malarial climate of the forest on the banks of the Irrawaddy River, in which the British had to fight.

Impi. The Zulus, though savages, had a very elaborate military organisation. Chaka, a Zulu king during the first half of the nineteenth century, divided his soldiers into 'impis,' roughly corresponding in size to British regiments, and established an extraordinarily high standard of savage military efficiency. In 1879 a Zulu force practically annihilated the greater part of a British column at Isandhlwana.

Pop. Ginger-beer; hence something very mild and innocuous.

Martinis. The Martini-Henry rifle was in general use in the British army from 1871 till 1888, when it was abandoned in favour of the Lee-Metford.

You broke the square. During the expedition against the Sudanese in 1884 under Sir G. Graham, an action was fought near Tamai in which the British troops advanced against the Sudanese in echelon of brigade squares. The Sudanese, helped by the uneven nature of the ground, broke into the leading square and temporarily captured the naval guns. See *The Light that Failed*, chap. ii., for a fine description of a charge of Sudanese who 'had not learned

AND OTHER VERSES

from books that it is impossible for troops in close order to attack against breechloading fire.'

SCREW-GUNS

Screw-guns are guns used in mountain warfare, made in light pieces which can be screwed together when the gun is to be used or packed separately on the backs of mules for transport. No piece must be longer than the length of a mule from neck to rump, or weigh more than 255 pounds. The whole gun is in five pieces. These can be unloaded, put together, and the first round fired within the space of one minute. Mules are employed in mountain batteries in preference to horses, as they are more sure-footed. Some details of the methods of warfare with screw-guns are given by 'the breech-piece mule of number two gun of the First Screw Battery' in 'Servants of the Queen' (*The Jungle Book*).

Stanza 2. *Naga.* The Nagas live among the hills of Upper Assam. They are a primitive people of aboriginal stock, and enthusiastic collectors of the heads of plainsmen, which they preserve. To get good specimens they will face any risks. If they have not time to take the whole head they take the scalp. Between 1854 and 1865 they raided the Indian plains nineteen times.

Looshai. The Lushai live to the south-east of the Nagas. Their principal industry is the plunder of weaker tribes in Kachar and Burma.

BARRACK-ROOM BALLADS

Afreedeeman. The Afridi are one of the most powerful Pathan tribes. They are much given to brigandage in private life, but in the Indian army prove loyal as well as brave, hardy and self-reliant. The following piece of history gives an insight into the Afridi character. Though professedly Mohammedan, they were at one time so irreligious that there were no 'mullahs' or priests in the whole tribe. Becoming a laughing stock for this reason among neighbouring tribes, they invited a mullah from Peshawur to do missionary work amongst them. The mullah strove to impress upon them the spiritual value of pilgrimages to the tombs of holy men. They had no shrines of their own to visit, as no Afridi had ever been a saint, and they could not visit the shrines of their neighbours, for every tribe's hand was against them. To overcome the difficulty they turned their living priest into a dead saint, and thus obtained the shrine they needed. There have been nine British campaigns against the Afridis between 1850 and 1909.

CELLS

Stanza 1. *Button stick.* A piece of flat wood, or more often metal, cleft down the middle, used by soldiers when they polish their buttons. It is placed between the button and the cloth, and thus saves the latter from being soiled by the metal polish.

Corporal's Guard. A party of three men under the command of a corporal, whose duty it is to parade the

AND OTHER VERSES

vicinity of the barracks and arrest drunken or riotous soldiers.

Clink. Regimental lock-up, in which prisoners are confined while awaiting sentence. The name is derived from that of a prison which used to be in Southwark.

Pack-drill. Drilling in full marching order, carrying rifle, knapsack, great-coat, etc.

C. B. Confinement to barracks. During the period of confinement the defaulter is not allowed to visit the canteen (regimental beer shop). He must answer to his name at the guard-room whenever the defaulter's call is sounded, attend all parades, and perform any fatigue duty assigned to him. The most unpleasant fatigue duties are usually performed by defaulters.

Stanza 2. *A dose of gin.* Gin mixed with beer makes a compound named 'Dog's Nose' that is far more intoxicating than either taken alone.

Stanza 3. *Stripes.* At the end of two years' service a soldier is granted the privilege of wearing a good conduct stripe, which carries extra pay, if during that time he has not committed any serious offence. After five years' service he gets a second stripe, and he may possibly get more if he serve long enough. The stripes are forfeited by serious, bad conduct. The offence in this case is not so much the drunkenness as having 'resisted the guard.'

Stanza 4. *Ord'ly room.* The Orderly Room. The

office of the commanding officer who will try the case and award the punishment.

GUNGA DIN

Stanza 1. *Bhisti.* Water-carrier. The 'bhisti' must not be confounded with the 'pani wallah,' who performs for Hindoos the service that the 'bhisti' performs for Mohammedans. The 'pani wallah' must always be a Brahman, so that Hindoos of all castes can accept water from him. The Mohammedan water-carrier is usually a very cheerful, obliging fellow, ready to turn his hand to any kind of camp work. The word 'bhisti' literally means 'heavenly one.' It is applied to him partly in chaff, partly in recognition of the value of his services in the hour of sore need.

Stanza 2. *Goatskin water-bag.* In the East from time immemorial water-carriers have carried their water in leather bags. In the Indian army goatskin is the material of which the bag must be made, as Mohammedans could not drink from a bag made of pigskin, and Hindu religious prejudice would be offended by the use of calf-skin.

Stanza 3. *'E didn't seem to know the use of fear.* It is difficult for those who have never heard shots fired in anger to realise the high degree of courage required in non-combatants on a battlefield. The soldier who is shot at has the satisfaction of shooting back at his enemy, but the non-combatant, such as

AND OTHER VERSES

the water-carrier or stretcher-bearer, is denied this relief to his feelings. The courage of the Indian 'bhisti' has become proverbial: at the siege of Delhi a bhisti named Juma, attached to the Queen's Own Corps of Guides, so distinguished himself for heroism during the performance of his duty that he received the star 'For Valour,' till recently the highest distinction that an Indian soldier could earn. In addition to this the men of the Guides petitioned that he should be allowed to join their ranks as a regular soldier. This was an extreme tribute to Juma's bravery, for the Guides are men of rank and position, and the social position of a bhisti is very low. Juma enlisted, became a commissioned officer, and again won the reward 'For Valour.'

Nut. Head.

Right flank rear. Behind the right hand side of the company to which he is attached.

Stanza 5. *Dooli.* A litter of canvas suspended from a wooden frame, in which the wounded are carried off the battlefield.

Canteen. Regimental beer shop.

Swig. Drink.

OONTS

Stanza 1. *Penk.* Beat feebly.

Commissariat camel, a camel used for the transport of food, etc., required by a column on the march.

Stanza 2. *Native follower.* A regiment on the

march in India has an exceptionally large number of camp-followers. The reason for this is primarily because it is necessary to allow soldiers in the native regiments to be attended by servants who perform for them necessary camp duties from which they themselves are precluded by religious prejudices. The climate makes it advisable to lighten the duties of the British soldier as far as possible, and, moreover, as the native soldiers are allowed to have servants, it would lower the prestige of the sovereign race if British soldiers were made to perform menial camp duties from which the native soldiers are exempted. Both British and native regiments, therefore, are attended by a large number of camp-followers. These are of three classes. Private camp-followers—officers' personal attendants, grooms, etc.—who are paid and rationed by their masters; regimental camp-followers —cooks, sweepers, water-carriers, etc.; and lastly, stretcher-bearers, mule-drivers, etc., paid and rationed by government.

Paythans. Pathans, Afghan inhabitants of the mountains on the North-West Frontier.

Socks. Whack, beat.

Stanza 3. *'E's blocked the whole division from the rear-guard to the front.* The mountain roads on the Indian North-West Frontier are very narrow, and, as fate would naturally arrange that a camel should choose the narrowest part in which to lie down, one beast could easily render a road temporarily im-

AND OTHER VERSES

passable. For a description of the confusion caused to a column on the march by a blocked road, see 'My Lord the Elephant' (*Many Inventions*).

Stanza 4. *'E'll gall an' chafe.* Get sores under his girths and saddle.

LOOT

Stanza 1. *'Aversack.* The haversack is a canvas bag in which a soldier carries such odds and ends as knife, fork, spoon, an oil-rag for cleaning his rifle, soap, razor, and one day's ration of biscuits. These last absorb a unique flavour from contact with the soap and oil-rag.

Clobber. Clothes.

Loot. A Hindustani word, meaning plunder, that has now become English. Looting is forbidden to the British soldier, but it is occasionally winked at by indulgent officers, who know that what the soldier leaves will very likely be plundered by the riff-raff that follow a column for the sake of what they may find. On one occasion, during the South African war, an officer whose duty it was to search a farm-house endeavoured not to see that his men busied themselves in catching the fowls. One soldier, however, chasing a hen round the corner of the house ran into his officer with such violence that the latter could not ignore the matter. He charged the soldier with intending to steal the hen, but Tommy hotly denied it and explained, 'That's a very vicious fowl, sir, and he'd

BARRACK-ROOM BALLADS

have pecked you in another minute if I hadn't headed him off!'

Stanza 3. *Cleanin'-rod.* A steel rod used for pushing the oil-rag through the muzzle of a rifle.

Baynick. Cockney pronunciation of bayonet.

Stanza 5. *A quartermaster* is a non-combatant honorary commissioned officer, whose duties are practically those of a housekeeper to his regiment. In barracks he assigns the men their quarters. On service he arranges the laying out of the camp, and in general he looks after the stores of food, forage, clothing, ammunition, etc. A quartermaster is usually a man of long service and ability who has risen from the ranks.

The Widow. The late Queen Victoria was thus affectionately referred to by her soldiers.

Mess-tin. A utensil in two parts, body and lid, that serves various purposes, such as soup-plate, teacup, and frying-pan. On the march the day's ration of meat is carried in it.

'SNARLEYOW'

Stanza 1. *The corps which is first among the women an' amazin' first in war.* The Royal Horse Artillery have the privilege of taking up their position on the right of the line at reviews and of preceding all other corps in marching past, though this proud position was recently at Aldershot yielded to the Army Flying Corps. The position of the Horse Artillery in

AND OTHER VERSES

the eyes of women is due, perhaps, to the exceptional splendour of its uniform, which is almost as glorious as that of the Life Guards.

Two's off-lead. The horse whose position in the harness of No. 2 gun was that of leader on the off-side. A Horse Artillery gun is drawn by six horses, harnessed in pairs, the near-side horse of each pair being ridden by a driver.

The wheel. The horses harnessed next to the gun. When the gun is wheeled they have to do the greatest part of the work.

Bombardier. An Artillery non-commissioned officer, ranking below a sergeant.

Stanza 3. *The limber.* The front of a gun-carriage, the hinder part being the gun itself. The limber consists of two wheels, axle-pole, and ammunition-case. When the gun is in action the limber is separated from and drawn up near it.

Stanza 5. *Sections.* A battery is divided into three sections of two guns each.

Stanza 7. *'Action front!'* The word of command given when a battery reaches its ground. The gun-carriages are wheeled round so that the muzzles of the guns which have been pointing to the rear on the march now point towards the enemy.

Monday head. A headache that follows too riotous enjoyment of the Sunday holiday.

Case. Case-shot, used at close quarters for firing 'into the brown' of an enemy. It is now super-

BARRACK-ROOM BALLADS

seded by shrapnel (see note, 'The Jacket,' stanza 2, p. 189).

THE WIDOW AT WINDSOR

The Widow, an affectionate nickname applied to the late Queen Victoria by her soldiers.

Stanza 1. *'Er nick on the cavalry 'orses.* Army troop horses are marked and numbered on the near fore-foot.

Stanza 2. *The Lodge that we tile, etc.* The allusion is masonic. To tile a Lodge is to guard it against the intrusion of unauthorised persons.

Stanza 3. *Bloomin' old rag.* The Union Jack.

BELTS

Stanza 1. *Revelly.* Reveille, the bugle call sounded in the morning as a signal to soldiers to get up. The various bugle calls have been set to words, not always seemly, that have become traditional in the army. The words set to the reveille call are, 'Rise—soldiers—rise—and put—your trou—sers on.'

They called us 'Delhi Rebels,' an' we answered 'Threes About.' A reference to an old regimental quarrel.

Stanza 4. *Liffey*, the river that flows through Dublin.

Stanza 5. *Side-arm.* Bayonet.

Stanza 7. *Clink.* The cells in which a prisoner awaits trial.

AND OTHER VERSES

THE YOUNG BRITISH SOLDIER

Stanza 2. *You shut up your rag-box.* 'Hold your tongue'; rag = tongue.

Stanza 4. *Go on the shout.* Treat comrades to drink. 'To shout' is to pay for a drink for some one else.

Stanza 6. *Fatigue.* Various forms of work which a soldier is liable to be called upon to perform outside the ordinary round of such duties as drill, mounting guard, cleaning stables, etc., are called 'fatigue' duties. These include such work as carrying coals, scrubbing barrack-room floors, unloading forage-waggons, etc. Men are chosen for the regular duties, such as guard-mounting, in rotation, but the sergeant warns as many men for fatigues as he thinks necessary, and is apt to give more than a fair share of work to a slacker.

Stanza 7. *If you must marry.* When a soldier marries by permission of the authorities he must have not less than seven years' service and two good-conduct badges to his credit. He must produce proof that he has at least £5, and satisfy his commanding officer that his wife is respectable. He will then be allowed quarters or lodging allowance, free medical attendance for wife and family, free transport when the regiment moves, and he will have an allowance in lieu of rations, fuel, light, etc. If his duties require him to leave his wife for a time, he will also have separation allowance. His wife will be permitted to earn money by washing in the regimental laundry for a proportion of men in her husband's company or squadron. Three per cent. of infantry men, four per cent. of cavalry and artillery, and fifty per cent. of the sergeants are allowed to marry. A man who marries without leave, and is thus unable to get his wife 'on the strength' of the regiment, is in a miserable position, as his expenses are heavier than they would be in civilian life, and he has less money with which to meet them.

Stanza 10. *Martini.* Martini-Henry rifle, in use in the army from 1871 till 1888.

Stanza 11. *When shaking their bustles.* The limber or forepart of a gun-carriage is attached to the gun itself only by a shackle, which allows considerable play. When, therefore, the gun-carriage is drawn over rough ground the gun bumps along behind, shaking from side to side very much as a bustle must have done if the wearer of one had ever been indiscreet enough to run in the days when they were worn.

Stanza 12. *Open Order.* Spread out so as to afford the enemy the least possible target.

MANDALAY

Stanza 1. *The old Flotilla.* The steamers of the Irrawaddy Flotilla Company.

An' the dawn comes up like thunder outer China 'crost the Bay! This line has been sometimes mis-

AND OTHER VERSES

understood by those who do not realise that it is *on the road* to Mandalay that the dawn comes up across the bay (the Bay of Bengal).

For a vivid description of the charm of Burma and the Burmese, see Rudyard Kipling's personal narrative in *From Sea to Sea*.

TROOPIN'

Stanza 1. *A Fourp'ny bit.* The fourpence a day paid to men when they are transferred to the Army reserve at the expiration of their period of service with the colours.

Stanza 2. *The Malabar's in 'arbour with the Jumner at 'er tail.* The Indian Government formerly possessed a fleet of six troopships, named the *Malabar*, *Jumna*, *Orontes*, *Euphrates*, *Serapis*, and *Crocodile*. The *Serapis* is mentioned in 'The Madness of Private Ortheris' (*Plain Tales from the Hills*).

Stanza 4. *New draf's.* Drafts of new recruits forwarded from the depots in England.

THE WIDOW'S PARTY

Stanza 1. *Lay.* Cockney slang for a trade or occupation of any sort. A pickpocket, for instance, who decided to try his hand at burglary might say that he would 'have a shot at a new lay,' or if he preferred to stay in his former profession he might tell a pal that he was 'still on the same old lay.'

Gosport. A fortified seaport on the shores of Ports-

BARRACK-ROOM BALLADS

mouth harbour, used to a great extent as a naval and military depot.

Stanza 3. *What did you do for knives and forks?* A reference to the regulation side-arms—that is, swords and bayonets.

Stanza 4. *Mess.* For convenience in the issue of rations the members of a company or troop are divided into different 'messes.' Food is issued in bulk to the representative of a mess, who carries it away for the members of his mess to divide among themselves.

Stanza 5. In India the work of carrying the wounded off the field of battle is performed by natives. The wounded are placed in canvas litters called 'doolies.'

FORD O' KABUL RIVER

These verses are founded on an accident that occurred to a squadron of British cavalry while fording the Kabul River during the Afghan War of 1879.

GENTLEMEN-RANKERS

Stanza 1. *Machinely crammed.* Educated more with a view to the successful passing of examinations than to the understanding on broad lines of the subject learned.

Stanza 2. *Stables.* The daily duty in a cavalry regiment of grooming and feeding horses and cleaning out the stables.

Kitchen slops. The daily routine of barrack life

AND OTHER VERSES

necessarily includes work that in private households is performed by domestic servants. Such work, of course, is extremely repugnant to a man who has been reared amid comfortable surroundings.

Rider. In each troop one man, who must be an expert horseman, is charged with the duty of taming refractory horses. He wears as a badge a spur worked in worsted on his sleeve. The rough-rider's rank does not entitle him to employ a servant, a privilege which is reserved for those above the rank of sergeant, but there is nothing in the Regulations to prevent his making a private arrangement with a comrade of his own rank to clean his boots and perform other menial services for him.

Stanza 4. *The Curse of Reuben.* When Jacob was on his deathbed he said to his eldest son, Reuben, 'Unstable as water, thou shalt not excel,' see Genesis, xlix. 4.

ROUTE MARCHIN'

Stanza 1. *Marchin' on relief.* Regiments in India are not kept long at one station. When one regiment moves out of a station and another comes to take its place, the latter is said to relieve the former.

Grand Trunk Road. One of the most famous highways in the world. It runs right across northern India from Calcutta to Peshawur. It is supposed to have been begun by Sher Shah, the Afghan usurper, who ruled Bengal before the Moguls. The Mogul

BARRACK-ROOM BALLADS

emperors improved it. It is shaded by avenues of trees, and there are wells and rest-houses at frequent intervals along its length, and a camping-ground for the use of troops at every ten miles. Every year a third of the area of each camping-ground is ploughed up so as to keep the soil wholesome. For a description of the varied life on this great highway see *Kim*.

Stanza 2. *A rifle-sling*. A band of white leather with which the rifle may be hung from the shoulder.

Stanza 3. *Revelly*. Reveille, the bugle call with which a camp is aroused in the morning (see note, 'Belts,' stanza 1, p. 40).

Stanza 4. *Open order*. On first leaving camp soldiers have to march at attention, their rifles at the slope on the left shoulder. Soon afterwards, at the word 'open order,' discipline is relaxed, the men may talk or sing and carry their rifles as they please, moving them from hand to hand or shoulder to shoulder, so that no one set of muscles gets unnecessarily tired.

Stanza 6. *Rookies*. Recruits.

If your 'eels are blistered. It is of the utmost importance that a foot-soldier should learn to take care of his feet. Parades are frequently ordered for 'foot inspection,' at which every man must take off his boots and socks and submit his feet for examination, lest neglected corns, blisters, etc., should lame him. A man who cannot march cannot fight.

Stanza 7. *Injia's coral strand*. A quotation from

AND OTHER VERSES

the well-known hymn 'From Greenland's Icy Mountains,' by Reginald Heber, Bishop of Calcutta from 1823 to 1826.

SHILLIN' A DAY

Stanza 1. *Revelly.* The first bugle call of the day (see 'Belts,' stanza 1, p. 40).

Birr to Bareilly, etc. Birr is in King's County, Ireland, Bareilly in the Rohilkhand division of the Indian United Provinces, and Leeds in Yorkshire. Lahore is the capital of the Punjab. Hong Kong is the easternmost military outpost of the British Empire. Peshawur is the capital of the Indian North-West Frontier Province. Lucknow is the headquarters of the 8th division of the northern army in India. Etawah, in the Agra division of the United Provinces of India, has ceased to be a military station, and only long-service men could boast of having been stationed there.

All ending in 'pore.' The Sanskrit *pura*, 'a town, city, or village,' is found in more or less its original form in several Indian languages, *e. g.* Bija*pur*, Berham*pore*, Punder*poor*, Avan*oor*, Tanj*ore*, Trichino*poly*, etc. The Greek *polis*, 'a city,' probably comes from the same root.

Cast from the Service. Invalided as being no longer fit for duty.

Stanza 2. *Ghazi.* The name given to Mohammedan fanatics who have taken a vow to exterminate 'unbelievers' with the sword. In action these men charge their enemy recklessly, believing that if they themselves are killed their souls will immediately be carried to Paradise. A charge by Ghazi fanatics is described in 'The Drums of the Fcre and Aft' (*Wee Willie Winkie*).

Commissairin'. Serving as a commissionaire or messenger. The Corps of Commissionaires was founded in 1859 by Captain Sir Edward Walter, K. C. B., with the intention of providing occupation for old soldiers who were unfit for heavy work. The fact that long service with the colours tends to incapacitate a man for any decently paid civil occupation is one of the main reasons why men do not care to enlist. It is a tragedy that many men of excellent character and intelligence, who have served their country well, can find no more dignified occupation on leaving the service than the opening and shutting of a hotel or restaurant door, or should be obliged to compete against small boys for posts as messengers. It is constantly urged that such posts as those of doorkeepers, etc., in the government offices should be reserved for ex-soldiers, but these posts are too frequently given to men who have no higher claim on their country than having served as butlers, footmen, or coachmen to successful politicians.

Grand Metropold. The names Grand and Metropole are favourite names for large hotels in the most important English cities and towns.

AND OTHER VERSES

THE BALLAD OF EAST AND WEST

Line 8. *Turned the calkins upon her feet.* Turned her shoes round so as to confuse any one attempting to follow the mare by her footprints.

Line 9. *The Guides.* The Queen's Own Corps of Guides, located at Mardan, one of the most famous corps in the Indian army. It was raised in 1846 by Sir Harry Lumsden by direction of Sir Henry Lawrence, who realised the Indian North-West Frontier's need—to protect outlying portions of the frontier, and to keep the tribesmen in check—of a thoroughly mobile force of troops, both horse and foot, composed of individuals able not only to fight but to act quickly and intelligently on their own initiative in times of emergency. It had at first one troop of cavalry and two companies of infantry. It has now 1400 men. Twenty-seven of its officers are British, the rest native. The corps is recruited from among the fighting races of the frontier, and in order to provide scouts with local knowledge in frontier wars, it alone among Indian regiments obtained permission to recruit men from beyond the frontier. Afridis, Yusufzai, Pathans, Khuttucks, Swats, Sikhs, Punjabi Mohammedans, Parsiwans (Afghan Persians), Dogras, Kabulis, Gurkhas, Turcomans, etc., serve in its ranks. Some Indian princes and several ex-outlaws have served as Guides. The corps is famous for the courage, loyalty, and intelligence of its individual members and for its efficiency as a whole. At one time no less than thirty-four of its members were entitled to wear the star 'For Valour,' until recently the highest reward that could be earned by an Indian soldier, and an exceptionally large proportion of its commanding officers have met soldiers' deaths. The Guides were the first to wear a loose-fitting, workman-like, dust-coloured (kharki) uniform instead of the showy and unserviceable uniform formerly in favour both in the British and the Indian army.

Line 11. *Ressaldar.* Native captain in an Indian cavalry regiment.

Line 13. *Abazai—Bonair.* Two frontier districts of the Punjab near the headquarters of the Corps of Guides. They are about forty miles apart.

Line 16. *The Tongue of Jagai.* The scene of the battle described in 'The Drums of the Fore and Aft' (*Wee Willie Winkie*).

Line 42. *' 'Twas only by favour of mine,' quoth he, 'ye rode so long alive.'* The Afghans have the greatest admiration for courage. When the Malakand garrison was surprised (July 1897) two officers, Lieutenants Rattray and Minchin, were playing polo there. It was the duty of these two officers to make the desperate attempt to get back to their station, an outpost named Chakdara, seven miles from the Malakand garrison. On their way there they met, and (as they held steadily on their way) were at the mercy of, the

AND OTHER VERSES

insurgent Afghans, who, admiring their pluck, instead of attacking them wished them Godspeed.

Line 82. *Peshawur.* The city in which is the principal military station of the North-West Frontier Province.

Line 86. *The wondrous names of God.* The real name of God is, according to Mohammedan belief, known only to prophets and apostles. Whoever knows it has power to raise the dead and perform other miracles. The Most Great Name of God being a secret, He is known by ninety-nine other epithets which are revealed in the 7th chapter of the Koran. The camel also knows the hundredth secret name of God. It was told him as a compensation for the hardships of his life on earth. He has never revealed it, but preserves a supercilious demeanour on account of his knowledge. Look at any camel for the truth of this!

Line 92. '*To-night 'tis a man of the Guides!*' The Corps of Guides has from time to time admitted outlaws to its ranks. The most notable of these was a Khuttuck robber named Dilawar, on whose head was a price of 1,000 rupees. Sir Harry Lumsden was so impressed with this man's enterprise, daring, and intimate knowledge of the country, that he sent a message inviting him to come under safe conduct to the Guides' camp and discuss matters. Dilawar came. Lumsden offered to recruit him in the corps, promising that if he refused the offer he should be hanged as soon as he could be fairly caught. Dilawar refused, and was, of course, allowed to leave the camp. Later he came in and enlisted. Years afterwards he confessed that his intention in so doing was to learn British methods of warfare and then return to brigandage. The integrity of the British so impressed him, however, that he became a loyal and devoted soldier. He rose to the rank of subadar (infantry captain). Trained originally for the Mohammedan priesthood, Dilawar always delighted in religious controversies, both with mullahs of his own faith and with Christian missionaries. Becoming dissatisfied with Islam, he became Christian in 1858, twelve years after he had joined the Guides. He died of cold and exposure in a mountain pass while on a secret and dangerous mission for the Government.

THE LAST SUTTEE

By the act of suttee, *i. e.* sharing her husband's funeral pyre, a Hindu widow believes that she not only makes atonement for her husband's and her own sins, but secures for herself reunion with him in heaven.

Stanza 1. *The Women's wing.* The wives of Rajpoots are jealously secluded from the sight of all men except their nearest relations.

Stanza 2. *Ulwar sabre and Tonk jezail,*
Mewar headstall and Marwar mail.
Every Rajpoot prince takes a pride in his armoury, in which beautiful and costly swords, matchlocks inlaid

AND OTHER VERSES

with mother-of-pearl and gold, rhinoceros-hide shields painted and enamelled in gold and silver, buffalo-horn bows, spears, daggers, etc., are carefully preserved. Ulwar, Tonk, Mewar, and Marwar are all Rajpoot States.

Stanza 3. *Boondi*—a Rajpoot State described in 'Letters of Marque' (*From Sea to Sea*). No Rajpoot may marry a woman who is not a Rajpoot.

Stanza 4. *Malwa*—a district to the east of Rajputana. *Abu*—a famous isolated mountain on the west of the desert of Rajputana.

Stanza 7. *Nautch-girl*—professional dancing-girl. Nautch-girls belong to a low class, and instead of being secluded in zenanas, as the women's quarters are called, go to one house or another as their professional services are required. Should, however, a man adopt one as his concubine he would seclude her in his house.

Stanza 10. *The Sun-born.* Some Rajpoots claim descent from a solar race, some from a lunar race, and some from a sacred fire once kindled on Mount Abu. The royal clans all belong to the military caste and are intensely proud of their race. Rajpoot literally means son of a rajah.

Stanza 17. *Thakur.* A title equivalent to 'lord' or 'baron,' from Sanskrit *Thakura*, 'honourable.'

THE BALLAD OF THE KING'S MERCY

Line 1. Abdhur Rahman was Amir of Afghanistan from 1880 till 1901. Before reaching the throne he had experienced many vicissitudes and had known danger and poverty. (In 'The Amir's Homily' (*Life's Handicap*) Abdhur Rahman tells his court how once he had earned money as a coolie.) During his reign he did as much for Afghanistan as King Alfred for England or Peter the Great for Russia. He ruled over a turbulent people who could be held in check only by fear. He was never safe from mutiny or assassination. His punishments were fiendish, but his self-sacrifice was splendid. So preoccupied was he with the enormous amount of work which he undertook, that he scarcely visited his harem more than two or three times in the year, preferring to eat and sleep in the room in which he transacted the business of the State. Every one in his kingdom had access to him. If a petition was sent to him by post marked 'Not to be opened by any one except the Amir,' no one dared tamper with it. Very often the Amir sent an answer in his own handwriting.

Durani. The dominant tribe in Afghanistan. It is pure Afghan stock, claiming direct descent from Jeremiah, son of Saul the first king of Israel.

Line 4. *Balkh to Kandahar.* Balkh is in the extreme north and Kandahar in the south of Afghanistan.

Line 5. *Before the old Peshawur gate.* Among the Semitic peoples of the East the neighbourhood of city gates has from time immemorial been used as meeting-places for administration of justice, discussion of pub-

AND OTHER VERSES

lic matters, and ordinary gossip. Cf. many references in the Old Testament. The theoretical reason for administering justice in the city gate is in order to afford ready access to all.

Kurd. The Kurds inhabit the high country that separates Asiatic Turkey from Persia.

Kaffir literally means one who denies—an infidel from the Mohammedan point of view. The word is in one sense restricted to the pagan inhabitants of the Hindoo Kush mountains to the north-east of Afghanistan. In another sense, in which it is used here, it means any non-Mohammedan. The Afghans are all Mohammedans.

Line 9. *There was a hound of Hindustan had struck a Eusufzai.* The Eusufzai are Afghan inhabitants of the district north and east of Peshawur. As the Afghans have for centuries regarded the inhabitants of India with contempt, the blow was unforgivable.

Line 17. *Daoud Shah* was at one time commander-in-chief of the Amir's army. In his autobiography Abdhur Rahman stated that Daoud Shah received 3000 sovereigns for inciting the mob to massacre Sir Louis Cavagnari and his party.

Line 25. *Abdhur Rahman, the Durani Chief, to the North and the South is sold.* An allusion to the idea prevalent at the time that Amir Abdhur Rahman intrigued equally with England and Russia.

Line 26. *Ghilzai.* A Pathan tribe of mixed Afghan and Persian stock. The Ghilzai revolted soon after

BARRACK-ROOM BALLADS

Abdhur Rahman came to the throne, and at the time that this poem was written seemed likely to revolt again.

Line 27. *Heratis.* People of Herat on the Afghan-Persian frontier, which has been ruled alternately, according to the fortunes of war, by shah and amir. They were always ready to revolt under Abdhur Rahman.

Line 28. *Abazai.* Part of the country near the Malakand Pass inhabited by the Eusufzai tribe.

Line 51. *Sungar.* A wall of stones erected to afford cover from rifle fire.

Usbeg. A tribe mostly Turkish in origin, inhabiting the country to the west of Balkh in Afghanistan as well as Bokhara and other parts of Central Asia. Abdhur Rahman's bodyguard, when he visited Lord Dufferin in 1885, was largely composed of Usbegs (see note, 'The Ballad of the King's Jest,' line 78, p. 58).

Line 52. *Zuka Kheyl.* The strongest and most warlike clan of Afridis of Pathan-Indian stock, occupying the vicinity of the Khyber Pass.

Line 54. '*See that he do not die.*' Abdhur Rahman displayed much originality in the invention of punishments. Many of them were sickeningly brutal, and most were devised with a certain terrible humour (see 'The Ballad of the King's Jest' for one of these).

Line 59. *Ramazan.* The ninth month of the Mohammedan year, throughout which every Moham-

AND OTHER VERSES

medan must fast, abstaining from water as well as food, from dawn till sunset of each day.

THE BALLAD OF THE KING'S JEST

Line 2. *Kafilas*—caravans. Some of the Ghilzai tribes are almost wholly engaged in the carrying trade between India and the northern states of Central Asia. For mutual protection against robbers the merchants with their families and flocks travel in bands under a military organisation. Some caravans will have as many as a thousand fighting men, besides women and children. As soon as the spring frees the mountain passes from snow, they leave their families and flocks in a standing camp and come down into India selling furs, drugs, shawls, carpets, madder, asafoetida, etc. On their return they carry back cotton piece-goods, tea, spices, etc.

Line 18. *Fort Jumrood* commands the entrance from the Indian side of the Khyber Pass.

Line 37. *Hookah*. A form of pipe commonly used in India, Arabia, Persia, etc., in which the tobacco smoke is cooled and purified by passing through water.

Line 43. *A grey-coat guard*. The Russians are called 'greycoats' in contradistinction to British 'redcoats.'

Helmund river during part of its length forms the boundary between Afghan and Persian Seistan.

Line 57. *Khuttuck*. The Khuttuck Pathans are

BARRACK-ROOM BALLADS

allied to the Afghans in speech and religion but not in blood. The full-blooded Afghan's contempt for the Khuttuck is due to the fact that the latter have frequently been raided by the more virile race. Placed in a difficult position between Afghanistan and India, the Khuttucks have had to hunt with the hare and run with the hounds.

Line 74. *In full Durbar*. A Durbar may be either a stately ceremonial or an ordinary council meeting for the discussion of State affairs.

Line 78. *Gholam Hyder, the Red Chief*. Gholam Hyder Ali, the Amir's Commander-in-Chief, a huge red-bearded, blue-eyed man, accompanied the Amir on his visit to Lord Dufferin in 1885. In Mr. Kipling's account of that event he describes Gholam Hyder's personal exertions on the platform of Peshawur station at midnight, when the railway authorities were trying to entrain the Amir's Usbeg bodyguard, 'eight hundred men and eight hundred horses, who had never seen a train before.' Gholam Hyder, Mr. Kipling asserts, almost threw the horses bodily into the trucks.

Line 81. *The face of the king showed dark as death*. Abdhur Rahman (see note 'The Ballad of the King's Mercy,' line 1, p. 53) was a man of extraordinary self-reliance and little apt to be disturbed by bad news. While he was at Rawal Pindi conferring with Lord Dufferin, then Viceroy of India, he was informed that the Russians had invaded his territory

AND OTHER VERSES

at Panjdeh. The news of an incident which nearly brought about war between England and Russia was received by Abdhur Rahman with perfect equanimity. He evidently regarded it as one of those irregularities which are bound to occur occasionally on a rough and unsettled frontier, too trivial to be noticed by any Central Asian ruler who desired to have any peace of mind at all.

Line 105. *Mowed*—grimaced.

Line 106. *As a sloth.* Sloths live for choice among trees, usually hanging, body downwards, from the branches.

WITH SCINDIA TO DELHI

These verses are based on the story of 'Salun the Beragun,' written by an orientalized Englishman (name unknown) under the *nom de plume* of 'Mirza Moorad Alee Beg,' some thirty years ago. Cf. M'Intosh Jellaludin's allusion to him in 'To be Filed for Reference' (*Plain Tales from the Hills*).

Stanza 1. *When we went forth to Paniput to battle with the Mlech.* Many battles have been fought at Paniput, near Delhi. The first recorded was in 1300 B. C., but the one which forms the subject of this poem was fought between Mahrattas and Afghans, in 1761. The Mahratta Confederacy was then at the height of its power. It ruled, or exacted tribute from, the whole of India as far north as the Indus and the Himalayas, until the Afghan invasion under Ahmed, king of Kabul. The battle of Paniput was waged for possession of the Jumna fords. The Afghans, though themselves in straits for want of food, evaded a pitched battle as long as possible, knowing that the more improvident and less hardy Mahrattas were less fitted to endure privation than themselves. At last the Mahrattas could endure the strain no longer. 'The cup is now full to the brim and cannot hold another drop,' said Sewdasheo Rao, the Bhao, who was in command. At night the last of the food was distributed, so that each man should have one full meal. Next morning the Mahrattas moved out to the attack (see also note to stanza 4, p. 61).

Our hands and scarves were saffron dyed. Knowing that they were to die, many of the Mahrattas, to indicate that they would accept no quarter, put on the *saffron robe*, disarranged their turbans, and anointed their hands and faces with a preparation of yellow turmeric. A man who yielded to the foeman after so doing would be utterly disgraced.

Mlech. A term applied by Hindoos to all who are not Hindoos.

Stanza 2. The Mahratta force amounted to 55,000 horse, 15,000 foot, and 200 cannon, besides many Pindharees or irregular troops, who received no pay but were allowed to accompany the army on condition that they shared their loot with the Mahratta generals. The Afghan forces with their Rohilla allies amounted to 41,800 horse, 38,000 foot, 70 cannon,

AND OTHER VERSES

and a large number of irregulars. The great cannon Zam Zammah, that stands before the doors of the museum at Lahore, and on which *Kim* was sitting when he first met his Lama, was captured from the Mahrattas at Paniput.

Damajee was the eldest son of Pilaji Gaekwar. He was pledged to maintain 10,000 horse and assist the Peishwa (Mahratta hereditary prime minister) when called upon. *Bhao* means literally brother or cousin. Sewdasheo Chimnajee Bhao was cousin to the Peishwa. *Mulhar Rao* belonged to the Dhangar or shepherd caste. He had begun life by herding his uncle's flocks, and had risen to power as a military adventurer. In the events preceding the battle Mulhar Rao had tried to run with the hare and hunt with the hounds.

Stanza 3. *Bhowani* is a war-goddess and wife of Siva. Sivaji, founder of the Mahratta power, had a sword called Bhowani, which after his death was placed in a specially built temple and worshipped annually by his descendants. The war goddess's spirit was supposed to reside in it.

Stanza 4. *Hills of Khost.* Mountains to the south-east of Kabul in Afghanistan.

Rohillas. Pathan allies of the Afghans.

The Mahrattas charged gallantly, and the Afghan leader was obliged to send his personal guards to the camp to drive out all who were shirking the battle. At a critical moment Wiswas Rao, the Peishwa's son, was killed. Sewdasheo Rao, the Bhao, sent a message to Mulhar Rao for help, but immediately afterwards descended from his elephant, mounted his Arab charger and fled. Mulhar Rao also fled, followed by Damajee. Then the whole Mahratta army became suddenly demoralised, and the Afghans advancing massacred them as they scattered. Only a quarter of the Mahratta forces escaped—the number of the slain being estimated at two hundred thousand. The headless body of the Bhao was found on the field, but Damajee and Mulhar Rao escaped. The battle of Paniput, by weakening the Mahratta power, furthered the British conquest of India.

Stanza 6. *Upsaras* are spirits of the clouds and waters. They are handmaidens of Indra and dance before his throne. When a battle is raging on earth they guide to paradise the spirits of those who have fallen, whose wives they then become. In Tod's *Annals of Rajasthan* there is a translation of a passage in the poems of Chand Bardai which describes the Upsaras preparing to receive the souls of the dead warriors and incidentally throws an interesting sidelight on the toilette of an Indian lady of the thirteenth century A. D. While the warriors anointed their bodies for the battle, the celestial Upsaras with ambrosial oils and heavenly perfumes anointed their silver forms, tinged their eyelids, and prepared for the reception of the heroes. 'The heroes gird on their armour, while the heavenly fair deck their persons.

AND OTHER VERSES

They place on their heads the helm; these adjust the corset. They tighten the girths of the war-steed; the fair of the world of bliss bind on the anklet of bells. Nets of steel defend the turban's fold; they braid their hair with golden flowers and gems. The warrior polishes his falchion; the fair tints the eyelid. The hero sharpens his dagger; the fair paints a heart on her forehead. He braces on his ample buckler; she places the resplendent orb in her ear. He binds his arm with a gauntlet of brass; she stains her hand with the henna. The hero decorates his hand with the tiger claw. The Upsara ornaments with rings and golden bracelets. The warrior shakes his ponderous lance; the heavenly fair the garland of love to decorate those who fall in the battle. The warrior strings his bow; the fair assume their killing glances. Once more the heroes look to their girths, while the celestial fair prepare their cars.'

A Rajput riding to battle wore a wreath on his head in preparation for his celestial bridal.

Other spirits that, according to Hindoo mythology, are interested in a battle are the Yoginis who drink the blood, and the Palcharas who eat the flesh, of the slain.

Bhagwa Jhanda. The standard of the Mahratta Confederacy.

Stanza 9. *Scindia.* Mahdaji Scindia was the son of a military adventurer who had risen from the post of slipper-bearer to the Peishwa to a command in his

BARRACK-ROOM BALLADS

master's bodyguard. He ultimately became one of the leading Mahratta chiefs. He attempted to carry on the fight at Paniput after Mulhar Rao had deserted.

Soobah. Leader of a troop of 625 horsemen.

Stanza 11. *Lalun.* In the story 'On the City Wall' (*In Black and White*) another Lalun, a member of the same ancient profession, sings a 'laonee,' sung by this Lalun on the eve of the battle of Paniput.

Stanza 13. *Populzai.* One of the clans of the Durani Afghans.

THE DOVE OF DACCA

Although 'The Dove of Dacca' is not included in the English edition of *Barrack-Room Ballads*, these notes are inserted here because the poem follows 'With Scindia to Delhi' in the *Collected Verse of Rudyard Kipling*.

Stanza 1. *The thorns have covered the city of Gaur.* The ancient capital of Central Bengal—long since ruined—is in the Maldah district, on a deserted channel of the Ganges. Gaur used to be between 20 and 30 square miles in extent. Now it is covered with jungle, and its ruins have been taken stone by stone for the building of mosques and palaces in Murshedabad.

Stanza 3. *Fire the palace, the fort, and the keep—*
Leave to the foeman no spoil at all.

On many occasions in Indian history women have performed the rite known as *johar*, *i. e.* self-sacrifice to

AND OTHER VERSES

avoid capture and rape by a conqueror. In 1294 A. D. twenty-four thousand women besieged in Jeysulmeer perished voluntarily by sword and flame when it was realised that the city could no longer be held. Their men-folk then performed purification ceremonies, donned the saffron robe (see note on 'With Scindia to Delhi,' stanza 1, p. 59), and marched out of the city to die. In 1303 the Pathan Emperor besieged Chitor in order to capture the famous beauty Pudmini. To avoid capture and the dishonour that would inevitably follow Pudmini and all her women, taking with them everything of value in the palace, shut themselves up in a subterranean room which they then set on fire. The rite of *johar* was most frequently performed by Rajpoots.

THE BALLAD OF BOH DA THONE

A Pretender to Theebaw's throne. Theebaw, King of Upper Burma, came to the throne in 1878, and, under the influence of Supi-yaw-lat, his queen, massacred all such of his relatives—men, women, and children—as he could catch. In so doing he followed the example of most of his predecessors, for, as the monarchy in Burma was confined to members of the royal family but was not hereditary, each successive king on reaching the throne endeavoured to exterminate all possible rivals. Such male members of the royal family as escaped took to dacoity (brigandage), partly for a livelihood and partly in order to have an armed force ready prepared in case events made feasible a forcible bid for the throne.

On 7th November 1885 King Theebaw ordered his subjects to drive the British out of Lower Burma, which had been a British province since 1867. Seven days later the British troops crossed the frontier and advanced to Mandalay, captured King Theebaw, and sent him a prisoner to Bombay. Theebaw's troops had not made any serious attempt to oppose the British advance, but had disbanded of their own accord and taken to the jungle, where they either joined existing bands of dacoits or formed new bands. Though none of them any longer had hopes of seizing Theebaw's throne, the various dacoit *Bohs* (captains) were disinclined to abandon dacoity, a profession which they had found lucrative, adapted to their tastes, and—until then—fairly safe. For two years the British troops were engaged in freeing the country from these dacoit bands. The war was prolonged, not by any particular valour on the part of the dacoits, but because the thick Burmese jungle makes the whole country one vast military obstacle. The dacoit gangs seldom stood their ground when attacked, and their flight was usually led by their Boh. 'A Conference of the Powers' (*Many Inventions*) and 'The Taking of Lungtungpen' (*Plain Tales from the Hills*) are stories of the Burmese war.

V. P. P. The value-payable parcels post, by which the value of the goods mailed is collected on delivery

AND OTHER VERSES

by the post office. The Indian Government was the pioneer in this postal development.

Senior Gomashta. Accountant in charge of Government bullock train.

Stanza 2. *The Peacock Banner.* The Burmese national flag.

Stanza 3. *From the Salween scrub to the Chindwin teak*—i. e. right across Burma from south-east to north-west.

Stanza 4. *He filled old ladies with kerosene.* It was the practice of the dacoits to torture their victims in order to make them confess where their money was hidden, and to mutilate those they killed in order to terrorise others. The Burmese are extraordinarily callous to the sight of suffering in others, and many of the tortures they devised were fiendishly cruel.

Stanza 10. *And his was a Company, seventy strong.* Owing to the thickness of the jungle and the difficulties of communication, the operation of large forces was impossible. Small flying columns were therefore set to patrol districts. The method of operations adopted was to surprise villages where dacoits were reported to be, and to attack if resistance were offered. The Boh usually left his followers to bear the brunt of an attack, and fled to recruit a new gang as soon as opportunity offered.

Stanza 33. *Babu.* (See introductory note, 'What Happened,' p. 5.)

Stanza 52. *Blade that twanged on the locking-ring.*

BARRACK-ROOM BALLADS

The locking-ring is the portion of the bayonet-joint that slips over a projection on the muzzle of the Martini when bayonets are fixed. The soldier was guarding the downward blow of a Burmese dah with his rifle and fixed bayonet.

Stanza 71. *Dammer.* (See note, 'The Rhyme of the Three Captains,' line 27, p. 72.)

THE LAMENT OF THE BORDER CATTLE THIEF

Stanza 1. *The Bar.* A term applied generally to the sandy wastes between the different rivers of the Punjab.

Shalimar. A village near Lahore.

Stanza 2. *Jezail.* A long, heavy match-lock gun, usually supported on an iron fork when in use.

Tulwar. A curved sword, the handle of which is often richly decorated.

Stanza 3. *Jat.* The Jats are a race of farmers and cattle-breeders living in the Punjab and Baluchistan. As peasants they are very hard-working and very patient under misfortune. When trained they make excellent soldiers.

Stanza 8. *Lowe.* Flame.

Stanza 9. *Abazai* and *Bonair* are two mountain districts of the Punjab about 40 miles apart across the Swat valley. The Khuttucks are a Pathan tribe allied to the Afghans in speech and religion but not in blood, and have often been raided by the Afridi Pathans.

Stanza 11. *The Zukka Kheyl* is the strongest and

AND OTHER VERSES

most turbulent clan of the Afridi Pathans (see note, 'Screw-Guns,' stanza 2, p. 31). They inhabit the mountains in the vicinity of the Khyber Pass.

Stanza 12. *And swing me in the skin.* The mere touch of pig's skin would be considered defilement by a Mohammedan.

THE RHYME OF THE THREE CAPTAINS

This poem is a contribution to a controversy conducted in the pages of the *Athenæum* in 1890 as to the treatment of English authors by American publishers. Mr. Rudyard Kipling's first contribution to the controversy was a statement in the *Athenæum* to the effect that a certain firm of American publishers had some years before published some of his stories in book form without asking his permission or paying him for the right to do so. The firm replied that they had bought the stories from Mr. Kipling's agent. To this Mr. Kipling rejoined that they had bought the serial rights only, not the right to publish in book form. In this letter he said, 'The real trouble, of course, is not with this or that particular picaroon across the water. The high seas of literature are unprotected, and those who traffic on them must run their chance of being plundered. If Messrs. . . . . . . had not taken my stories, some other long or short firm would have done so. Only, a pretentiously moral pirate is rather more irritating than the genuine Paul Jones. The latter at least does not waste your time and ink.' A fortnight later a letter appeared in the *Athenæum* signed by Walter Besant, William Black, and Thomas Hardy. Referring to Rudyard Kipling as 'a certain author,' these well-known novelists said that they could not judge of his case, but that they had found the conduct of the firm in question 'just and liberal' to the foreign author, whose interests 'the American law not only fails to protect, but entirely ignores.' This poem, in which 'the three captains' typify the three above-mentioned authors, was Rudyard Kipling's rejoinder. The real Paul Jones, formerly a slaver, fought in the American Navy during the War of Independence, and harassed British shipping in English waters. The accusation brought against him by the British that he was a pirate was always hotly denied by the Americans.

Line 3. *Admiral of the North.* The scenes of the most popular of William Black's novels are laid in Scotland.

Line 4. *Lord of the Wessex coast.* Thomas Hardy's speciality is description of the countryside in 'Wessex' —Dorsetshire and Wiltshire.

Line 5. *Master of the Thames.* Walter Besant was a great authority on London life and the history of London, the Fleet Prison, etc. At the time when this poem was written he was Chairman of the Society of Authors, a trade-union of writers founded to secure legal protection for their work. Although he took in this controversy the side of the publisher against the

AND OTHER VERSES

author, no man did more than Besant to obtain just treatment for authors from English and American publishers. (See note on line 88, p. 74.)

Line 7. *In the sheer.* From deck to waterline.

Line 11. *Light she rode.* She was light in the water because she had been robbed of her cargo.

Line 12. *Scuttle-butt.* A cask containing drinking water kept on deck for general use.

Line 15. *Laccadives.* Islands in the Indian Ocean formerly infested by Arab pirates.

Line 16. *Tack.* Alter the course.

Prow and *junk.* The prow is a distinctive type of vessel used by Malay seamen, as the junk is the typical Chinese craft. Piracy was formerly rife in both Chinese and Malayan waters.

Line 18. *Lime-washed Yankee brig.* Trans-Atlantic slave-ships had to be constantly lime-washed for the sake of disinfection. Slavers usually stuck to the one evil trade, but as they were fast vessels manned by blackguard crews they occasionally indulged in piracy when safe opportunity offered.

Line 20. *From Sandy Hook to the Nore.* Sandy Hook is the point from which ships outward bound from New York take their departure. *The Nore* is a sandbank at the mouth of the Thames, at the point where the river broadens into the estuary.

Line 21. *Rovers' flag.* When the pirates dared they flew a black or red flag on which a skull and cross bones in white was depicted.

BARRACK-ROOM BALLADS

Line 22. *The Gridiron*—the flag of the United States of America, so called because of the red and white stripes that it bears. *The Jack*—the Union Jack, the national flag of Great Britain.

Line 23. *Crimped*—pressed. During the Napoleonic wars, British ships were liable to be overhauled by British men-of-war on the high seas and compelled to surrender a number of their men. Nowadays to 'crimp' a seaman means to make him drunk or otherwise temporarily helpless and put him against his will on board an outward bound vessel.

Line 26. *Shaddock*. A fruit akin to the grape-fruit of the West Indies and Florida.

Line 27. *Dammer*. A kind of resin made from a pine (*Dammara orientalis*) that grows in Amboyna and the Moluccas. It is used for making varnish and for rendering packages water-tight.

Line 29. *Boom*. A spar used to extend the foot of a mainsail. The boom on any vessel is much smaller than the same vessel's foremast.

Line 30. *Yahoo*. Contemptible person. The word was coined by Swift and applied to an imaginary race of men whose intellect and passions were on a level with those of the lowest animals.

Shoe-peg oats. A story is current to the effect that an astute American having manufactured a larger number of wooden shoe-pegs than he could sell, ran the unsaleable stock through a machine which tapered their ends and sold the result as oats!

AND OTHER VERSES

Line 32. *Hulled.* Shot him in the hull.

Line 36. *Bilgewater.* The water that collects in the bilges, the lowest internal part of a ship's hull. It is usually foul on account of the rats that have drowned in it and for other reasons.

Line 42. *Spitted his crew on the live bamboo.* A recognised form of torture in China.

Line 43. *Mangroves.* Trees that grow in foul-smelling tidal mud in the tropics.

Line 45. *Lazar.* Leprous, covered with sores (derived from Lazarus).

Line 58. *Seventy-three.* A vessel carrying seventy-three guns, and thus too formidable to be attacked by a pirate.

Line 59. *A ship of the Line*—a battleship.

Line 61. *Cocos Keys.* Low lying islands off the north coast of Cuba. The Keys in the Gulf of Mexico were the favourite haunt of the buccaneers.

Line 70. *Chaplain of the Fleet.* One of Walter Besant's novels is so called. Until 1753 many unscrupulous parsons, dwelling within the liberties of the Fleet Prison in order to be beyond the reach of ordinary law, lived by performing irregular marriages without banns or licence for whoever was foolish enough to employ them. They were utterly conscienceless, and were ready to degrade any ceremony of the Church for a few shillings.

Line 74. *A jury coat* is a makeshift coat; a Joseph's coat, besides being a coat of many colours (see Genesis xxxvii. 3), is the name given to an overcoat formerly worn by a woman when riding.

Line 75. *Halliards*—the cords leading from the masthead to the deck by which flags are hoisted. The *bunting*—the flag, so called from the thin worsted stuff of which flags are made.

Line 78. *Lascar crew.* All Oriental, and especially Indian, seamen are called Lascars.

Lines 79-81. '*Mainsail haul*' and '*Foresheet free*' are two orders given when a ship 'tacks' or is put about to run on a new course.

Line 85. *Pluck*—heart, liver, and viscera generally. *Mizzen-truck*—the top of the aftermost mast.

Line 86. *Dipsy-lead.* Deep-sea lead, used for sounding in deep water.

Line 87. *Fore-sheet home.* The fore-sheet was free (line 81) when the ship was putting about. Now that she is sailing on a new tack it is hauled 'home' and made fast.

Line 88. *The bezant is hard, ay, and black.* A punning reference to the names of the three authors—Besant, Hardy, and Black—whom the poem attacks.

Line 89. The *Kling* and the *Orang-Laut* (*i. e.* 'men of the sea') are fishermen inhabiting the Malay Archipelago. The latter are described by de Barros as 'a vile people, living by fishing and robbing.' Challong, the amphibious man, in 'The Disturber of Traffic' (*Many Inventions*), was an Orang-Laut.

Line 92. *Dip their flag.* Vessels passing each

AND OTHER VERSES

other at sea salute by 'dipping' their flag and hauling it up again.

THE BALLAD OF THE 'CLAMPHERDOWN'

Stanza 1. *The bleached Marine*. Though a marine is a soldier enlisted for service at sea, he need not be unduly ashamed of being sea-sick, as in point of fact he serves a large part of his time on land.

Stanza 2. *Stays*. Wire ropes supporting masts and funnels.

Stanchions. Iron bars built into the ship's deck or side to support the boat-deck, awnings, etc.

Stanza 3. *A cruiser light*. Cruisers are faster and less heavily armoured than battleships. They are intended for scouting rather than fighting (see note on 'Cruisers,' p. 199).

Hotchkiss gun. A light quick-firing machine gun.

Stanza 5. *Botch*. Tinker up.

Make it so. The customary term in which a naval officer assents to a suggestion from a subordinate.

Stanza 7. *The helpless ram*. The ram is the machine that rams the projectile and charge into the gun. At the date when this poem was written it was worked by steam, which would fill the turret if the ram got out of order.

The twisted runners. The runners are the steel rails on which the gun is turned.

Stanza 8. *Thresher*. A kind of shark that attacks and sometimes kills whales.

BARRACK–ROOM BALLADS

Stanza 10. *Lie down, lie down, my bold A. B.* A. B. is the recognised term for a man rated as 'able-bodied seaman.' When a seaman first enters the navy he is called a 'boy'; he is promoted from that rank to ordinary seaman, and then to able or able-bodied seaman. He is told to lie down, as otherwise the force of the contact when the ships collide will knock him down. 'Lie down' is an order that always accompanies the order 'prepare to ram.'

Stanza 11. *Nordenfelt.* Quick-firing machine gun.

Stanza 12. *We have emptied the bunkers in open sea.* The coal is exhausted because the *Clampherdown* has been at sea so long without re-coaling.

Stanza 15. *The waist.* The middle of the ship.

Stanza 16. *Conning tower.* The shot-proof pilot-house of a man-of-war.

THE BALLAD OF THE 'BOLIVAR'

Stanza 1. *The Ratcliffe Road* has now disappeared from the map of London. It used to run at the back of St. Katherine's Docks and the London Docks. It was inhabited principally by seamen and the crimps, boarding-house keepers and others who lived on seamen. Its reputation was a most unsavoury one.

Sign away. A seaman hired for a voyage has to sign an agreement in the presence of a Board of Trade official before sailing.

The Bay. The Bay of Biscay.

Stanza 2. *Loaded down with rails.* Rails are as

AND OTHER VERSES

bad a cargo as a ship can carry. It may easily shift in bad weather, and should it do so, the work of securing it again is highly dangerous.

The Start. A signal station on the most southerly point of Devonshire.

Stanza 3. *Smokestack white as snow, i. e.* by reason of encrusted salt left by the spray that has dried there.

All the coal adrift adeck. For economy's sake most tramp steamers outward bound from England carry coal enough for both the outward and the homeward voyage. As there is not room in the bunkers for so large a supply, the balance is carried on deck. Until this is used up, it impedes the movements of the crew even in fine weather.

Stanza 4. *Coal and fo'c'le short.* Short of coal and short-handed.

The Wolf. A lighthouse midway between Lizard Point and the Scilly Islands.

A two-foot list to port. Lying over on her left side.

Stanza 5. *Threshed.* Steamed against the wind.

Stanza 6. *Hog* and *sag*. When a ship 'hogs' from the strain of the seas, her deck rises amidships like a hog's back; to *sag* is the direct opposite. She tends to hog on the crest of a wave, and to sag in the hollow between two waves.

Raced. When by pitching badly a steamer lifts her propeller clear of the water it 'races' furiously. The vibration thus caused strains every bolt and rivet in her hull, and strains the engines severely.

BARRACK-ROOM BALLADS

Strake. Side. Technically, a strake is one breadth of planks or plates forming a continuous strip (or streak) from stem to stern.

Plummer block. The heavy metal box that keeps the propeller-shaft in position. If this should work seriously loose, the driving power of the propeller would wreck the engines.

Stanza 7. *Iron decks* are cheaper than wooden ones, and are commonly found on tramp steamers.

Bilges. (See note in 'Andrew's Hymn,' line 22, p. 112.)

Stanza 8. *The money paid at Lloyd's.* The insurance premium paid by the ship's owners. The *Bolivar* was leaky and was so old that she was not worth the expense of keeping in repair. Her owners had therefore sent her to sea with a dangerous cargo in winter, in the hopes that she would founder and enable them to collect the sum for which she was insured. (See 'The "Mary Gloster,"' line 18, p. 167.)

Stanza 9. *Took it green.* A light wave comes aboard in the form of white spray; a heavy one, crashing over the side, has a green colour by reason of the light shining through it. A wave that is green as it comes aboard will throw many tons of water on to the deck.

Watched the compass chase its tail. A ship's compass is considerably affected by the ship herself, and sometimes by her cargo. While the ship is being built the hammering on her iron plates will make these to a certain extent magnetic, though the influ-

AND OTHER VERSES

ence thus caused tends to decrease as the ship gets older. The ship's compass is even affected by the position with regard to the equator in which the ship was built. In the case of the *Bolivar* the pounding of the seas, causing the ship to vibrate, increases the magnetism latent in her cargo of rails, and thus makes the *Bolivar's* compass practically useless.

Stanza 11. *The wheel has gone to hell.* The steering-gear having smashed, it became necessary to rig yokes on the rudder-head and steer with a tackle carried to the aft steam-winches, a cumbersome and difficult process.

Stanza 12. *Bilbao.* A Spanish port on the south coast of the Bay of Biscay. It imports rails for the network of railways of which it is the centre.

Euchred. In the game of euchre a player who, having had the advantage of declaring what suit shall be trumps, fails to score, is said to be euchred.

Bluffed. (See note, 'The Three Sealers,' line 54, p. 127.)

THE SACRIFICE OF ER–HEB

The gods mentioned in this poem have no place in any particular cult, and the story contained in it is based on no particular legend: the incidents recorded, however, are such as might happen among almost any barbaric people who have attained a certain stage of mental culture. Human sacrifice is a feature of most primitive religions. It may have a variety of ob-

BARRACK-ROOM BALLADS

jects. Sometimes a victim is sacrificed merely in order that he may carry a direct verbal message to the gods, in which case a slave would suffice. Sometimes he is sacrificed because God, the life-giver, must be nourished with life lest his power fail and the crops suffer, in which case the victim would have to be physically perfect, and would be worshipped as divine prior to the sacrifice. In this case Bisesa is sacrificed because Taman, the god above all gods, is angry at having been neglected and must be propitiated. The victim therefore must be desirable.

> 'By my wealth and love
> And beauty, I am chosen of the God.'

Before her death they 'loosed her hair, as for the marriage-feast,' to prepare her for her union with the god, Taman.

She must also be beloved by those who sacrifice her. She is the daughter of 'the first of all Er-Heb,' and is also 'plighted to the Chief in War.'

They burned her dower, killed her favourite bull, and broke her spinning-wheel, as otherwise she could not have taken these with her to the Other World.

THE GIFT OF THE SEA

The death-bed observances here referred to belong to Yorkshire and other parts of the North Country. At the moment of death windows and doors are

AND OTHER VERSES

thrown wide open and strict silence is maintained so that nothing shall hinder the flight of the soul. Before death neighbours come into the death-chamber to pray. This observance is called 'The Passing.' The most famous of the passing songs is a quaintly beautiful hymn, usually called the Lyke-Wake Dirge, one stanza of which runs:

> 'If ever thou gavest hosen and shoon,
> *Every night and alle,*
> Sit thee down and put them on;
> *And Christe receive thy saule.*'

EVARRA AND HIS GODS

The gods here described have no place in any special pantheon, but are such as are commonly made and worshipped by the common folk of India. The god of 'gold and pearl' might be made by a rich man after the likeness of the god or goddess to which his family was specially devoted. Indian peasants often make idols out of any peculiarly shaped stone, tree, or root that takes their fancy as suitable for the purpose. They paint and deck these with leaves, and then venerate them. It is a general but not universal rule, that whoever makes an idol makes it more or less after his own image.

THE CONUNDRUM OF THE WORKSHOPS

Stanza 6. *We have learned to bottle our parents twain in the yelk of an addled egg.* See the subject of

BARRACK-ROOM BALLADS

'blastoderms' in any work on embryology, or 'The Conversion of Aurelian M'Goggin' in *Plain Tales from the Hills*.

THE LEGENDS OF EVIL

The second of these two poems follows very closely a Mohammedan legend recorded by John Lockwood Kipling in *Beast and Man in India* (chap. iv.). In consequence of the donkey having introduced the devil into the ark, though the fault should obviously be ascribed to Hazat Nuh (Noah), the stubborn animal's descendants are compelled to bray whenever they see the Father of Evil.

The former poem touches on a common Indian belief that monkeys could speak if they chose. Hanuman, the Hindoo monkey god, is thought by many scholars to be meant to represent the aboriginal tribes of southern India.

THE ENGLISH FLAG

On 27th March, 1891, during an important trial of Irish political agitators, the court-house at Cork caught fire. Political feeling at the time was at fever-heat, and the crowds outside the building laughed and cheered as the building burned, especially when the flagstaff fell with the Union Jack still flying from it. The crowd, in the words of the *Times* correspondent, 'seemed to see significance in the incident.' If so, they must a few days later have been impressed by

AND OTHER VERSES

the fact that, when the ruins were examined, the flag was found uninjured, though the flagstaff and halliards had been destroyed. It had been caught in falling in an unburnt angle of the wall.

Stanza 3. *Bergen.* A Norwegian port of call for the Dundee whalers.

Disko. An island off the west coast of Greenland.

The Dogger. A shoal off the coast of Northumberland, ranking next to the Newfoundland Banks as a fishing-ground for cod.

Stanza 5. The *musk-ox* ranges farther north than any other land animal except the polar bear.

Stanza 6. *The Virgins.* A group of islands, mostly British, in the West Indies.

Sea-egg. The sea-urchin. It may be found at any depth from between tide-marks downwards. Sea-eggs are often vivid orange, purple, or blue in colour.

Stanza 7. *Keys.* Low islets or shoals. The word is used almost exclusively in the West Indies, where it is also spelt 'cays' (from Spanish *cayo*).

Stanza 9. The sunfish is a deep-sea fish found in all temperate and tropical seas, and seldom seen near a coast. In fine weather it comes to the surface and basks, its dorsal fins standing high above water. The albatross, which breeds at the Crossets and at Tristan da Cunha, is only seen in the Southern Ocean.

Stanza 10. *Kuriles.* A chain of islands between Japan and Kamchatka. The name is derived from the Russian *kurit* ('to smoke'), on account of the dense fogs which prevail there.
Praya. A word used in the East for a wharf or esplanade.
Kowloon. A peninsula on the Chinese mainland opposite Hong Kong, ceded to Hong Kong in 1860.
Stanza 11. *Hoogli.* The river on which Calcutta is built. 'The Hoogli once rose and played with men and ships till the Strand Road was littered with the raffle and carcasses of big ships'—'On the Banks of the Hoogli' (*From Sea to Sea*).
Stanza 13. The *wild ass* (kiang and onager) and the *white* or snow *leopard* have their home in the mountains of Central Asia.
Stanza 15. *They bellow one to the other, the frighted ship-bells toll.* During fog steam-driven ships constantly blow their sirens; sailing ships toll their bells.

CLEARED

In 1887 the *Times* published a series of letters which accused C. S. Parnell of being privy to the murders in Phœnix Park, Dublin, of Lord Frederick Cavendish, Chief Secretary for Ireland, and of Thomas Burke, the Permanent Under Secretary. The letters also accused Parnell and other Irish Nationalist Members of Parliament of inciting men to crime for political purposes. As an outcome of the libel suits

AND OTHER VERSES

that followed, a Commission was appointed in 1888 to inquire into the charges made by the *Times*. The Commission reported that some of the charges, including the main one, were false, some true, and some not proved.

Stanza 3. *The surgeon's knife.* Cavendish and Burke were murdered with amputating knives. The latter had obtained information of an important political conspiracy that had murder for its object. The Commission acquitted Parnell and the other respondents of insincerity in denouncing the murders.

Burk—stifle. The word is derived from the name of a murderer, executed at Edinburgh in 1829, who smothered many victims in order to sell their corpses for purposes of dissection.

Stanza 5. *Moonlighters* were men who committed outrages with the object of terrorising those who did not support their political agitation. The Commission reported that the charge that the respondents made payments for the purpose of inciting to crime was not proved, but that they did pay for the defence of criminals and for the support of criminals' families, and compensated men who had been injured while committing crimes.

Stanza 6. *They only said 'intimidate,' and talked and went away.* The Commission reported that the respondents did not incite to crime but incited to intimidation, and that the consequence of that incitement was that crime and outrage were committed by the persons incited.

Stanza 8. *They only took the Judas-gold from Fenians out of jail.* The Commission reported that the respondents did accept subscriptions from a known advocate of crime and of the use of dynamite, and also took money from the Clan-na-Gael, an American-Irish Fenian organisation.

Stanza 11. *Tups.* Rams.

Stanza 16. *Than take a seat in Parliament by fellow-felons cheered.* Parnell was cheered when he first took his seat in the House of Commons after the Report of the Commission.

Stanza 17. *You that 'lost' the League accounts.* The Commission inquired into the receipts and payments of the Land League, a political organisation with which many of the respondents were concerned. It was found that over £100,000 of its expenditure was unaccounted for.

AN IMPERIAL RESCRIPT

On 4th February, 1890, the German Emperor issued a rescript to 'those Powers that dominate the world's market,' in which he proposed a conference 'with a view to coming to an understanding as to the possibility of complying with the wants and wishes of labourers as manifested by them during recent strikes.' The project was generally received with sympathy, though many regarded the rescript as a trick to ap-

AND OTHER VERSES

pease the German Social Democratic party and thus influence impending elections in Germany. The Emperor had expressed a hope that means would be found of forcing the conference's recommendations on the world at large, but this sanguine hope was abandoned even before its first meeting. After sitting for a fortnight and passing some resolutions as to the restriction of Sunday labour and the employment of women and children, the conference dissolved.

TOMLINSON

Line 22. *A Prince in Muscovy.* Leo Tolstoy passed through many phases of religious thought and finally evolved a religion of his own, which he sought to propagate by means of his books and by his manner of life.

Line 30. *A carl in Norroway.* Henrik Ibsen was remarkable for his candid and clear delineation of human society and his power of showing the soul at war with circumstance. Tolstoy declared that he wrote books for the healing of nations. Ibsen, on the other hand, diagnosed the moral diseases that affect society without suggesting any remedy.

Line 49. *O'er-sib.* Too closely related.

Line 74. *And this I ha' got from a Belgian book on the word of a dead French lord.* The Marquis de Sade, a writer of licentious novels of a peculiarly offensive type.

Line 85. *Empusa,* in Greek mythology, was a goblin in the service of Hecate, Queen of Hell.

BARRACK-ROOM BALLADS

THE LONG TRAIL
(L'ENVOI)

Stanza 2. *The Tents of Shem.* Noah blessed Japheth (from whom, according to the old school of ethnologists, the European races are descended) by promising that he should 'dwell in the tents of Shem' and have Canaan (the reputed ancestor of the negro races) for his servant. See Genesis ix. 27.

Stanza 3. *The Golden Gate.* The entrance to San Francisco harbour.

Bluffs. (See note, 'Rhyme of the Three Sealers,' line 54, p. 127.)

Stanza 4. A *beam-sea* is a swell parallel to a ship's course. Such a swell causes a ship to roll. She will pitch when the course of the swell is at right angles to her own course.

A *tramp* steamer is a cargo steamer that, unlike a liner, is not confined to a trade between a definite series of ports, but tramps the sea picking up a cargo wherever she can.

With her load-line over her hatch. The load-line is the Plimsoll mark, a line on a ship's side to mark the depth to which her proper cargo causes her to sink. A ship's *hatch*, the opening to her hold, is above the level of the deck. As the load-line is normally at or just above the water-line, a roll that brings it above the level of the hatch would occur only in a very heavy sea.

AND OTHER VERSES

Dago. The seaman recognises three classes of races apart from British and American—Dutchmen, Dagoes, and niggers. All Teutonic and Slavonic races are lumped together as Dutchmen or 'square-heads.' Frenchmen, Spaniards, Italians, and all Levantines are Dagoes. The remainder of the races of the world are classed as niggers. Dago is a corruption of the common Spanish and Portuguese name 'Diego.'

Stanza 5.
There be triple ways to take, of the eagle or the snake,
Or the way of a man with a maid.

Cf. Proverbs xxx. 18 and 19: 'There be three things which are too wonderful for me, yea, four which I know not: The way of an eagle in the air; the way of a serpent upon a rock; the way of a ship in the midst of the sea; and the way of a man with a maid.'

The North-east Trade. The wind that blows regularly from 35° north of the equator to 3°N. South of the equator the direction of the trade wind is south-east.

Racing screw. (See note, 'Ballad of the "Bolivar",' stanza 6, p. 77.)

Ships it green. (See note, 'Ballad of the "Bolivar",' stanza 9, p. 78.)

'Scends. Drops down the slope of a wave that has passed.

Stanza 6. This stanza describes the last moments

at the wharf side of a vessel that is on the point of departure. The *Blue Peter*, a blue flag with a white square in the centre, is hoisted at the foremast head to notify all concerned that the ship is about to sail. The funnels quiver with the pressure of the as-yet-unused steam that from time to time must be let off through the safety-valve. The last crates of cargo are taken on board. Then the gang-planks by which passengers have come aboard are hoisted up and in. The ship is warped through the dock gates. The second mate, at the stern, signals 'all clear aft,' *i. e.* that all hawsers have been cast off and the last connection with the land has been severed.

Fenders. Bundles of rope or baulks of timber suspended from the ship's rails to protect her side from contact with the wharf.

Derricks. Spars that serve the purpose of cranes to lift cargo from the wharf and lower it into the ship's hold.

Tackle. The rope suspended from a pulley at the head of the derrick. It has a hook at the lower end to catch the slings in which the crates are placed.

The fall rope. The other end of the rope which passes from the pulley to the winch which supplies the hoisting power.

Sheave. The wheel of the pulley over which the fall rope runs.

Hawsers. Heavy rope cables.

Warp. Move a vessel by hauling on ropes or

AND OTHER VERSES

hawsers attached to some fixed object, such as a buoy, an anchor, or a bollard on a wharf.

Stanza 7. In this stanza, after being delayed by river-fog, during which the pilot has to feel his way by having a man in the chains to take soundings with the lead, the ship passes out of the Thames. The *Lower Hope* is just below Gravesend and Tilbury. It is the last reach through which an outward bound vessel will pass, for below it the river broadens out into the Thames estuary. As soon as the Lower Hope is passed the *Gunfleet Sands*, which skirt the Essex coast to the north-east, come into view, and the *Mouse*, a lightship almost in mid-stream, is right ahead. The ship passes this, rounds the North Foreland, and comes into view of the *Gull Light*, which is between the Goodwin Sands and the coast of Kent.

Sirens. A ship's steam whistle is ironically called a siren, because the noise it makes is exceedingly unmusical. It is blown constantly during a fog. Near a harbour mouth, in foggy weather, sirens may be heard in all directions.

Lead. A weight attached to a line marked off into fathoms with pieces of leather, rag, and twine. The lead is dropped overboard by a seaman, who ascertains the depth by seeing how much line he must pay out to allow the lead to reach bottom, and calls out the result to the pilot. The ship goes at her slowest speed when it is necessary to take soundings. The working of the 'dipsy' (*i. e.* deep-sea) lead is more elaborate.

BARRACK-ROOM BALLADS

Stanza 8. *The scared whale flukes in flame.* Under certain conditions the sea gleams with myriad sparks of phosphorous wherever it is disturbed, such as where the wave rises from the ship's bows, in the white water churned up by the propeller, in the wake of the porpoises that play about the ship's bows, or in the splash made by a whale when in diving it throws its 'flukes' —the whaler's name for its tail—into the air.

Taut with the dew. The effect of moisture on ropes is to tighten them. Dew is always heavier at sea than on land, and in the tropics heavier than in the temperate regions.

Stanza 8. *Comb*—break. A comber is a wave that breaks not on a shoal or rock but by its own weight in deep water.

Stanza 9. *The Foreland*—a point on the coast of Kent. *The Start*—a point on the south coast of Devonshire. From the Foreland to the Start is practically the whole length of the English Channel.

The Seven Seas

TO THE CITY OF BOMBAY

Stanza 8. *'Mother of cities to me.'* Rudyard Kipling was born in the city of Bombay, where his father, John Lockwood Kipling, the illustrator of *Kim* and *The Second Jungle Book*, was in charge of the Art School. When Rudyard Kipling was ten years old his father was appointed curator of the museum at Lahore, the museum visited by the Tibetan lama in the first chapter of *Kim*.

Stanza 10. *Touch and remit.* Homage is paid by native princes in India by the offer of gold mohurs, which the Viceroy or his representative merely touches as a sign that he accepts the spirit of the tribute.

A SONG OF THE ENGLISH

Stanza 1. *Fair is our lot—O goodly is our heritage!* Cf. Psalm xvi. 7 (Prayer Book version): 'The lot is fallen unto me in a fair ground: yea, I have a goodly heritage.'

THE COASTWISE LIGHTS

Stanza 1. *Spindrift.* Spray blown from the crests of waves.

THE SEVEN SEAS

Skerry. A rock scarcely large enough to be called an island.

Voe. An inlet or creek, a term used in the Shetlands.

Stanza 2. *Siren.* (See note, 'The Three-Decker,' stanza 8, p. 165.)

By day the dipping house-flag and by night the rocket's trail. Vessels, not fitted with wireless telegraphy, who wish their owners to know their position signal to some lighthouse that is in telegraphic communication with the shore; in the day-time by showing their house-flag, the recognised flag of their owners, and at night-time by coloured rockets.

Stanza 4. *Clippers* (see note, 'The Mary Gloster,' line 31, p. 168). A clipper under full sail is one of the most beautiful sights at sea, and a *cargo-tank*, or vessel in the design of which the utmost possible cargo capacity was made the first consideration, is one of the least beautiful.

THE SONG OF THE DEAD
PRELUDE

Hide-stripped sledges. When all better food is exhausted, hide or leather, shredded and soaked, can be eaten as a last resource.

The warrigal. The Australian dingo or wild dog.

Sere river-courses. Rivers in the Australian interior run only after heavy rain. For the greater part of the year they are nothing better than chains of stagnant ponds, some of which are far apart, and between these their beds are as dusty and dry as a parade-ground.

Kloof. African-Dutch for a deep rocky ravine.

The Barrens. The vast tracks of land in the north of Canada where no timber will grow. They are ranged by herds of caribou (reindeer) and musk-ox.

Wolverine. An animal of the weasel kind; the American glutton or carcajou, found in Arctic Canada. It is exceptionally bold and exceptionally cunning. It robs traps of the animals snared in them, and robs the caches, or stores of food made by hunters. It will steal things that are of no possible use to it, and has been known to rob a hut of blankets, kettles, axes, and knives.

I

On the sand-drift—on the veldt-side—in the fern scrub. Sand-drifts are a feature of the Australian deserts. South African plains are called veldt. The fern scrub is found in New Zealand.

When Drake went down to the Horn. On his famous voyage round the world Drake sailed through Magellan Straits, but strong winds afterwards blew him southwards as far as Cape Horn. His discovery of this cape was of immense political importance. If the Magellan Straits had been the only gate to the Pacific, Spain might have held it for long against all

THE SEVEN SEAS

comers, but she could not hold the open sea that Drake found beyond the Horn. Drake's voyage was far more than a mere privateering expedition, more even than a voyage of exploration. It was England's refutation of Spain's claim to exclusive rights in the Pacific, and an assertion that wherever an English keel could float was English water.

II

Sheering gull. The flight of a sea-gull is very curious. It flies for the most part in broad circles, but every now and again suddenly swerves or 'sheers off' to one side.

The Ducies. One of the uttermost outposts of the British Empire. They form part of the Paumotu Archipelago in the South Pacific, and lie about midway between New Zealand and South America.

The Swin. The Channel by which ships outward bound from London reach the North Sea.

Golden Hind. The 100-ton galleon, first named the *Pelican*, that served as flagship of the fleet with which Drake embarked on his voyage round the world, and the only one of his five ships that completed the voyage.

THE DEEP-SEA CABLES

The wrecks dissolve above us. Ships that founder in very deep water are said never to reach the bottom of the sea, because the water at great depths, owing to the weight above it, has a density greater than

THE SEVEN SEAS

that of the materials of which ships are made. They hang midway between the surface and the uttermost deeps.

THE SONG OF THE SONS

From the whine of a dying man, from the snarl of a wolf-pack freed,
Turn and the world is thine.

The reference is to the Irish party and to the waning political influence of the late W. E. Gladstone.

THE SONG OF THE CITIES

BOMBAY. *Royal and Dower Royal.* The town of Bombay was founded by a king. It passed into British hands as part of the dowry of the Infanta Catherine of Portugal on her marriage to Charles II.

CALCUTTA. *The sea-captain.* Calcutta was founded in 1686 by Job Charnock, a merchant seaman who became an 'agent' in the service of the East India Company. The town was sacked by Suraj-ud-Dowlah in 1756 and held by him until recaptured by Clive six months later. It is built on silt thrown up by the river Hoogli, and thus typifies foreign dominion in Asia—power on an insecure foundation. The site of Calcutta was chosen by Charnock for its military and commercial rather than its sanitary advantages. (For a vivid description of the lack of these see 'The City of Dreadful Night' in *From Sea to Sea*.) The Nilghai quotes a song about Charnock in chapter viii.

THE SEVEN SEAS

of *The Light that Failed*. The author of the song is unknown.

RANGOON. *Shwe Dagon*. (See note, 'Buddha at Kamakura,' stanza 8, p. 226).

HONG KONG. *Praya*. Wharf. The allusion is to the typhoons that occasionally sweep the harbour.

HALIFAX. Natural advantages and extensive fortifications combine to make Halifax, which has never been attacked, one of the strongest positions in the British Empire.

QUEBEC and MONTREAL. *A whisper rose*. The reference is to the trouble between the United States and England that arose out of the dispute as to the boundary between Venezuela and British Guiana.

CAPE TOWN was founded by the Dutch in 1652, captured by the British in 1795, handed over to the Batavian Government in 1803, recaptured by the British in 1806, and finally ceded outright to the British by Holland in 1814. The Lion's Head, a spur, over 2000 feet high, of Table Mountain, overhangs the town. British dominion extends from Cape Town northwards to Tanganyika. Had not the territory north of Tanganyika, which was ceded by the Congo State to Britain, been abandoned to Germany in 1890, British dominion would now extend without a break from Cape Town to Cairo.

BRISBANE. *Stirp*—family. *Suffer a little*. A large part of Brisbane was destroyed by floods in 1893. The whole of Queensland at that time, and for

THE SEVEN SEAS

years afterwards, suffered from acute financial depression.

HOBART. *Man's love first found me; man's hate made me Hell.* The legend is that Abel Tasman, who discovered Hobart, had undertaken his voyage for love of the daughter of Anthony Van Dieman, governor of Batavia. It was first used as a penal settlement for the most unmanageable of the convicts from Sydney.

ENGLAND'S ANSWER

Draw now the threefold knot firm on the ninefold bands. The threefold knot is the Union of England, Scotland, and Ireland, typified by the rose, thistle, and shamrock in the Royal Arms. The ninefold bands are (1) Canada, (2) Australia, (3) South Africa, (4) New Zealand, (5) India, (6) the West Indies, (7) Newfoundland, (8) the Tropical Dependencies in the East, and (9) the South Sea Islands.

This for the waxen Heath, and that for the Wattle-bloom,
This for the Maple-leaf, and that for the southern Broom.

The heath, the wattle, the maple, and the broom are characteristic of South Africa, Australia, Canada, and New Zealand respectively.

THE FIRST CHANTEY

A Chantey is a song sung by sailors while at heavy work so that they may haul in unison. Most chanties

THE SEVEN SEAS

have been handed down by several generations of seamen, but few have been put into print, partly perhaps because they are generally crudely constructed, but principally because most of them are grossly indecent. In chapter viii. of *The Light that Failed*, the 'Nilghai' sings part of one of the respectable ones, a chantey that was popular in the Royal Navy in Nelson's time, and offers to sing one of the other kind. Some others are recorded in *Captains Courageous*. Most of the chanties have a boisterous and sometimes meaningless chorus. The song 'Frankie's Trade,' in *Rewards and Fairies*, is in the true Chantey style. (See also note on the chorus of 'The Merchantmen,' p. 103.)

Stanza 1. In the dawn of the world's history a man customarily obtained a wife by capturing her from a neighbouring clan, if we can judge by customs recently surviving among the Australian blacks, the Masai, the Dog-rib Indians, and other primitive peoples.

Stanza 3. So far as it is possible to judge, the history of the evolution of the boat has been as follows, First, the floating log giving support to the swimmer, then the canoe hollowed out of a single log, then the dug-out canoe with its sides raised by the addition of a long plank to break the force of the waves and partially prevent their coming aboard, until the boat built of planks strake above strake was perfected.

THE SEVEN SEAS

Stanza 7. In *Lectures on the Early History of the Kingship*, Prof. J. G. Fraser has authoritatively shown how among primitive peoples men credited with supernatural powers tend not only to become kingly priests but are often regarded as divine.

THE LAST CHANTEY

For meaning of Chantey see note, 'The First Chantey,' p. 99.

Rev. xxi. 1: 'And I saw a new heaven and a new earth: for the first heaven and the first earth were passed away; and there was no more sea.'

Stanza 2. *Barracoot'*. The Barracuda is a voracious perch-like fish in the West Indian seas that attains a length of ten feet.

Stanza 6. *Picaroon.* It has been suggested that in using this word, Rudyard Kipling departed from his usual accuracy, and confused the words 'picaroon' and 'barracoon.' The latter means a shed in which slaves were imprisoned until they could be taken on board the slave ships. However, as picaroon means a pirate, and has been extended in colloquial language to mean pirate-ship or any ship engaged in an allied trade, the use of the word here is perfectly justifiable.

Stanza 7. *Once we frapped a ship.* To frap a ship is to pass turns of a cable round the middle of her hull in order to keep her from breaking asunder under the weight of the seas. H. M. S. *Albion* was frapped after the battle of Navarino. *Sir Patrick Spens*, an old Scots ballad, describes the frapping of a ship:

> 'They fetch'd a web o' the silken claith,
> Another o' the twine,
> And they wrapp'd them round that gude ship's side,
> But still the sea came in.'

Acts xxvii. contains the account of the frapping of the ship in which St. Paul was wrecked.

Stanza 9. *The gentlemen-adventurers.* The Companies of Gentlemen Adventurers of the Tudor period were the forerunners of the great chartered companies, such as the Honourable East India Company, the Hudson Bay Company and others, which made the British Empire. Their original quarrel with Spain arose from their vigorous refusal to recognise Spain's right to a monopoly of trade in the New World. Thus when Hawkins, representing a syndicate of London merchants, first took a cargo of slaves to the West Indies, he was debarred from trading by a prohibitive customs duty, until, by landing a hundred armed men, he persuaded the authorities to reduce the tariff. The Spanish Government revenged itself by confiscating two of his ships that fell into its power. Thereafter English trading ventures to America became practically piratical expeditions, and consequently the few English seamen that fell into the hands of the Spaniards were sent to the Inquisition or the galleys. The dealings of the English with the

THE SEVEN SEAS

Spaniards were red enough, but the former would have hotly denied iniquity.

Stanza 10. *A gray Gothavn 'speckshioner.* Gothavn is the seat of the government of Northern Greenland. The highest official there is an inspector, who, besides fulfilling magisterial duties, regulates the whaling industry. Dundee is the port from which most British whaling vessels sail.

Flenching. The cutting up of a whale's blubber.

Ice-blink. A peculiar shimmer in the air reflected from distant ice.

Bowhead. The Greenland whale. Its home is among floes and on the borders of the ice-fields, and has never been found south of the limits of winter-ice.

Stanza 11. *The windless, glassy floor.* Cf. Rev. iv. 6: 'And before the throne there was a sea of glass like unto crystal.'

Stanza 13. *Spindrift.* Spray blown from the crests of waves.

Fulmar. The molly-mawk, the North Atlantic species of the petrel. It boldly accompanies whalers and seal-fishers for the sake of what offal it can get.

THE MERCHANTMEN

Stanza 1. *King Solomon drew merchantmen.* Cf. 1 Kings x. 22: 'For the king had at sea a navy of Tharshish with the navy of Hiram: once in three years came the navy of Tharshish, bringing gold, and silver, ivory, and apes, and peacocks'; and 1 Kings v. 8, 9:

THE SEVEN SEAS

'And Hiram sent to Solomon, saying, . . . I will do all thy desire concerning timber of cedar. . . . My servants shall bring them down from Lebanon unto the sea: and I will convey them by sea in floats unto the place that thou shalt appoint.'

Chorus. *Flaw.* Sudden unreliable gust of wind coming from an unexpected quarter. The trade wind is regular both in force and direction.

Lay your board and tack again. A vessel beating against the wind advances on a zig-zag course at rather less than a right angle to the direction of the wind. When she has sailed as far as is expedient in the one direction, she 'tacks' or goes about and sails away at an acute angle to her previous course. Her 'board' is the stretch she makes on one tack.

Paddy Doyle. A reference to a well-known chantey. In hoisting a sail the work becomes heavier as it progresses, and the pulls which the seamen give necessarily shorter. At the last, when they are finally 'sweating-up,' they can give only short pulls. For these, special chanteys have been adopted. One of these is as follows:—

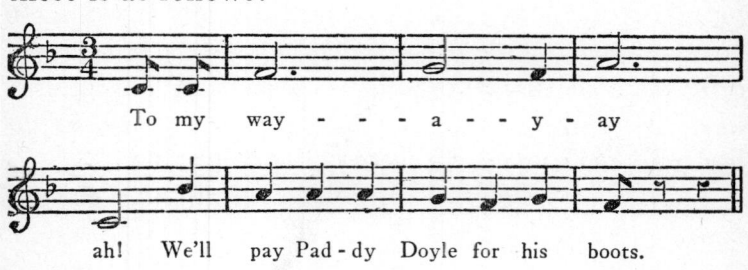

To my way - - a - - y - ay ah! We'll pay Pad-dy Doyle for his boots.

THE SEVEN SEAS

Mr. W. B. Whall, Master Mariner, who has preserved this in his valuable little book, *Ships, Sea Songs and Shanties* (Brown & Son, Glasgow), says that he never heard this particular one used except for bunting up a sail in furling. Who the original Paddy Doyle was is not recorded; probably a seaman's outfitter, who allowed some seaman to have a pair of sea-boots on credit. Such an event would be sufficiently rare to be worth chronicling. Usually an outward-bound seaman pays for his kit with an 'advance note' that no one but the outfitter will cash, and the outfitter takes good care not to lose on the bargain!

Stanza 3. *And light the rolling homeward bound.* The pretence that the victim was robbed in her own interest because she was dangerously low in the water, is typical of the humour of Elizabethan buccaneers. In the contemporary narrative of Drake's voyage round the world, it is recorded that a party from the *Golden Hind*, landing on the coast of Chili for water, met a Spaniard driving a train of eight llamas, each carrying a hundred pounds of silver. 'We could not endure,' says the chronicler, 'to see a gentleman Spaniard turned carrier so, and therefore, without entreaty, we offered our services and became drovers: only his directions were not so perfect that we could keep the way he intended; for almost as soon as he had parted from us we were come to our boats.'

Stanza 4. *Walty.* Cranky, tottering like a sprung spar.

THE SEVEN SEAS

Kentledge. Pig-iron used as permanent ballast laid on the kelson plates and fitted between frames.

Kelson. A piece of timber in wooden ships (or in iron vessels a bar or a combination of iron plates) placed on the floor of a ship's interior and parallel with the keel, to which it is bolted.

Slings. The tackle that holds the yard to the mast.

Galley. Cook-house, in a sailing ship usually a small wooden house standing on the deck.

Boom. A long spar used to extend the foot of the aftermost sail or 'spanker' over the stern.

Mossel Bay. In Cape Colony.

Stanza 5. *Texel.* An island to the north of Holland. The sea here is shallow, and the swell very awkward and choppy.

Awash with sodden deals. Ships outward bound from Baltic ports often carry cargoes of deal planks. As these are very light, to get a load the timber-ships not only fill their holds but stack planks on their decks to a height of ten or twelve feet. In heavy weather the seas that come aboard will almost float these and set them moving in spite of the stout cables with which they are lashed to the body of the ship. There is then great danger of the deck-load becoming unmanageable. Should it shift a few inches the load becomes heavier by many tons on the side towards which it has shifted. It is no uncommon thing for a timber-laden ship to stagger into port with her scuppers on one side level with the water.

THE SEVEN SEAS

Norther. (See note, 'The Explorer,' stanza 5, p. 211.)

Ratched. Beat against the wind.

Crossets. An uninhabited group of islands, far south in the Indian Ocean. They lie near the course of sailing-vessels outward bound to New Zealand.

Agulhas Roll. All along the coast of South Africa, from Cape Agulhas eastward, a heavy swell comes in from the Southern Ocean. The suddenness with which it rises before a gale is the chief danger of that coast (see note 'The Native Born,' stanza 8, p. 121).

Stanza 7. *Vane* and *Truck*. The truck is the topmost part of the mast, and the vane is the weathercock attached to it.

The Dutchman. The legend of the Flying Dutchman is that a Dutch navigator named Vanderdecken beat about the Cape of Good Hope for nine weeks without being able to round it (cf. Marryatt's 'Flying Dutchman' in his *The Phantom Ship*). He blasphemously swore on a relic of the True Cross that he would beat to the Day of Judgment rather than give in. Ever since, his vessel has been doomed to haunt the Southern Ocean. She may be recognised by the fact that she always sails, with all sail spread, dead against the wind—an impossible feat for a natural ship. Vessels that sight her meet with disaster, and those rash enough to speak with her are never heard of again.

THE SEVEN SEAS

Stanza 8. *Bunt.* The middle part of a square sail which when furled is tossed up on to the centre of the yard.

Gasket. The cord with which the square sail when furled is lashed to the yard.

The Isle of Ghosts is peopled by the spirits of men whom pirates murdered and buried with their treasure in order that their ghosts might guard it from looters. When ships pass the island the restless spirits, hoping to be carried to their own homes, board the ship and help to work it, but their doom always drags them back to the treasure they were set to guard.

M'ANDREW'S HYMN

A young marine engineer, known to a friend of the writer of these notes, once asked if Rudyard Kipling ever delivered lectures on marine engineering subjects, as he proposed, if that were the case, to miss a voyage in order to take advantage of them. It transpired that he knew nothing of Kipling's fame as an author but had read *The Day's Work*, three of the stories in which, 'The Ship that Found Herself,' 'Bread upon the Waters,' and ".007,' show the author's intimate and accurate acquaintance with the structure both of a ship and a railway engine, and he had formed the opinion that Kipling must be a Professor of Engineering and that his lectures would be worth attending. This testimony to the extraordinary range and accuracy of Kipling's knowledge of engineering subjects is endorsed by all qualified to give an opinion. No attempt will be made in the notes on this poem to explain the meaning of such technical words as 'crosshead-gibs' or 'follower-bolts.' Such explanation would serve no useful purpose, for they could not be made intelligible, even with the aid of diagrams, to those unacquainted with a ship's engine-room, whereas those familiar with marine engines will not need them. It should be said, however, that wherever he has chosen onomatopoetic words to suit the sound made by the various parts of the engines, such as 'The crank-throws give the double-bass, the feed-pump sobs and heaves,' 'My purrin' dynamos,' etc.—Mr. Kipling shows the same uncanny accuracy that he displays in all his works, whether they be of steam engines, Hindoo customs, sailing ships, or the habits of seals. To appreciate the poem thoroughly, it should be read in a ship's engine-room when the engines are doing their work and under the guidance of an engineer who knows them well and has the gift of intelligibly explaining their different functions. The idea of the poem originated in a personal experience of the author's. When it was first published in *Scribner's Magazine* for December, 1894, it was prefaced by an extract from a private letter:—

'And the night we got in, sat up from twelve to four with the chief engineer, who could not get to sleep either . . . said that the engines made him feel quite poetical at times, and told me things about his past life. He seems a pious old bird; but I wish I had known him earlier in the voyage.'

Line 4. *Predestination.* The doctrine that God has from all eternity unalterably fixed whatever is to happen. It was taught (though not originated) by Calvin.

Line 6. *My 'Institutio.'* M'Andrew means that he has learned his faith from his engines. He borrows the word from the title of the work (*Christianae Religionis Institutio*) in which Calvin expounded his doctrines. M'Andrew amplifies his meaning in the lines (153 to 167) where he speaks of the 'orchestra sublime,' in which each component part of his engines at its appointed time and in its appointed order does its appointed work; in which all the parts are dependent on all the others and perform a task that has been 'foreseen, ordained, decreed,' thus teaching the lesson of 'Law, Order, Duty and Restraint, Obedience, Discipline.'

Line 9. *Race.* In bad weather the pitching of the ship will occasionally lift the propeller partly or wholly out of the water. Being freed from the resistance of the heavier element, it will then 'race' at greatly increased speed, jarring the whole ship and the engines in particular.

Line 13. *A full-draught breeze.* A steamer's engines are affected by the direction and force of the wind, as a fresh current of air in the stoke-hole enables the furnaces to burn freely.

THE SEVEN SEAS

Ushant out of sight. Well into the English Channel, the southern side of the entrance to which is marked by the Ushant light.

Line 15. *Seventy—One—Two—Three.* Ferguson, the engineer, on coming on watch, has increased the speed of the engines from seventy to seventy-three revolutions of the crank-shaft per minute.

Line 18. *Elsie Campbell.* It is the Scotch custom to refer to a dead woman by her maiden name—*e. g.* 'Mary Moffat, wife of David Livingstone,' is carved on Mrs. Livingstone's tomb.

Line 19. *The Year the 'Sarah Sands' was burned.* In 1857 the *Sarah Sands* was on her way to India with troops. She took fire 1000 miles from land. She carried a large quantity of powder, which volunteers attempted to get out of the magazine while the rest of those on board took to the boats. At the last possible moment those in the powder magazine abandoned their task and joined the others in the boats. An explosion soon afterwards took place, and although her afterdeck and a great part of her side were blown out, the *Sarah Sands* did not founder. Those in the boats boarded her again and eventually succeeded in extinguishing the fire. Then on very short rations, and in a badly crippled condition, the *Sarah Sands* was worked to port.

An account of the disaster was contributed by Rudyard Kipling to the 1898 Christmas number of *Black and White.*

THE SEVEN SEAS

Line 20. *Maryhill, Pollokshaws, Govan,* and *Parkhead* are all on the outskirts of Glasgow.

Line 22. *How's your bilge to-day?* The bilges of a ship are the parts between the 'floors' (or frames at the bottom of a ship, where they are made deep and strong to support her weight when docked). Sir Kenneth probably meant 'How is your bilge-water?' In his anxiety to bring his conversation down to the level of M'Andrew's intelligence, he has misused an expression that itself is more often found in popular fiction than heard at sea.

Line 24. *The auld Fleet Engineer.* The chief of all the engineers employed in the company's ships.

Line 27. *Ten pound was all the pressure then.* A pressure on the boilers of ten pounds per square inch. An idea of the improvement of marine engines during M'Andrew's day may be gathered from the fact that whereas, when he was a 'boiler-whelp,' it needed from seven to nine pounds of coal on the grate to obtain a horse-power hour of work, at the present day a cargo ship (built for economy rather than speed) can carry a ton freight a mile on the heat developed by half an ounce of coal on the grate.

Line 48. *Jane Harrigan's an' Number Nine, The Reddick an' Grant Road.* The places here referred to are well known, either from personal experience or by repute, to most seamen, but are not mentioned in any respectable guide-book. Number Nine, despite its English name, is in a Japanese port. A vivid and

THE SEVEN SEAS

painful description of Gay Street in Hong Kong is given in *From Sea to Sea.*

Line 58. *The Chief.* Though the first mate of a ship is often called the 'Chief Officer' especially on passenger vessels, the simple title 'the Chief' is always reserved for the chief engineer.

Line 59. *Sumbawa Head* is in the Malay Archipelago. It appears later in the poem that M'Andrew, at the time of which he is speaking, was on a ship whose run lay along the coasts of Sumatra and Java, and through the East Indian islands to Queensland, passing Deli, Sumbawa, and Torres Straits, and skirting the Barrier Reef. Nowhere is the beauty of the Tropics greater than on this run. Islands clothed with palms and dense vivid green scrub are in sight for days together. The air is soft and warm, but not too warm, and even the water in the morning-bath has somewhat of the 'spicy, garlic smell' of the East.

Line 65. *Broomielaw* is part of the Port of Glasgow, a neighbourhood as different from Sumbawa as any place on earth.

Line 66. *Fetich.* Idol.

Line 75. *The sin against the Holy Ghost?* See Matthew xii. 24 to 32.

Line 78. *Third on the 'Mary Gloster.'* The *Mary Gloster's* third engineer.

Line 82. *We dared not run that sea by night.* As the Barrier Reef is over a thousand miles long, the work of surveying and charting it occupied many years. The dangers of this part of the Queensland coast were exemplified by the wreck of the *Quetta*, a British India steamer, on an uncharted rock right in her usual course.

Line 83. *The hatch* is the covering of the opening in the deck through which cargo is lowered to the hold. It is a favourite place on which to lie in warm weather, partly because being covered with tarpaulin it is softer than the deck, and partly because any one lying there is out of the way of those who need to pass forward or aft.

Line 84. '*Better the sight of eyes that see than wanderin' o' desire!*' Cf. Ecclesiastes vi. 9: 'Better is the sight of the eyes than the wandering of the desire.'

Lines 99-105. In '*The Mary Gloster*' M'Andrew is referred to as 'chief of the Maori Line.' The ships of both the lines that serve New Zealand from England (the New Zealand Shipping Company and the Shaw Savill and Albion Company) go outward round the Cape and homeward round the Horn. Their course for a large part of the voyage lies along little-frequented sea-lanes. Usually the ships of both lines make Hobart a point of call between Cape Town and Wellington, and thus traverse a sea-highway part of which is used by two other lines (the Lund's Blue Anchor Line and Rennie's Aberdeen White Star Line), but the route between Cape Town and Wellington lies far to the south of most traffic routes—it lies, in fact, as close to the Antarctic ice as the captain cares to go. The best chance for any ship disabled on this route—and that would be very slender—would be to 'speak' (*i. e.* sight and get into signalling communication with) a whaling ship.

The shaft of a steamer which connects the propeller with the engines is its most vital part. Practically any other part of the engines could be mended or replaced from spare parts carried on board, but the welding of so huge a piece of steel as a propeller-shaft requires appliances too big to find a place in a ship's workshop. A case is on record of a ship's propeller-shaft being mended at sea by her own crew, but the feat was an exceptional one. The jiggers or small sails carried by modern passenger steamers serve little purpose except to steady the ship in rough weather. Of so little value are they that their use is gradually being discarded. A ship that depended only on such sails would scarcely move through the water at all. An accident to a steamer's shaft forms the subject of the story 'Bread upon the Waters' (*The Day's Work*).

Line 103. *Steamin' to bell for fourteen days o' snow an' floe an' blow.* The sea being thick with floating ice, M'Andrew would be standing by his engines all the time to slow, back, or stop as ordered by bell from the bridge. Steaming to bell is a nerve-racking performance for all hands.

Line 104. *Kelpies.* Water sprites.
Girn. Snarl.

THE SEVEN SEAS

Line 106. *Hail, Snow an' Ice that praise the Lord.* Cf. the passage in the *Benedicite*, 'O ye Ice and Snow, bless ye the Lord: praise Him and magnify Him for ever.'

Line 112. *The tender.* The small vessel that takes passengers and mails from steamers that have reached harbour but are not to lie alongside a wharf.

Line 119. *A snifter-rod 'ross.'* The French for both nightingale and snifter-rod is *rossignol*. Probably M'Andrew stopped short at 'ross-' from doubts how to pronounce the rest of the word.

Line 121. *To lie like stewards wi' patty pans.* At the end of a voyage the chief steward will replace whatever material in his department has been lost, broken, or worn out. Very often he has an arrangement with the supplier of these articles by which he gives a written order for more than he needs, and tells the supplier verbally how much he must actually sell him. The supplier and the steward will then share the difference between the actual cost of the goods supplied and the cost as shown in the steward's written order.

Line 124. *Clink the fire-bars.* Clog the fire-bars with 'clinkers' or unburnable refuse from the patent-fuel-bricks.

Line 125. *Wangarti.* Coal from Wangarti in New South Wales, which would be bought in Wellington for the homeward run.

Line 143. *Spar-decked yachting-cap.* The peaked

flat cap that is worn as part of a ship's officer's uniform, and therefore adopted by those who, not being professional seamen, like to appear nautical.

Line 147. *Manholin'*. Creeping through manholes which are only just large enough to be squeezed through by a broad-chested man.

Line 157. *Hear that note?* A competent engineer learns to superintend his engines rather by ear than by eye. Anything that needs attention—a loosened bolt or a bearing that needs oiling—will declare itself by altering the tone or rhythm of the beat of the engines. On small ships in which the chief engineer takes a watch, it is his privilege to spend his four hours, if he so choose, on the deck instead of in the engine-room, out of sight of, but within hearing of, his engines. The average marine engineer would be awakened from sleep if the engines began to run hard.

Line 161. *To work . . . at any tilt.* To work at any angle to which they may be brought by the pitching or rolling of the ship.

Line 163. *The Mornin' Stars.* Cf. Job xxxviii. 7: 'When the morning stars sang together, and all the sons of God shouted for joy.'

Line 165. *Not unto us the praise.* Cf. Psalm cxv. 1 (Prayer-Book version): 'Not unto us, O Lord, not unto us, but unto thy Name give the praise.'

Line 168. *Try-pit.* The pit in which the engines were tested.

THE SEVEN SEAS

Line 170. *Trip hammer.* Large hammer used in ironworks and worked by machinery.

Line 175. *Declarin' all things good.* Cf. Genesis i. 31: 'And God saw every thing that He had made, and, behold, it was very good.

Line 177. *The Artifex.* The mechanic, inventor, maker.

Line 178. *Scale.* The incrustation that gathers on boilers.

Slip. The loss of power caused by the fact that a ship's propeller operates not on a solid but on a fluid body, in which the screw does not progress to the full amount of its pitch. When the propeller is lifted wholly or partly out of the water, as often happens in rough weather, there is more 'slip' to be reckoned with than when the water is smooth.

Line 183. *The 'Stand by' bell.* The signal from the bridge to the engine-room to warn the engineer to 'stand by' his levers ready to alter the ship's speed. The pilot, who has been cruising about off the English coast in a small sailing vessel waiting for a job, has seen a liner approaching and has lit a flare to indicate who he is. The officer on watch on the ship's bridge therefore warns the engineer to be ready to stop the ship in order to pick him up.

Line 185. *Pelagian.* The doctrine of Pelagius was practically the converse of that of Calvin. Calvin taught that God has foreordained who are to be saved; Pelagius that it is the human will

THE SEVEN SEAS

which is the determining factor in the salvation of the individual.

THE MIRACLES

Stanza 1. *Lost Atlantis.* A legendary continent long since sunk beneath the sea, and now, if it ever existed, forming the bed of the Atlantic Ocean.

Stanza 4. *I stayed the sun at noon.* The position of a ship is always ascertained at noon by an observation of the sun's altitude, if it is visible.

I read the storm before it fell. I. e. by means of the barometer, which gives warning of bad weather.

Stanza 5. *Ere my rocket reached its height.* As soon as a ship comes within touch of a signal station on the land she is approaching, she signals her name by means of flags or rockets, and the news of her arrival is immediately telegraphed inland. This poem was written in 1894, before wireless telegraphy had been brought into practical use.

THE NATIVE BORN

In England the term native is usually applied, by those who have no respect for their mother tongue, to any one with a dark skin. In the British overseas dominions it is applied to any one of English blood born in that dominion.

Stanza 1. *God bless her!* These words always accompanied the toast of Queen Victoria's health, as

THE SEVEN SEAS

'God bless him' is always said by English people when the health of King George is drunk.

But he does not understand. Cf. in 'The English Flag,' 'What should they know of England who only England know?'

The Cross. The Southern Cross, which after midnight declines towards the west.

Of obligation. The toasts of obligation are the loyal toasts drunk to the health of the Sovereign, the Royal Family, etc.

Stanza 5. Galvanised iron is the roofing-material in common use throughout Australia. At the end of the dry season the grass is burnt over wide areas to ensure a fresh growth when the rains come, and for weeks at a time the sky is dimmed by the haze caused by these bush fires. On the great black-soil plains, which cover the greater part of New South Wales and Queensland, it is found unnecessary to shoe working horses, whose hoofs become naturally adapted to the soft stoneless soil over which they range.

Stanza 6. This stanza refers to New Zealand, which is free from long periods of drought and sudden floods, such as Australia periodically experiences.

Stanza 7. On the level treeless Canadian prairies it is possible to drive a plough, without deviating from a straight line, right across a large farm from one boundary to another. Both space and labour are thus economised. The furrows on some Canadian wheat farms are as much as eight miles long.

THE SEVEN SEAS

Stanza 8. Exceptionally severe hail and thunder storms are experienced throughout Cape Colony. Otherwise its climate is fine, dry and bracing, and of especial benefit to all whose lungs are weak. The great combers that roll in from the Southern Ocean and break on the coasts of Cape Colony vividly impress all who see them. At Sea Point, on the outskirts of Cape Town, they are especially magnificent. In the calmest weather they are ten feet or more in height, and break with a splendid roar, throwing their spray almost into the verandahs of the hotels. The swell on this coast is referred to in 'The Merchantmen'— 'the dread Agulhas Roll.' The 'baked Karoo' desert is infinitely more attractive than it sounds. Its climate is fine, dry and bracing, but it is its wonderful blend of colours that impresses it on the memory. The plains are dotted with low ranges of kopjes, between which grow stunted mimosa, wild pomegranate, and wax heath, all of which during the dry season is seen through a veil of limpid blue atmosphere. After the early rains the landscape becomes glorified with gorgeous purple and yellow blossoms and vivid greens. The Karoo is technically desert because of the absence of running water, but the areas that have been irrigated are as productive as any part of South Africa.

Stanza 9. In Natal it is no uncommon thing for white children in outlying districts to speak Zulu before they can speak English, and even the children

THE SEVEN SEAS

of well-educated parents often for several years speak English with the characteristic Zulu intonation, and with occasional quaint renderings into English of Zulu metaphors.

Stanza 11. *Your foot on the table.* It is an old and excellent Scottish custom to drink toasts to those whom it is especially desired to honour, with one foot on the chair and the other on the table.

THE KING

Stanza 1. *The Cave-men.* The Palæolithic Prehistoric Age (see notes on the first stanzas of 'In the Neolithic Age' and 'The Story of Ung') is divided into two periods. In the earlier period lived the 'river-drift men,' whose remains have been found beneath beds of gravel, sand, or clay deposited by the Thames, the Somme, and other rivers; in the second period lived 'the Cave-men,' so called because their remains have been found in caves in various parts of Europe.

The Gods of Hunt and Dance. If we may infer the religious beliefs of prehistoric men from those of primitive people of our own day (see note 'In the Neolithic Age,' stanza 5, p. 160), we may suppose that the gods of palæolithic man were hunting gods, and that they were propitiated by ceremonial dances. The Red Indian idea of Heaven is a Happy Hunting Ground, and the Snake Dance of the Moquis, the Sun Dance of the Sioux, the Ghost Dance of the Paiute, the

THE SEVEN SEAS

Greencorn Dance of the Iroquois, all have a religious significance. Dancing as a religious ceremony was handed down from the ancient Greeks even to the early Christians, who made special provision for dancing in the choir. Methods of hunting the kangaroo and the gorilla are imitated in the ceremonial dances of the Australians and some of the West African negroes. A British Columbian Indian will pray to a mountain-goat to stand still and allow itself to be shot, and the licentious dances of the Bushmen are intended to propitiate He-Whom-we-know-with-the heart-but-cannot-see-with-the-eyes.

Stanza 2. *The Lake-Folk.* (See note 'In the Neolithic Age,' stanza 7, p. 161.)

Stanza 3. *The arquebus*, the father of the musket and grandfather of the rifle, and the *culverin*, the progenitor of the modern field-gun, were not among the earliest types of firearm, but came into use during the sixteenth century (siege-guns first came into use in the fourteenth), when the development of the use of gunpowder was making the bow and the cross-bow obsolete, and thus revolutionising methods of warfare.

Stanza 4. *The known and noted breezes.* The scientific mapping out of the prevailing winds of the world was begun in Germany at the beginning of the nineteenth century, and was soon taken up in England and America. At the present day charts are obtainable which lay down not only the regular winds but the tracks of recent storms and the courses they

THE SEVEN SEAS

may be expected to take in the near future. The great maritime explorers of the fifteenth and sixteenth centuries had to trust to luck more than to science, but it seems that Columbus, before undertaking his historic voyage, evolved a theory, which proved to be correct, as to the general trend of the North Atlantic winds.

Stanza 7. *The reeking Banks.* The Banks are shoals to the south of Newfoundland, where fog prevails during a great part of the year. The fog is especially dangerous in that the Banks are frequented by the Newfoundland fishing fleet, and lie in the course of vessels bound from New York and the St. Lawrence to Liverpool, Southampton, Cherbourg, Hamburg, and other European ports. For a vivid description of the dangers of the Banks see *Captains Courageous.*

THE RHYME OF THE THREE SEALERS

Lines 14-29. At the time of which this poem treats there were about twenty schooners engaged in seal-poaching. They made Yokohama their base, but sailed under the colours of any nation, according to the needs of the moment. Their ostensible trade was to hunt the valuable but almost extinct sea-otter. When they could not find unguarded seal-rookeries to rob, their plan of campaign was to land on a seal-island, fraternise with the Cossack guard, and, if they could, make them drunk and rob the warehouses in which

THE SEVEN SEAS

the furs were stored. It was reported of one sealer caught by the Russians, a man named Maclean, that he was sentenced to work underground chained to a fellow-convict, and fed by means of a basket lowered down the shaft of the mine. His fellow died, and Maclean remained chained to the corpse for three days before he could communicate with those on the surface. The story lacks official confirmation, but shows the dread that seal-poachers had of the Russians. The 'Yokohama pirates,' as they were called, were dispersed or driven into more lawful livelihoods about the year 1886.

The seal-islands belonging to Russia are Robben Island in the Sea of Okhotsk and the Komandorski (Commander) Islands in the Bering Sea. The latter are by far the more valuable. Bering Sea is called the *Smoky Sea* on account of the dense fogs that prevail there throughout the summer months, and on account of the smoke that drifts there from the volcanoes of the Kurile Islands. The *blue fox* has been introduced into many of the Bering Sea islands, where it can be bred more successfully than on the mainland, as it cannot there interbreed with the commoner and valueless red fox. The *kit fox*, the smallest of all foxes, is commoner and less valuable than the blue fox. Its skin is worth from one-and-threepence to five-and-sixpence, whereas that of the blue fox is worth thirty-four to one hundred and ninety-five shillings.

Matka, a word applied to a she-seal, is the Russian

word for 'mother.' As the Russians were the first to exploit the Bering Sea seal-fisheries, the terms used in the industry, such as *holluschickie,* the young unmated seals, and *sea-catchie,* the full-grown males, are Russian. The movements of the seal herds are very regular, and the date of their arrival on the breeding-grounds can be foretold almost to a day.

During the breeding season the full-grown bulls lie on the rocks near the shore, never leaving land till September. The young seals—whose fur alone is valuable—sleep and play among the sand-dunes farther inland, except when they visit the sea. The full-grown males leave paths between the sea and the inland dunes, and the holluschickie use these as much as they like, but should one venture on to a rock that a bull had reserved for himself and his cows, he would be roughly mauled. As the holluschickie are as easy to drive as sheep, seal hunters, instead of killing them where they find them, drive them in droves to convenient places near the beach before clubbing and skinning them. (See also note on the Envoy, p. 132.)

Line 38. *Weighed.* Weighed or hoisted in her anchor.

Line 41. *Vladivostock.* The chief Russian naval station in the Pacific, to which vessels confiscated by patrol cruisers would be taken.

Line 42. *Whins.* Gorse.

Line 44. *Hatches.* The panels that cover the

THE SEVEN SEAS

hatchway through which cargo is lowered into a ship's hold.

Line 48. *There was no time to man the brakes, they knocked the shackle free.* Reference to the notes on the 'Anchor Song' (p. 140) will indicate what a long and tedious process is that of weighing anchor. Rather than be captured the crew of the *Northern Light* sacrificed their anchor and all the cable they had out by parting the latter at a point where one length of cable was joined to another by means of a shackle. This could be done in a few seconds. The brakes are the handles of a machine that in some ships is used instead of a capstan for weighing the anchor.

Line 49. *Goose-winged*, in the case of a 'fore and aft' schooner (that is a schooner carrying no square sails), means with mainsail and foresail extended over opposite sides of the ship. 'Fore and aft' rigged vessels adjust their sails thus when running dead before the wind. The *Northern Light* would naturally choose to run before the wind, as she had no particular course to steer and no object at the moment except to get away with all speed from what she believed to be a Russian cruiser.

Line 51. *The Mines of mercury.* See note on lines 14-29.

Line 53. *Threw her up in the wind.* Turned her head to the wind so that she came to a standstill.

Line 54. *Bluffed—raised out on a bluff.* In the

THE SEVEN SEAS

game of poker a player often pretends, by raising the stakes, to have a better hand than he really has. If his opponent has not confidence enough to bet an equally high stake he retires 'raised out' from the gamble. The first player then takes all the money that is on the table, winning by cunning what he could not have got by the value of his cards. The trick, which is allowed by the rules of poker, is called 'bluffing.' The crews of both the *Northern Light* and the *Stralsund* 'bluffed' by faking their ships to resemble Russian cruisers.

Line 65. *With a double deck to play.* With two packs of cards.

Line 69. *Boom.* The spar that extends the foot of the mainsail over the schooner's stern. It creaks against the mast as it swings to port or starboard.

Line 70. *Bitt.* A strong post, standing upright on the deck, to which cables are made fast.

Line 71. *Pelts.* Skins.

Line 72. *Flenching-knife.* Skinning-knife.

Line 82. *Bend*—a curved rib of the ship's framework. *Butt*—the end of a plank in a vessel's side where it meets the next plank.

Line 83. *Sparrow-dust.* Small shot.

Line 90. *Joss.* Pidgin-English for a heathen god. The etymology of the word is curious, as it is a corruption of the Portuguese *Deus*. The word appeared in English literature as long ago as 1711.

Line 95. *Chock.* A block of wood wedged against

THE SEVEN SEAS

a boat, cask, or anything secured on deck to prevent it from shifting when the vessel rolls.

Cleat. A piece of wood bolted to the deck or the ship's side to which a rope may be made fast.

Line 98. *Fundy Race* is between Nova Scotia and New Brunswick. The tide has here a range of between 60 and 70 feet, exposing miles of foreshore, at low water.

Line 99. *And see the hogs from ebb-tide mark turn scampering back to shore.* The sight of pigs scampering to the shore is a common sight also on parts of the coast of Normandy, where the tide runs out two miles and more and comes in very rapidly. The pigs follow the tide as it goes down, grubbing in the mud for cockles. As soon as it turns they race back to the mainland lest they should be cut off and drowned.

Line 108. *A warlock Finn.* Seamen credit the Finns with magical powers. In Dana's *Two Years before the Mast* a case is recorded of the master of a ship ill-treating a Finn member of his crew because he thought that the unfortunate man had maliciously caused the bad weather that the ship encountered.

Line 110. *Topping-lift.* A rope running from the masthead to the outer end of the boom. As Tom Hall was standing at the quarter-rail near the wheel, the topping-lift would be about on a level with his head.

Line 113. *Holluschickie.* Young seal; the word literally means 'bachelor.'

Line 120. *The sea pull drew them side by side.* Just as the earth draws lighter bodies towards itself, so two ships unanchored and becalmed near each other are slowly drawn towards each other. As the force exerted in the latter case is slight the movement is slow. In the case of a very large ship, however, it is a force to be reckoned with.

The *gunnel* is the upper edge of the ship's side.

Line 121. The *sheerstrake* is the uppermost layer of the planks that form the ship's side. Technically the strake is one breadth of planks (or plates in an iron or steel ship) forming a continuous strip (or streak) from stem to stern.

Line 129. *Sun-dogs.* In the Arctic there sometimes appear to be three or more suns in the sky. One of these is the true sun. The others, which are called sun-dogs, are reflections of the sun from off the ice.

Line 134. *To weather and to lee.* The weather side of a ship is the side from which the wind or the swell of the waves is coming. The opposite side is the lee.

Line 136. *Headsails* are all sails set forward of the foremast.

Line 137. *Sheet.* The sheets are the lines attached to the lower corners of the sails to hold these in position.

Line 142. *Oh, there comes no good o' the westering wind that backs against the sun.* In good weather, north of the equator, when the wind shifts it 'veers' regularly from east to south, south to west, west to north, etc., as do the hands of a clock, following the course of the sun. When it shifts in the opposite direction, against the sun's course, it is said not to 'veer' but to 'back.' Bad weather always follows the backing of the wind. It is perhaps from this natural law that the widespread fear of making any circular movement, such as passing wine decanters round a dinner-table, *widdershins* (that is in the opposite direction to the sun's course), has arisen.

Line 145. *Tolstoi Mees* (Thick Cape). The easternmost point of St. George in the Pribyloff Islands. Of these islands, St. George and St. Paul, named after the ships in Bering's fleet that discovered them, are those on which the seal breed. They formerly belonged to Russia, but were ceded, together with Alaska, to the United States. They contain the largest seal-rookeries in the world, which are carefully preserved by the United States Government.

Line 146. *Shoal water*. Shallow water near land as opposed to 'the deep,' the open sea.

Line 147. The four hours at a time during which a sailor is on duty is called his *watch on deck*. His four hour period of leisure is called his *watch below*. The time during which it is his duty to steer the vessel, which seldom exceeds two hours at a time, is called his *trick* at the wheel.

Line 151. *Tell the Yoshiwara girls to burn a stick*

THE SEVEN SEAS

for him. Both the Chinese and Japanese venerate the dead by burning sticks of incense (called joss-sticks in Pidgin-English; see note on line 90) before the images of gods, saints, etc. Yoshiwara is the quarter of Yokohama where the prostitutes live.

Line 153. *Carry him up to the sand-hollows to die as Bering died.* Vitus Bering, the Danish navigator, explored the Bering Sea on behalf of the Russian Government in 1728 and again in 1741. (See note on line 145.) On the latter voyage he was shipwrecked on the island in the Komandorski Group which now bears his name. Bering was very ill with scurvy at the time, and his crew laid him down on the sand, which soon drifted round him, partially covering him. When his crew would have cleared it away he told them to leave it, as he said it helped to keep him warm. The last resting-place of his life thus became his grave.

Envoy. Constant fogs in the Bering Sea make navigation very difficult, as it is rarely possible to take an observation of the sun. Navigators rely principally on the lead, which gives them the depth and the character of the sea-bottom below them for comparison with the chart. For the rest they must depend on guess work and luck. The islands on which the seal breed may, however, be approached with confidence, as their situation is revealed by the 'deep seal-roar,' which day and night throughout the breeding-season goes up from the seal-rookeries—it is composed of the bellowing of bulls (*sea-catchie*) challenging each other, of the mother seals (*matkie*) calling to their pups, and the pups (*kotickie*) bleating for their mothers. It has been compared by H. W. Elliot, author of *An Arctic Province*, the standard work on the seal-islands, to the booming of Niagara Falls, and to the roar of a Derby Day crowd by Roger Pocock, who, in *The Frontiersman*, gives an account from personal experience of a voyage made on a seal-poaching schooner. The noise rises above the thunder of the surf and the roar of the fiercest gale. As it can sometimes be heard six miles out to sea, ships approaching the islands hear it and can find their way through the fog by its guidance.

The habits of the seal while on the breeding-grounds are intensely interesting. Each full-grown bull has as many cows as he can control and keep. The average is thirty cows to each bull. Some have been known to have as many as a hundred, but weaklings have to be content with one or two. The bulls haul ashore on the seal-islands before the cows arrive. They select resting-places for the season, choosing situations near the sea for preference, so that they may watch for the cows when they arrive and secure as many as possible. Until the cows come they spend their time fighting each other for the best places. A month after the bulls have hauled ashore the cows begin to arrive. The bulls, on seeing them, swim out to meet them, each endeavouring to drive as many as possible to his own reservation. While a bull is collecting his seraglio, other bulls will try to steal his cows and he will have to fight for them. Very often, while two bulls are fighting for a cow, a third bull will come on the scene, seize her, taking the scruff of her neck between his teeth, and drag her away to his own camping-ground. The cow will not be hurt unless a fourth bull seizes her by the tail and tries to pull her in another direction. The cows have to be guarded so vigilantly that the bulls do not sleep for more than a few minutes at a time during the three months that they are on shore. The strongest and heaviest bulls that have won stations near the shore, and are thus able to watch for the arrival of the cows, get the biggest seraglios. Those bulls that have had to put up with stations farther inland have to be content with such cows as they can steal while other bulls are fighting. A comprehensive and accurate account of the habits of seals is given in 'The White Seal' (*Jungle Book*).

THE DERELICT

Stanza 2. *Whom now the currents con, the rollers steer.* On board ship the officer of the watch *cons* the ship, giving his directions to the steersman.

Stanza 3. *The gear . . . answers the anguish of the beams' complaining.* As the ship is not being held to a course, the wind will not fill her sails and keep her yards steady. The *gear* (rigging) therefore creaks with every roll of the abandoned ship.

THE SEVEN SEAS

Stanza 4. *My hawse-pipes guttering wail.* The hawse-pipes are the holes in the ship's bows through which the anchor-cables pass. Each time the derelict pitches, the water will come spluttering up through these holes, swishing down them again as her head rises before the next wave.

Watches. Time is kept at sea by 'watches' of four hours each.

Stanza 6. *Comber.* A great curling wave.

Stanza 7. *Where the bergs careen.* A ship that is being careened (see note, 'The Song of Diego Valdez,' stanza 4, p. 205) is made to lie over on one side. Owing to the fact that they are constantly melting, icebergs lean over on one side more and more until they topple over.

Strake on strake. A strake is one breadth of planks in a ship's side forming a continuous strip from stem to stern.

THE SONG OF THE BANJO

Stanza 1. *Pack.* Carry on the back of a pack-horse.

Tails. Straggles.

Stanza 2. *So I play 'em up to water and to bed.* One of the last duties in camp before settling down for the night is to water horses.

Stanza 4. *Dung-fed camp smoke.* In treeless country the scarcity of fuel creates a problem for travellers that is sometimes difficult to solve. The sun-dried dung of horses, cattle, antelopes, etc., gives, however, a good heat and burns with a clear glow. The main drawback to its use is the labour entailed in collecting it.

Stanza 6. *Rowel 'em.* Spur them.

Stanza 7. *Blooded*—initiated. In many primitive initiation ceremonies neophytes are smeared with blood. The ceremony is still sometimes performed in the English hunting field on a youngster who is 'in at the death' for the first time.

The shouting of a backstay in a gale. A backstay is a wire rope that supports the mast of a ship, extending from the topmast head to the bulwark. In a high wind its vibrations give out a clear resonant note.

Stanza 8. *Hya! Heeya! Heeya! Hullah! Haul!* These are cries used by sailors when hauling to ensure that all shall pull in unison. Usually the boatswain or one of the leading seamen, such as the captain of the mainmast, gives the time to the others. Such cries are usually preceded by a verse of a chantey (see 'The First Chantey,' introductory note, p. 99).

Sign and sail. A seaman has to 'sign on' the ship's articles before he is allowed to sail in her.

Johnny Bowlegs. There is here an allusion to the Cape-Dutch song, 'Pack your kit and trek, Johnny with the limping leg.'

Kit. Luggage, outfit.

Trek. This is a word that has wandered far from

its original meaning. It literally means 'pull,' and in this sense is used by a Boer waggon-driver to his oxen. The word was subsequently applied, both as noun and verb, to a Boer migration by waggon in search of unoccupied land, and has now come to mean travel of any kind.

Stanza 9. *Many shedded levels.* Where railways run among mountains above the snow-line, as for instance in the Canadian Rockies, it is necessary in many places to protect the line from snow-drifts and avalanches by building long sheds above it.

The Song of Roland. This is the song that Taillefer, William's minstrel, sang as he rode to his death at the battle of Hastings. He had been granted permission to strike the first blow, and as he rode forward singing he tossed his sword in the air and caught it again so that the Saxons wondered at his skill. Roland, the hero of the song, commanded Charlemagne's rear-guard in the retreat from Spain. Attacked by an overwhelming Saracen force, Roland refused to summon Charlemagne to his assistance, as he might have done by sounding his horn, until all but sixty of his men were killed. Then he blew it. He fought on till he was the last survivor, then blew his horn a second time, so fiercely that his temples burst. Charlemagne, thirty leagues away, heard the blast, and before he died Roland heard his answering battle-cry. The story of his exploits has grown in the telling, but Roland (or Hruodland) was an historical char-

THE SEVEN SEAS

acter. 'The Song of Roland' is the great epic of the Middle Ages.

Stanza 15. *The Stealer.* Hermes, the patron god of merchants and thieves, began his career of crime on the day he was born by stealing the oxen that Apollo tended (Hor. *Od.* i. 10). He invented the lyre, which he made out of a sea-shell and ultimately sold to Apollo, the god of music and poetry.

Stanza 16. *From Delos up to Limerick.* Delos was the island which Neptune raised from the sea to afford a birthplace for Apollo. Limerick is a town in Ireland that has given its name to a particular kind of five-lined burlesqued epigram. According to the *New English Dictionary*, the form of the modern limerick has existed in Ireland for some considerable time. From Delos up to Limerick therefore covers all time from the most ancient to the most modern, and every class of song from the divine music of Apollo to the popular music-hall rhyme.

THE LINER SHE'S A LADY

A 'liner' is a passenger boat that plies regularly between certain ports. The cargo steamer, in sea slang called a 'tramp,' on the other hand, never knows where her next voyage will take her. She may go to West Africa for a cargo of oil or rubber in January, and in June be dodging ice in the White Sea on her way to Archangel for timber, and a month or so later may be loading cotton in New Orleans or lying in

THE SEVEN SEAS

Rangoon on the chance of getting a load of rice. Very often she is out of touch with her owners, and her captain solicits custom from port to port. The earnings of a cargo steamer plying an uncertain trade therefore bear comparison with those of unfortunate women who hang about Portsmouth Hard by the Royal Dockyard waiting for sailors who have been paid off or granted liberty ashore.

Fratton is a suburb of Portsmouth.

MULHOLLAND'S CONTRACT

Stanza 2. *I had been singin' to them to keep 'em quiet there.* Prairie or bush bred cattle are very wild when first herded and driven towards market. At night time they are liable to stampede at any sudden noise, even that of a stick breaking beneath a horse's hoofs. It is therefore the duty of a stockman or cowboy who rides round a herd at night to sing continuously, whether he has any musical ability or not. The cattle learn to associate the sound of singing with the men who drive them and to whom they get accustomed. Therefore when they are on a cattle ship their natural fear at the unaccustomed noises of the sea will be modified if, above the din of the gale, they can hear the strains of the 'Swanee River' or 'Yip-i-addy.'

Stanza 6. *Stanchion.* Any upright post or bar, such as the post of a cattle-pen or the iron pillar between decks that supports the deck above.

Stanza 11. *An' turned my cheek to the smiter exactly as Scripture says.* Cf. Luke vi. 29: 'And unto him that smiteth thee on the one cheek offer also the other.'

ANCHOR SONG

In this song are contained in their proper order the words of command that the master of a sailing vessel might use in getting his ship away to sea. The process of getting up an anchor varies so greatly in different ships, however, and has undergone so much modification as machinery improved, that many seamen might question the accuracy of the directions contained in this song. Some of the words used, moreover, are now almost obsolete. It should be mentioned, therefore, that all the terms here used, and the order in which the commands are given, have the authority of Dana's *Sailing Manual*.

Stanza 1. All sails being so arranged that they can be let go at short notice, the cable is hauled in by means of the capstan—weary back-breaking work that requires all hands and may take two or three hours if much cable is out, for the cable comes in literally inch by inch. The men walk round and round the capstan, turning it with long handspikes placed in sockets at the head of the drum round which the cable is passed. When the cable is *heaved short* —that is, when all the slack has been hauled in—the drum of the capstan is kept from slipping back by a *pawl* or steel wedge that locks into the cogged wheel at the base of the capstan. The men then go aloft to loosen the sails. The yards are braced *aback and full*—that is the foreyards are braced aback, a position which tends to send the vessel astern, and the afteryards are braced full to the wind, a position which tends to send her ahead. Thus the sails, though spread, neutralise each other and the wind holds the ship in one spot until the work of getting up the anchor is completed. As soon as the anchor loses its hold on the ground the ship will drift. Before it is broken out, therefore, the *jib* must be hoisted. This will make the ship *pay off*—that is, her head will come round until the wind is at an angle that will start her on her course.

Stanza 2. *Mother Carey.* A term of endearment applied to the open sea. Its history is peculiar. From the early days of Christianity the Virgin Mary was regarded as the especial patroness of sailors, and was invoked under various appellations, one of which was 'Mater Cara' (Dear Mother). The name Aves Matris Carae (The Dear Mother's birds) was given to the stormy petrels, as these friendly birds warn sailors of the approach of bad weather. When Latin became a dead language the name Aves Matris Carae became in French 'Oiseaux de Notre Dame' and in English 'Mother Carey's chickens.' From the name Mother Carey's chickens, applied to the seabirds, comes the term Mother Carey applied to the sea.

Stanza 3. Everything being in such order that the ship will be under control directly she loses her hold of the bottom, the men return to the capstan and again heave away. Soon the anchor is *apeak*, that is, directly under the ship's bows, the cable stretching vertically downwards. With a strong heave it is *broken out* of the ground. The work then becomes lighter and proceeds more rapidly. When the anchor comes to the surface of the water the mate signals to the captain that it is '*awash*.' ('Clear' means that it has come up clear—that is not fouled with the cable.) As it is the *starboard bower*—the anchor on the right hand side of the ship's bow—that has been holding her, the ship *casts* or turns to *port* as soon as the anchor leaves the mud.

Stanza 4. Having severed their last connection with the land, the men feel that they are *paying with the foresheet* any debts they may have contracted ashore. Australian miners have a somewhat similar expression; when they leave a mining field without settling up with the storekeeper, they say that they 'pay by the mile.'

Ballast. Heavy material—iron, lead, sand, or stone—placed in the bottom of the hold to keep the ship steady. When a ship has little or no cargo to carry she is loaded with some comparatively worthless material as extra ballast. This will be thrown overboard when space is wanted for a more profitable cargo. As British imports—grain, wool, timber, etc.

—are on the whole more bulky than her exports of manufactured articles, it is inevitable that a number of ships must leave England 'in ballast.'

Hawser. The cable attached to the anchor.

Bitt. A perpendicular baulk of timber standing up from the deck, to which ropes, etc., are made fast. As soon as the anchor is clear of the water the men leave the capstan. Others who have been hauling in the slack of the cable as it passed the capstan-drum then make it fast to a bitt to prevent it slipping back.

Foresheet. The line used to keep the foresail in position.

Stanza 5. The ship now comes on her course and begins to forge ahead. The first thing to do is to secure the anchor on board. When first lifted clear of the water it hung from the hawse-hole—the hole in the bows through which the cable runs. It must now be hoisted *handsomely* (*i. e.* carefully) to the *cathead*— a thick beam that projects from the bows and is perforated at the end to hold a revolving pulley. This pulley is connected to a block now attached to the ring of the anchor. The free end of the rope that passes through both block and pulley is termed the *fall.* The seamen *tally* on to the *fall* (*i. e.* catch hold of it) and haul away, walking aft as they do so—the cable from the hawse-hole being simultaneously slackened—till the ring of the anchor is up to the cathead. The rope that passes through the sheave of the cathead is not strong enough permanently to take the weight of the anchor, so it is now secured by means of a *stopper*, a heavy chain that is passed through the ring of the anchor. As this cannot easily be knotted, the stopper is made fast to the ring and stock of the anchor by *seizing* or lashing it with cord. The fluke of the anchor is still hanging downwards, and this also must be secured. A *davit* or fish-hook-shaped iron in the bows to the end of which a block is attached, similar to those with which a ship's boats are hoisted and lowered, is swung outwards. From its block dangles a rope, at the lower end of which is a hook. This hook is so swung that it catches in the fluke—the process is sufficiently like angling to justify the term *fish*. When the hook has caught the fluke it is hauled up till the stock of the anchor is parallel with the ship's side. The forward support or *guy* of the *davit* is then eased, with the result that the davit swings inward like a crane, carrying the fluke with it. The fluke is then lowered on to the gunnel of the ship, where it will remain until the anchor is again required.

Stanza 6. All hands then go aloft and unfurl the square sails by loosening the *gaskets*, the slender ropes with which these sails when not in use are secured to the yards. The ship is now forging ahead and losing sight of one harbour landmark after another.

Dropping light on light. When a ship leaves a landmark so far astern that it disappears below the horizon, she is said to 'drop' it. When, on the other hand, she comes within view of it, she is said to 'lift'

THE SEVEN SEAS

it (cf. 'The Rhyme of the Three Sealers,' 'And if the light shall *lift* aright to give your landfall plain'; and 'The Three-Decker,' 'You'll never *lift* again our purple-painted headlands').

Stanzas 7 and 8. Soon the ship is clear of the harbour and can be put on her course. The wind is against her and the ship must *thrash* or beat against it in a series of zig-zag tacks instead of sailing straight ahead as she would if she had a side wind or a fair wind (*i. e.* a wind behind her). As the prevailing wind in England is the south-west, it is usually the fate of ships outward bound down the Channel to have a head wind. The order is given to the helmsman, '*wheel, full and by.*' He is to keep the ship as close to the wind as possible consistently with the sails being kept full or distended. The ship thrashes her way down Channel, passes the whirling Ushant light that marks the south side of the English Channel, and sees the lights of Brest Harbour in the distance. Then these flicker out and she is alone in the open sea.

Red Ensign. The flag of the British mercantile marine. It is a red flag with the Union Jack occupying one corner. The flag of the Royal Navy is the White Ensign.

All she'll stand. All the sail that can safely be spread.

The dirty scud to lee. Low thin clouds flying swiftly before the wind. 'Dirty' here does not refer to the colour of the clouds. In sea language bad

THE SEVEN SEAS

weather is called 'dirty' weather. Hence scud that indicates bad weather is dirty scud. The Ushant light is to the *lee* of the ship (*i. e.* on the opposite side to that from which the wind is blowing), because she was beating against the wind when she passed it.

THE LOST LEGION

Stanza 2. *The Wallaby track.* In the Australian bush a man in search of work, or who makes a pretence of wishing to get employment an excuse for living on the hospitality of the squatters, tramps from one station to another with his swag, *i. e.* a bundle consisting of a spare suit of clothes wrapped up in a blanket, on his back, and in his hand a billycan or 'billy' in which to boil meat and make tea. Such a man is called a 'traveller,' a 'sundowner' (because he usually turns up at a station at sundown, when it would be churlish to refuse him hospitality), or a Murrumbidgee-whaler (because when not on the road he often ekes out a precarious living by fishing in the Murrumbidgee or other river, and is apt to tell lies about the 'whales' he has caught). When on the road, a sundowner is said to be 'humping his swag,' 'humping Matilda,' or 'humping bluey' (a swagman's blanket is usually coloured so that it will not stain easily). He is also described as being 'on the Wallaby track.' (The wallaby is a small kind of kangaroo.)

Sarawak. The State of Sarawak in Borneo was founded by one of the most famous members of 'the

Lost Legion,' Sir James Brooke, who at his own expense equipped a ship and trained a crew with which to enforce order among the Dyaks of North Borneo. In acknowledgment of his services, the Sultan of Borneo made him rajah of the State which is still governed by a member of his family.

The Fly. The Fly River in British New Guinea. It attracts the hardier types of gold prospectors.

Tucker. Food.

Masai. A people of Eastern Equatorial Africa, who have a strong prejudice against work. Cattle looting used to be their chief industry, and the robbing of Swahili caravans their principal form of recreation.

Stanza 3. *The Islands*. The South Sea Islands, owing to their warm climate and the absence of conventional society, have a great attraction for the class of man who likes to wear pyjamas all day. The industries open to white men are trading for beche-de-mer (sea-slug) for the Chinese market, and copra (dried cocoanut), pearl-fishing, and, with limits that are constantly growing more restricted, 'black-birding,' or kidnapping recruits for the indentured labour market.

The Bay. The Gulf of Carpentaria, to the north of Australia, locally known as 'the Bay.' The centre of the pearl fishery in these waters is at Thursday Island in Torres Straits.

We've shouted on seven ounce nuggets. In the early days of all the chief gold-fields, scarcity of currency necessitated payment for everything bought locally in raw gold. Small payments were made in pinches of gold-dust—'a nib' (of gold) for a 'nobbler' (of drink) was formerly a common Australian expression —but men who wished to celebrate a lucky strike would *shout* drinks for all-comers with a fair-sized nugget. A seven ounce nugget of Australian gold would be worth about £25, enough to buy ten drinks apiece for at least twenty-five people, even at the highest gold-fields' prices. Many stories are current of extravagance on the early gold-fields. Revolver practice at bottles of champagne was sometimes adopted as a pastime by those who were tired of 'shouting' for every thirsty loafer in sight, and it was a common practice to place glasses of champagne on a dancing-floor, and make any dancer who upset one 'shout' a case of champagne to be shared among the dancers. A wily Mohammedan camel-driver on the Coolgardie gold-field used to plead religious scruples when a miner offered to treat him, and ask that his camels should be shouted for instead: to assuage a camel's thirst was an expensive business with water at half a crown a gallon.

A Seedeeboy's pay. Seedee (Hind. *Sidi*) was a name originally given in India to African Mohammedans, many of whom formerly held positions of trust under Deccan rajahs. Later it came to mean negroes in general. Now, in its corrupted form of 'seedeeboy,' it is applied to natives of Africa (Zanzibaris, etc.)

THE SEVEN SEAS

who work in the stokeholds of ships. The fact that many of the seedeeboys are Krumen from the coast districts of Liberia in West Africa, has given rise to the untenable derivation of 'seedee' from C. D. (*i. e.* Coast Districts).

Sayyid Burgash. Sultan of Zanzibar and the adjoining African coast from 1870 to 1888. He leased a part of his mainland territory—a strip of coast-line ten miles broad—to Sir William Mackinnon, from which concession grew what is now British East Africa.

Loben. Lobengula, chief of the Matabele from 1870 to 1894. He conceded the mineral rights throughout his dominions to the British South Africa Company for a number of rifles and ammunition and a sum of £100 a month, which he spent principally on bottled Bass. He did not, however, cede his privilege annually to raid the Mashonas. His assertion of this right—his warriors actually killed Mashona servants of the Chartered Company's pioneers in the streets of Victoria—led to the Matabele War, the destruction of the royal kraal near what is now Buluwayo, the flight of Lobengula towards the Zambesi, and the extension of the Chartered Company's power in Matabeleland. Lobengula's eyes were 'smoke-reddened' because Matabele huts are not provided with chimneys, and Lobengula spent most of his time indoors towards the end of his reign, as he had become too corpulent to walk.

Stanza 4. *An I. D. B. race.* For many years the chief industry in Kimberley, next to diamond mining, was I. D. B. (*i. e.* illicit diamond buying). In spite of the utmost precautions, natives employed in the mines often smuggled diamonds out of the compounds and sold them for a twentieth part of their value to speculators. In consequence, in 1882, the Diamond Trade Act authorised a penalty of fifteen years' penal servitude for any one found in possession of an unregistered diamond. The mine-owners employed an immense number of detectives, and many of these, to earn their wages, did not scruple to offer an innocent stranger a diamond over a friendly glass of beer, and arrest him as soon as he had taken it into his hand. The detective might even drop it into his pocket unobserved, and then exercise his power of search. Cases are recorded of men hiding diamonds in the houses of men against whom they owed a grudge, and then informing the police where to find them. The methods taken in Kimberley to suppress I. D. B. were so much disliked in parts of South Africa, outside Cape Colony, that an I. D. B. thief was safe as soon as he crossed the border. The Orange Free State border being only a few miles from the town of Kimberley, many I. D. B. thieves sought to escape by racing for the frontier on dark nights mounted on thoroughbred horses. The frontier was of course constantly patrolled by mounted police. In Kimberley itself, owing largely to the methods of the detectives, I. D. B. was regarded as a very venial offence. A genial adventurer once told the writer of these notes that on one occasion, being under suspicion of I. D. B., his lawyer urged him to state frankly in confidence whether he had ever bought diamonds. His reply was, 'If you ask such damned silly questions I shall go to another lawyer. Don't all of us, and you yourself, buy diamonds when we get a chance?'

Stanza 6. *Foreloopers.* The leading pair of oxen in a South African waggon-team, unlike Australian teams that obey the driver's voice, are usually led by a Kaffir boy, called a forelooper, who pulls them to the near side or the off side by means of a rheim of hide fastened to their horns.

'*Regards,*' '*Hurrah,*' '*Here's How,*' and '*Salue*' are expressions used by men who pledge each others' healths, equivalent to the common 'Here's luck.' 'Regards' is an abbreviation of 'Here's my regards.' 'Here's How' is Canadian. According to Mr. E. B. Osborn (*Morning Post*, 14th March, 1913), 'How' was the signal given by the leader of a party of buffalo hunters for his men to close in on the herd. 'Here's a how' therefore has come to mean 'Let the fun begin.' 'Salue' is South African.

The Australian goes back to the '*swag and billy*' (see note on stanza 2 of this poem). Packhorses are not used to any great extent in South Africa, and the Australian talks about the 'track,' not the 'trail.' It is therefore the Canadian who goes back to the *trail*

THE SEVEN SEAS

and packhorse. The South African goes back to the *trek and the lager.* 'Trek' in this case means journey (see note, 'The Song of the Banjo,' stanza 8, p. 136). A lager is a camp formed by drawing up waggons so as to form a square. This camp formation was adopted originally by the early Dutch voortrekkers as a means of defence against native attacks. It is still used in country where there is danger from lions. The oxen are confined inside the square, and the men with their families sleep in the waggons.

THE SEA–WIFE

Stanza 3. *For since that wife had gate or gear,*
Or hearth or garth or field.
The words here used are north country words. *Gate* means the right to pasture horses or cattle on common land. *Gear* means property of any kind. A *garth* is a small piece of enclosed land, such as a yard, paddock, or orchard.

HYMN BEFORE ACTION

The words of this poem are adapted to the music of the well-known hymn 'The Church's one Foundation.'

TO THE TRUE ROMANCE

Stanza 5. *Who wast or yet the Lights were set,*
A whisper in the Void.
Cf. Genesis i. 1, 2: 'In the beginning God created

THE SEVEN SEAS

the heaven and the earth. And the earth was without form, and void; and darkness was upon the face of the deep.'

Stanza 10. *Wrack*—damage, wreck. *Scaith*—harm.

THE FLOWERS

Stanza 3. Muisenberg, Constantia, and Wynberg are villages lying at the foot of Table Mountain. The writer of these notes, having five days to spend at Cape Town after living five years in the Queensland bush, devoted the whole of his spare time to wandering among the lanes between these villages, because the countryside reminded him so much of England. The resemblance would not probably have been so striking to one fresh out from home.

The tilted wain. Throughout South Africa waggons provided with tilts or tent-like canvas coverings are in common use. An old-fashioned farmer likes to use his waggon as a dwelling-place when away from home, even when he visits a town where hotels are available. The tilt affords shelter for his bed and gear as well as privacy when he is asleep.

Stanza 4. The Otway district of Victoria, where the magnificent Australian gum-trees are seen at their best, has been reserved as a State forest, an act of national forethought appreciated as much by mere holiday-makers as by those who wish to study Australian flora in its primeval conditions.

Stanza 5. The *kowhai* (Sophora tetraptera) is a New Zealand shrub with light foliage and bright yellow flowers. It flowers at the turn of midwinter before it bursts into leaf. Parts of the shores of Lake Taupo in North Island are covered with it, and as the season advances its petals drop on to the surface of the water. The kowhai was introduced into England in 1765 by Sir Joseph Banks.

The windy town is Wellington, the capital of New Zealand. There is a local joke to the effect that no man in Wellington is ever seen with both hands in his pockets, as one is always needed to hold on his hat. The wind sweeps down from an amphitheatre of hills, the sides of which are golden with gorse and broom, that lie at the back of Wellington.

The Bell-bird. One of the honey-eaters. Its note is most musical, and resembles a chime of bells.

Ratas. The climbing rata (*Metrosideros florida*) has a profusion of orange-scarlet flowers that make beautiful masses of colour against the dark green of the bush. Another rata (*M. lucida*) is a tree that grows to a height of sixty feet. 'Rata' is from a Maori word meaning 'red-hot,' an allusion to the colour of its flowers.

Fern and *Flax* are the two most characteristic of New Zealand plants. The latter grows in large swampy areas. The tree-fern, perhaps the most exquisitely graceful of all plants, is common in the forests.

THE SEVEN SEAS

THE LAST RHYME OF TRUE THOMAS

What we know about True Thomas—Thomas of Erceldoune, the Rhymer—is more legendary than historical. He lived in the thirteenth century, on the Scottish side of the Border. According to a popular legend, Thomas, lying one day on Huntlie Bank, was accosted by a lady gay, the Queen of a realm not 'in heaven, paradise, hell, purgatory, nor on middel-erthe.' Thomas mounted behind the Queen on her milk-white steed and rode along the road to fair Elfland.

> 'For forty days and forty nights
> He waded through red blood to the knee,
> And saw neither sun nor moon
> But heard the roaring of the sea.
> . . . . . .
> And till seven years were past and gone
> True Thomas on earth was never seen.'

While in fairyland the Queen gave Thomas an apple, saying:

> 'Take this for thy wages, True Thomas:
> It will give thee the tongue that can never lie.'

Two commonplace reasons may be assigned for the belief that the real Thomas of Erceldoune visited fairyland. The first is that he often used to disappear mysteriously for long intervals—commentators suggest to rest and meditate in a monastery. The second is that on one occasion he so nearly died that a superstitious people may have supposed him to have visited another world. He was in an English prison so ill that the jailer, believing him to be dead, threw him over the walls on to the castle rubbish-heap. Here he was found by an old nurse, who carried him away, and while preparing him for burial found that he was not dead.

The Eldon Tree Stone, a large boulder still lying by the wayside near Melrose, is said to mark the spot where True Thomas disappeared with the Fairy Queen.

Stanza 3. *Knowes.* Hillocks.

Stanzas 4 and 5. Under the feudal system knighthood was an honour reserved for those who held land, and were thus able to place a number of armed retainers at the disposal of their sovereign in time of war. So many men of this class impoverished themselves in order to equip troops for the Crusades, that it became the custom for monarchs to confer knighthood on men who deserved it but had lost the means of suitably supporting the honour. Sometimes a monarch when creating a new knight would confer on him land sufficient to support his new dignity, also a keep (castle), tail (property reserved to the holder and heirs of his body), seizin (freehold land), the right to administer justice, a blazon (coat of arms), etc., thus placing him in all respects on an equality with those who could claim knighthood by virtue of the land they held.

THE SEVEN SEAS

There were two ceremonies by which knighthood was conferred. On the battlefield the ceremony was as simple as at the present day, and consisted merely of a touch with the sword or a light blow from the hand, combined with an exhortation to knightly conduct from the giver to the receiver. The other, less common, ceremony was far more elaborate. The prospective knight began by being shaved and having his hair cut. He then took a bath, and while he was in it two 'ancient and grave knights' instructed him 'touching the order and feats of chivalry,' and made the sign of the cross with water on his naked shoulder. The candidate for knighthood was then dressed, refreshed with wine, and left in the chapel, where he spent the night in prayer, his arms and armour having previously been placed on the altar. In the morning he confessed and received the Sacrament. Afterwards he rode, attended by his future squire, to the hall where he was to receive knighthood. Two knights buckled on his gold spurs (only knights might wear gold spurs—squires wore silver), making the sign of the cross on his knees as they did so. Then he who was to dub him knight buckled on his sword, struck him on the neck, bade him be a good knight, and kissed him. Lastly, all went to the church, where the new knight laid his sword on the altar and vowed to defend the church.

Each knight was entitled to be attended by a page and a squire—two boys of gentle birth who would

THE SEVEN SEAS

themselves eventually become knights. A knight's attendant would be a page on entering his service and become a squire at the age of about sixteen, after which he accompanied his master in the battlefield.

Stanza 28. *Birred* and *brattled* are two Scottish words. The former represents the sound made by a spinning-wheel, the latter that of horses cantering.

Stanza 31. *The eyass stooped upon the pye.* The hawk swooped down on the magpie.

IN THE NEOLITHIC AGE

The Stone Age is the period in the world's history before man had learned the use of metals, and therefore made his tools and weapons of wood, horn, and stone. It is divided into two periods, the Palæolithic or 'old-stone' age when his stone implements were roughly chipped, and the Neolithic or 'new-stone' age when they were highly finished and polished. The date of the Stone Age varies in different countries. In Egypt the Neolithic Period ended some six centuries B. C., whereas the Australian aborigines, the South African bushmen, and other peoples were still in the Neolithic stage, and the Tasmanians still in the Palæolithic stage, when first discovered by Europeans.

The scenes of the following stories are laid in England of the Neolithic Period, 'The Knife and the Naked Chalk' (*Rewards and Fairies*), 'How the First

Letter was written,' and 'How the Alphabet was made' (*Just-so Stories*).

Stanza 2. *Troll and gnome and dwerg.* Supernatural dwarfish inhabitants of hills and caves and the bowels of the earth.

Stanza 3. *Solutré.* In the Solutré cave at Saone-et-Loire (France) many relics of the Stone Age have been found. They include stone spear-heads, flint knives and saws, and barbed spear-points, as well as bone and horn implements. They are associated with gnawed bones of over forty thousand horses.

A mammothistic etcher. That there were wonderful artists among the men of the Stone Age is evidenced by the life-like etchings of mammoths, horses, fish, chamois, etc., that have been found engraved on bones and by relief carvings on horns of this period. Admirable paintings in three colours of boar and bison have been found in the cave of Altamira in Spain. They are said to be fifty thousand years old, and it is remarkable that they must have been made by artificial light. Neolithic man seems to have been more materialistic and practical than his Palæolithic ancestors, for, although his tools were better, his art was greatly inferior to theirs.

Stanza 4. *I stripped them, scalp from skull.* Scalping a dead enemy is a very ancient custom, not confined to North American Indians. Herodotus describes the practice among the Scythians, and the

Franks and Anglo-Saxons took scalps as late as the ninth century A. D.

Stanza 5. *But my Totem saw the shame.* The worship of Totems, almost universal among savage peoples, is too vast a subject to treat in a note. Briefly it may be said that a man, a family, a clan or a tribe chooses some object for a totem and venerates it. The object is usually an animal, such as beaver, an emu, a crocodile (as Simeon means a wolf, Caleb a dog, etc., some authorities believe that the ancient Israelites were totem worshippers; other authorities say they were not), but such objects as the north-west wind, sea-foam, and even the ends-of-things have been adopted as totems. In most cases a man will not eat the flesh of an animal that he has adopted for his totem, though he would not object to others doing so. In some cases a man can marry any woman who has a different totem from his own, in other cases the opposite is the rule. Many North American Indians carve the ridge-poles of their houses with representations of their totems. Among the duties of a totem are those of visiting his worshipper in dreams and giving him good advice. Although it is practically impossible for us to know anything definite about the religious beliefs of Neolithic man, Rudyard Kipling is on fairly safe ground in supposing that he was a totem worshipper, for innumerable cases have been found of primitive peoples holding religious beliefs that were current amongst races thousands of miles

THE SEVEN SEAS

away and thousands of years before. The theories among the modern Maoris with regard to the creation, for instance, are strikingly similar to those of the primitive Greeks, and the Greeks in their mysteries used an instrument, the rhombus, that the Australian blacks, who call it a turndun, still use in their initiation rites.

Stanza 6. *Certified by Traill.* Henry Duff Trail, himself a minor poet as well as a critic and reviewer, was at the time of the publication of this poem a contributor to the *St. James's Gazette* and the *Saturday Review*.

Stanza 7. *Allobrogenses.* A Celtic tribe of southern Gaul that came into contact with Rome in 121 B. C.

Our only plots were piled in lakes at Berne. The prehistoric inhabitants of Switzerland lived in villages built on piles near the shores of lakes. Traces of over a hundred of these villages have been found, the most perfect example being one on Lake Moosseedorf near Berne. It was 70 feet long, 50 feet wide, and connected with the shore by a gangway of faggots. The relics that have been found there include stone axes with horn handles, a flint saw, harpoons of barbed horn, awls, needles, chisels and fish hooks of bone, and a skate made out of a horse's leg bone.

The *plot* of any literary work is its main outline.

Stanza 9. *The wildest dreams of Kew are the facts of Khatmandhu.* Khatmandhu, the capital of Nepal, is noted for its beauty, fertility, and equable climate, so that what is grown at Kew Gardens with great labour and trouble can be grown there without any trouble at all. A great spring festival is held there annually.

The crimes of Clapham chaste in Martaban. The district of Clapham in London earned a reputation for piety when the 'Clapham sect,' which included William Wilberforce, Zacchary Macaulay, and other philanthropists lived there. Martaban is a town near Moulmein in Burma, a land east of Suez, where, according to Kipling's 'Mandalay,' 'there aren't no Ten Commandments.'

THE STORY OF UNG

Ung belonged to the later period of the Palæolithic or 'old-stone' age. Men of this period lived a life almost identical with that of the Eskimo of to-day—it is suggested, indeed, that the modern Eskimo are their lineal descendants—except that later Palæolithic men lived mostly in caves. Contemporary European animals included the cave-bear, the cave-hyena, the cave-lion, the mammoth, the sabre-toothed tiger, the hairy rhinoceros, the hippopotamus, the musk-ox and musk-sheep, the Irish elk, the wild horse, the glutton, the reindeer, and the aurochs.

Stanza 5. The *mastodon* was a prehistoric elephant. The most obvious difference between it and the mammoth was that the former's tusks were straight whereas the tusks of the latter were curved almost into the form of a circle.

The *bowhead* is a variety of the Arctic right-whale never found far from the floes and ice-barriers. As the normal life of a whale extends to many hundred years, he has not yet had time to modify his shape.

Stanza 8. *Ouches*. Brooches (see note on 'Dordogne,' stanza 13, below).

Stanza 9. *Trammels*. Nets.

Stanza 13. Near *Dordogne* in western France are caves in which have been preserved a large number of relics of Palæolithic man. These include awls, lance-heads, hammers and saws of flint, bone needles, arrowheads, harpoons, the gnawed bones of mammoths, cave-lions, cave-bears, horses, reindeer, ibex, and musk-sheep, and representations of animals—oxen, reindeer, horses, bison, etc.—either sculptured on horn or engraved on stone or ivory. One of the most remarkable of these is a figure of a mammoth engraved on a piece of mammoth ivory. In one place the artist seems to have made a false stroke (no erasure of a line was possible to him), but the whole figure is far better drawn than most modern untrained men could draw. The proportions of the great animal, his shaggy hide and small eye, his life-like position, are delineated with great skill. On the walls of the cave of La Mouthe are three pictures of hunting scenes: one represents bisons and horses, one a primitive hut, a bison, reindeer, ibex and mammoth, and one a mammoth, hinds, and horses.

THE THREE DECKER

The old wooden three-decker ships are as extinct as the three-volume novel. They became obsolete when ships were built of iron. They were staunch vessels, though. The *Victory* was forty years old when she carried Nelson into action at Trafalgar, and is still afloat in Portsmouth harbour.

Stanza 1. *A watch.* Half the ship's crew (see note, 'The Second Voyage,' stanza 5, p. 204).

Packet. Strictly a ship sailing regularly to a definite destination instead of tramping now to one port, now to another.

Stanza 2. *Able Bastards.* This expression refers to the general tenor of the early Victorian novel, when the apparently low-born hero turns out to have been changed at nurse. Hence 'Wicked Nurse confessed.'

Islands of the Blest. An earthly paradise on the rim of the western ocean inhabited by mortals to whom the gods have given immortality. No wind blows there and perpetual summer reigns. In this case they typify the regions of romance.

Stanza 3. Some readers see in this stanza a punning reference to the well-known tourist agencies of Gaze and Cook and to the Inman line of passenger steamers, now incorporated with the American Line.

Stanza 4. *Zuleika* was, according to the Koran,

THE SEVEN SEAS

the name of Potiphar's wife who tempted Joseph (Yussuf). The Old Testament story is related in the 39th chapter of Genesis.

Stanza 5. *Fo'c's'le.* The forecastle of a ship, in which the common seamen are quartered.

Stanza 6. *County-folk.* The aristocracy of an English county consists mainly of families that have been long established on the land and are called 'county people.' A newcomer requires good introductions if he is to be received into this class. The old type of three-volume novel seldom concerned itself with people of lower than county rank. The works of Dickens did much to break this convention.

Stanza 7. *Lift* (see note to 'Anchor Song,' stanza 6, p. 144). *Purple-painted.* The colour lent by distance to a landscape.

Lordly keeps of Spain. To build 'Castles in Spain' is an expression, borrowed from the French, for weaving magnificent fancies.

A ram-you-damn-you-liner. A passenger steamer that does not care how many small craft she sinks, being solely concerned with maintaining her advertised speed from port to port.

Bucking-screws. High-speed propellers that shake the ship when they race.

Stanza 8. *Sirens.* The Sirens of classical mythology were sea-nymphs whose voices were so ravishing that none could resist them. The hooters that modern steamers blow at regular intervals when

THE SEVEN SEAS

steaming through fog are satirically called sirens, because the noise they make is so hideous.

Boom out the dripping oil-bags. In very bad weather bags of oil are suspended on long booms over the weather side of the ship. The oil dripping into the water gives the oncoming waves a temporary oily coating, with the result that they do not break as badly as they otherwise would.

Stanza 9. *Threshing.* Beating against the wind.

Drogue. A sea-anchor made of planks, oars, etc. A crippled vessel in tempestuous weather must ride out the gale head to wind; if she presented her side to the waves she would be swamped by the seas that would break over her. A bundle of planks is thrown overboard and attached to the ship's bows with a cable. As the ship will drift faster to leeward than the planks, the drogue will hold her head towards the wind.

The Flying Dutchman. This phantom ship sails calmly in the teeth of the fiercest gale (see note, 'The Merchantmen,' stanza 7, p. 107).

Truck to taffrail dressed. Adorned with flags along the full length of the signal halliards from the masthead to the stern.

Stanza 10. *Poop-lanterns* went out of use at the beginning of the nineteenth century.

Stanza 11. *Hull down.* The ship is so far off that her hull is below the horizon and only her masts are visible.

All's well. The customary cry of the man on

THE SEVEN SEAS

watch at night each time that the hour or half-hour is struck on the ship's bell.

AN AMERICAN

Stanza 1. *Avatar.* The earthly form in which a deity or spirit manifests itself.

Stanza 4. *Stoop*—veranda. The word was introduced into America, as it was into South Africa, by early Dutch colonists. At the time when this poem was written the average immigration into the United States from various European countries was over half a million per annum. It has become even greater since then.

THE 'MARY GLOSTER'

In the last chapter of his book *Master Mariners,* Mr. John Spears shows that the history of modern shipbuilding is carefully followed in this poem.

Line 9. *Master, i. e.* master-mariner, the correct designation of the officer in charge of a ship in the British mercantile marine. Such an one is not, strictly speaking, entitled to be called 'captain,' as this is a title reserved for the Royal Navy.

Line 10. *Freighters*—cargo ships. A ship that regularly carries passengers is a liner.

Line 18. *Ran 'em or opened the bilge-cocks.* The effect of opening the bilge-cocks of a ship is to let water into the hold. If left open the vessel will fill and founder. Dishonest shipowners, finding that a

THE SEVEN SEAS

vessel belonging to them is too old to be profitable or in too bad repair to be worth mending, sometimes instruct her master to find an opportunity of sinking the vessel at sea in order that they may get the money for which the ship is insured. The master who consents to the crime must, of course, be liberally rewarded, as he risks his life (and that of his crew) in the first place, and secondarily risks his liberty if the fraud should be discovered.

Line 31. *Clippers*. Clipper-built ships, properly speaking, are sailing-ships built with bows raking forward and masts raking aft. They are designed for speed. At the time when sail was still competing with steam for the mastery of the sea, clipper-built sailing-ships carried cargoes—such as tea from China and wool from Australia—the owners of which wished to get their goods on the market as speedily as possible. The freights earned by the owners of such ships was greater than that charged by slower vessels. Some of the clippers made remarkably fast passages. The *Rainbow* in 1843 sailed from London to Canton in ninety-two days and returned in eighty-eight. In 1860 the *Dreadnought* ran from Sandy Hook across the Atlantic to Queenstown in nine days seventeen hours (cf. *Captains Courageous*, where her exploits are sung). The *Lightning* established a world's record by sailing 436 miles in one day of twenty-four hours, which would be a good day's steaming for a modern P. & O. boat. The average modern tramp-steamer

THE SEVEN SEAS

steams about 200 miles in the twenty-four hours. The passage here, however, refers to fast cargo-steamers entitled to be called clippers on account of their speed. The fastest sailing-ships could not be depended upon to make such runs as those exceptional ones mentioned above, and more reliable fast cargo-steamers gradually took their trade.

Line 47. *The Lines were all beginning.* The Cunard, the P. & O., and the Pacific Steam Navigation Company started in 1840. There was no further important development till 1850, when the Inman line began. The Leyland started in 1851. The Allan, the African Steamship Company, and the Ocean Company began in 1852; the Union Steamship Company in 1853; and the British India in 1855.

Line 50. . . . *And a Social hall.* This would appear to have been one of the earliest names given to the first room aboard a passenger liner which was neither the Saloon nor the Smoking-room—the ancestor, so to speak, of all 'lounges', etc., of the mammoth modern liner.

Line 54. *I'd given my orders for steel.* The construction of steel ships began between 1870 and 1875. Between 1875 and 1880 twenty-six steel steamers were built in the United Kingdom, and three hundred and sixty-two iron steamers. In 1906 six hundred and sixty steel steamers were built in Great Britain, and only one iron steamer. In 1907 no iron steamers were built at all.

THE SEVEN SEAS

Line 55. *First expansions.* In modern steamers the cylinders are quadruple expansion.

Line 86. *Galley.* Ship's kitchen.

Line 128. *Hundred and Eighteen East and South just three.* This point is in Macassar Strait, in the channel between the Little Paternosters and Celebes, a little to the south-east of the former.

Line 131. *M'Andrew, he's chief of the Maori Line.* From 'M'Andrew's Hymn' it appears that M'Andrew was once third engineer on the *Mary Gloster;* later he was on a ship running out to New Zealand via the Cape and homewards round the Horn.

Line 141. *In Ballast*—without cargo. Steamers are ballasted with water in tanks (see note on 'Anchor Song,' stanza 4, p. 142). *A lively ship*—a ship that rolls and pitches a good deal.

Line 145. *'Ouse-flag.* The flag of Sir Anthony's Company—presumably bearing the device of a Red Ox.

Line 174. *But I wouldn't trust 'em at Wokin'.* Sir Anthony had evidently purchased a family vault from the Woking Necropolis Company, but had his doubts of being able to regain his wife from a situation so far inland.

Line 180. *She trims best by the head.* To trim a vessel is to adjust her ballast so that she will float upright. Sir Anthony means that the *Mary Gloster* balances best when so ballasted that her bow is slightly lower in the water than her stern.

THE SEVEN SEAS

Line 185. *That was the after bulkhead.* The bulkheads are the partitions between the water-tight compartments of a ship. As a vessel sinks these burst one after another with the pressure of water and imprisoned air.

SESTINA OF THE TRAMP ROYAL

A sestina is a poem of six stanzas of six lines each, with an envoy containing the author's parting words. The line endings of the first stanza are the line endings of each of the other stanzas but in different order. This form of poem was first used by the troubadours. It has been described as a dangerous experiment, on which only poets of the first rank should venture.

WHEN 'OMER SMOTE 'IS BLOOMIN' LYRE

Stanza 1. *'E went and took—the same as me.* Since Mr. Rudyard Kipling thus frankly admits his indebtedness to the work of others, there is no indiscretion in indicating a few of the phrases that he has borrowed. The title *Many Inventions* is from Ecclesiastes vii. 29, and several of these notes call attention to passages in the Bible of which he has made use. *Traffics and Discoveries* is part of the full title of *Hakluyt's Voyages—The Principal Navigations, Voyages, Traffiques and Discoveries of the English Nation made by sea or overland to the Remote and Farthest Distant Quarters of the Earth at any time within the compass of these 1600 Yeares.* The words *their lawful*

THE SEVEN SEAS

occasions come in the general prayer for those at sea in which security is prayed for 'such as pass on the seas upon their lawful occasions'—a prayer obviously designed to exclude pirates. *Captains Courageous* is from Mary Ambree, *Reliques of Ancient English Poetry*, vol. ii., where the words are spelt 'captaines couragious.' *A Fleet in Being* was a phrase coined by Admiral the Earl of Torrington. In a despatch to the Council of Regency in 1690 he said that 'whilst we had a fleet in being they (the French) would not dare to make an attempt' to invade. The phrase has come to have a technical meaning, and is applied to a fleet that has a certain definite degree of efficiency. The key to the origin of the title *Rewards and Fairies* is given in the first story of Puck of Pook's Hill. Puck sings a song, the first line of which (though he would not sing it, as he had an objection to the word 'fairies') runs 'Farewell Rewards and Fairies.' The song was written by Richard Corbet, poet, bishop, and boon companion of Ben Jonson. It would be impossible to catalogue all the government reports, journals of learned societies, old records, etc., from which Mr. Rudyard Kipling has drawn the material for his stories.

'BACK TO THE ARMY AGAIN'

In the British army a man who has served his time 'with the colours,' that is, has undergone a period of service with his regiment, either in barracks or on active service, is transferred from the active list to the reserve. In the reserve he is free to follow whatever occupation he likes and to live where he likes, his only obligation being that he must return to his regiment and his former duties when called upon in a time of emergency. While in the reserve he draws pay at the rate of 4d. a day. In some circumstances a man is allowed to continue with the colours instead of joining the reserve, but as a rule he is transferred whether he wishes it or not. The theory underlying this regulation is that by keeping men with the colours for short periods only, and then compelling them to give place to fresh recruits, the largest possible amount of men are trained to arms at a minimum cost. A man is not allowed to re-enlist, for by doing so he upsets the purpose of the regulation. If he does re-enlist, therefore, he must fraudulently pretend that he has not served before.

Stanza 1. *Ticky.* Lousy.

Goose-step. The first drill taught to a recruit. He has to stand on one leg holding out the other in front of him until at the word of command he lowers the latter and raises the former. The purpose of the drill is to teach him to balance himself properly on his feet as a first step towards teaching him to march in a soldier-like fashion instead of shambling and shuffling. A man undergoing the goose-step drill is apt to look supremely ridiculous.

Stanza 2. *Back pay.* A lump sum of money

THE SEVEN SEAS

given to a man on leaving the colours with which to tide over the time between the cessation of his pay as a soldier on the active list and his finding some civilian employment.

Right about turn. This apparently simple action needs three definite movements—(1) the right foot is drawn back till its toe touches the left heel, (2) the body is swung round on the heels, (3) the left foot is advanced so that its heel touches the heel of the right foot. No one could do this in approved military fashion without being taught to do so.

Stanza 3. *Dress.* Sidle up to neighbour. During marching-drill a space of about an inch is preserved between each man and his neighbour. When the squad halts, lest there should be any gaps in the ranks each man 'dresses by the left' (or by the right as the case may be), *i. e.* he moves to the left (or right) until he can just feel his neighbour's sleeve touching his own. As this must be done immediately a squad is halted, a trained man will do it instinctively, whereas an untrained man, though he may realise that he ought to be nearer his neighbour, will not know without being told whether he should sidle up to the man on his right or the one on his left.

Stanza 4. *'Shun.* If a command is to be obeyed smartly it is necessary that the word of command should be as short as possible. The command, 'attention'—at which a soldier straightens his body, brings his heels together, and adopts an attitude of alertness generally—has therefore been boiled down into the monosyllable ' 'shun.' No untrained recruit could come to attention by the light of nature, for the position necessitates that the head, knees, shoulders, arms, hands, fingers, and eyes should each be held in a particular way. If, therefore, a man who pretends to be untrained comes to attention without making a mistake in one or other of these particulars, his pretence is fairly sure to be suspected.

Rookies. Recruits.

Carry an' port. Two positions in which the rifle is held. *Carry*—sloping across the body, and resting in the hollow of the left arm. *Port*—held in both hands across the body in such a position that the breech may be examined by an inspecting officer.

Stanza 5. *The Jumner.* See note 'Troopin', stanza 2, p. 43.)

Stanza 6. *Slops*—clothes. A soldier's uniform is issued to him ready-made. He takes them to the regimental tailor for necessary alterations.

Stanza 7. *A swagger cane.* A light cane carried by all soldiers, except such as are required to carry riding-whips, when out for a walk in uniform. Fashion is rigid in the matter, each regiment having its own pattern of cane with the regimental crest on the handle. The Regulations do not require that a man should carry a cane, but the unwritten law of the army does. If a sergeant met a man outside barracks who was not carrying a cane, he would probably tell him that he had not finished dressing himself.

Stanza 8. *'Oo's there?* 'Who's there,' or 'who goes there,' is the regulation question put by a sentry when challenging any one who approaches him.

'BIRDS OF PREY' MARCH

Stanza 1. *Eyes Front.* It is not considered seemly for soldiers who are marching through a town to stare about them. Should a man turn his head to look at something he will be called to order by the nearest sergeant with the command 'eyes front.' In passing some one entitled to a salute, the command 'eyes right' or 'eyes left' will be given. On a long march the command 'open order' is given, when discipline of this sort is relaxed.

Colour-casin's. The waterproof covering of the regimental colour or flag.

Stanza 2. *Keep your touch.* When a number of men abreast wheel round a corner, the outside man has to move faster than the inside man. This tends to make the men separate, and to counteract this tendency, each man should close in to his neighbour towards the inside man, who is the pivot on which they are wheeling.

Mark time. Keep the feet moving, but without advancing. Wheeling checks the normal speed of the march. After the corner is well passed, therefore,

THE SEVEN SEAS

the leaders mark time for a moment to allow the rear ranks to close up.

Stanza 4. *Slingers.* Rolls of army bread dipped in tea to make them more palatable when butter, jam, etc., are not available. The following derivation is supplied by a gunner in the R. H. A.: 'It's like this: at the canteen, when a man as can't sing gets up to sing, the men takes an' slings slingers at him.'

'Tween-decks. The lower deck on a troopship.

Stanza 5. *Kit.* Luggage.

Stanza 6. *'Eavy marchin'-order.* Carrying all the kit that would be carried on active service—greatcoat, knapsack, water-bottle, mess-tin, haversack, etc.

'Alt. Fall in. In mounting the gangway of the troopship and passing along its narrow alley-ways, the men have to break their ranks. Before they are dismissed and assigned to their quarters on the ship, therefore, they 'fall in' or re-form in line on the deck.

The pessimistic note of the last stanza is probably largely due to dislike of the prospect of a long and uncomfortable voyage on a densely crowded ship, and the present discomfort and wearisomeness of marching, halting, marching again, missing a meal, and being generally 'messed about.' Those who regulate the movements of troops seem to find it expedient, in order to prevent any possibility of delay, to call them out several hours before it is really necessary.

THE SEVEN SEAS

'SOLDIER AND SAILOR TOO'

Stanza 1. *The Ditch.* The Suez Canal.

Regulars. The regular army troops, so called to distinguish them from the now abolished 'Volunteers,' or the existing 'Territorials.'

Jolly. A marine. The origin of the term is not complimentary. The sailors gave the name to the marines because they considered that their relative importance as compared with the seamen was as that of the yawl or 'jolly-boat' to the ship itself. Marines are soldiers, either infantry or artillery, who serve on board ship. The idea of sending soldiers to sea originated in 1664, at a time when seamen in the king's ships were pressed men, and, consequently, badly disciplined—the function of the marines was then to keep the seamen in order and to 'stiffen' them during an engagement. At sea the principal duty of the marine is to mount guard in parts of the ship where sentries are considered necessary. His fatigue duties are much the same as those of the seamen. Seamen of the Royal Navy do not consider the marine officers hard worked. The answer to the naval riddle, 'Who works harder, the chaplain or the captain of marines?' is 'The chaplain, because he does nothing and has no one to help him, but the captain of marines does nothing and has two officers to help him.'

Harumfrodite. Hermaphrodite, having a dual function.

THE SEVEN SEAS

Stanza 2. *Cosmopolouse.* Cosmopolitan.

Stanza 3. *A double fatigue.* (See 'The Young British Soldier,' stanza 6, p. 41.)

Bernardmyo. A station in Burma named after Sir Charles Bernard.

Procrastitues. Procrastinators, idlers.

Stanza 4. *You may say we are fond of an 'arness-cut, or 'ootin' in barrick-yards,*
Or startin' a Board School mutiny along o' the Onion Guards.

Some little time before these verses were written a regiment was guilty of organised misconduct and was sent to Bermuda, a very unpopular station, as a punishment. As the staple product of Bermuda is onions, the regiment for a while got the nickname of the Onion Guards. Harness-cutting is the usual method adopted by soldiers who wish to call attention to grievances, such as the issue of bad rations, of which their orderly officers refuse to take notice.

Stanza 5. *Cover.* Something to protect one when fighting, such as a rock, gully, wall, ant-hill, or tree-trunk.

Birken'ead. In 1852 the troopship *Birkenhead* went down between the Cape of Good Hope and Cape Agulhas. She was loaded with troops for the 'Kaffir War' against the Gaikas. Many of the soldiers on board were youngsters who had never seen active service, yet the conduct of all under exceptionally trying circumstances was admirable. The *Birken-*

THE SEVEN SEAS

head was insufficiently provided with boats. The men were paraded on deck to wait their turn to be taken off, and when the ship sank, those who were still on board preserved their formation, and cheered as the ship sank. The report of their exemplary conduct created a great impression in England and on the Continent.

Stanza 6. *The sinkin' Victorier.* In 1893, when the Mediterranean fleet was manœuvring in two columns off the coast of Syria, Admiral Tryon made the signal for the course to be inverted, the ships to turn inward in succession. During the execution of the manœuvre the *Camperdown* collided with the *Victoria*, Admiral Tryon's flagship, and sank her. Admiral Tryon together with 355 officers and men were drowned. The captain of the *Camperdown* was exonerated from blame, as he had carried out explicit orders. Tryon had a reputation for ordering risky manœuvres, and it was pointed out at the time that the facing of risk is an essential part of a naval officer's training.

Widow. Her late Majesty Queen Victoria.

SAPPERS

The rank of sapper is the lowest rank in the Corps of Royal Engineers, corresponding to private or trooper in the infantry or cavalry. During the first half of the nineteenth century there was a corps entitled 'The Royal Sappers and Miners'; it was distinct from

THE SEVEN SEAS

the Corps of Royal Engineers, but its officers belonged to that corps. After the Crimean War the two corps were amalgamated. The primary duty of a military engineer is the construction of fortifications and siege-works, but most of the work to which the growth of science has given a military importance—such as telegraphy, railway making, etc.—has been entrusted to the Engineers.

Stanza 3. *Fatigue.* (See 'The Young British Soldier,' stanza 6, p. 41.)

Stanza 9. *The Line.* Infantry, foot-soldiers (not Guards).

Stanza 11. *Under escort.* Much of the work of the sappers must necessarily be done under fire. This fire is checked as far as possible by an escort of riflemen stationed near where the sappers are at work. Nevertheless it requires courage of a very high order to proceed calmly at such work as the building of a pontoon bridge, or blasting rocks, while bullets are flying, without the satisfaction of retaliating.

Stanza 14. *They grudge us adornin' the billets of peace.* This is the soldiers' point of view. The civilian opinion is given in 'Public Waste' (*Departmental Ditties*).

Stanza 15. *Our Colonels are Methodist, married or mad.* That the Engineers are Methodist, married or mad, is an old saying in the army, the origin and reason of which it is hard to trace. (Their 'madness' is perhaps due to the fact that they have to pass stiffer examinations than officers in other branches of the army.) They are better paid and can therefore afford to marry earlier. Some famous engineer officers, such as General Gordon, have been noted for their piety.

THAT DAY

Stanza 2. *Sove-ki-poo.* Tommy's rendering of the phrase 'sauve-qui-peut' (save himself who can).

Stanza 7. *We was put to groomin' camels.* Withdrawn from fighting duties and sent to the lines of communication, where such necessary but comparatively safe duties as guarding convoys, handling camels, etc., would be assigned to them.

'THE MEN THAT FOUGHT AT MINDEN'

Stanza 1. *Minden.* A battle in the Seven Years' War (1759) in which the French cavalry were routed by British infantry.

Rookies. Recruits.

Maiwand. A disastrous battle in which a British Indian Brigade was routed by Afghans. The Afghans outflanked the Brigade, the artillery ran out of ammunition, and the native portion of the British Indian force got out of hand. The troops were scattered and had to get back to Kandahar as best they could. The battle and the retreat that followed are notable for the many acts of daring and self-sacrifice performed by individual officers and men.

THE SEVEN SEAS

Stanza 2. *Fatigue it was their pride, and they
would not be denied
To clean the cook-'ouse floor.*

Besides parades, musketry practice, and other military duties, soldiers necessarily have to do all the domestic work, from weeding the barrack-yard to carrying coals, that life in barracks necessitates. Such non-military duties are called 'fatigues,' and are exceedingly unpopular with the men (cf. *Many Inventions*, in which Mulvaney's objection to being told off to carry tents gets him into trouble). It may be doubted whether the soldiers who fought at Minden were any fonder of fatigue duties than the soldiers of the present day, but the old hand, who is here advising recruits, is justified in holding them up for admiration at the expense of strict historical accuracy.

Stanza 3. *'And-grenades.* Hand-grenades were weapons used in addition to other arms by some British and foreign regiments during the seventeenth and eighteenth centuries. They became obsolete in the nineteenth century, but were used in the twentieth by the Japanese during the siege of Port Arthur. It was at one time the custom to form in each English battalion a company of picked men to use grenades. The Grenadier Guards have for their badge a bursting grenade.

Clubbed their field parades. When a company wheels in line if one man moves at the wrong pace the whole line will be thrown out and 'club' or bunch in

THE SEVEN SEAS

the middle. Such an act of clumsiness would be a greater offence, because more conspicuous, at a field parade than at an ordinary parade.

Stanza 4. *Grouse.* Grumble.

Stanza 5. *Musketoons.* Clumsy, large bore, short-barrelled match-lock guns.

'Alberdiers. Halberds—weapons that consisted of a long staff that had at its end an elongated pike-head with an axe on one side and a pick on the other—were almost obsolete by the time Minden was fought. They were still, however, carried by sergeants in some infantry regiments.

Stanza 8. *Rooks.* Rookies, recruits.

Stanza 10. *Core.* Corps.

CHOLERA CAMP

Stanza 3. *Nullahs.* Water-courses, ravines.

Stanza 4. Under normal conditions a major commands each wing of a battalion, a captain commands a company—about 120 men—and a lieutenant half a company. Lance in this case means a lance-corporal (the lowest grade above private) acting as sergeant. Eight file consists of eight men in the front and the same number in the rear rank—sixteen in all—whereas a sergeant should command a section of thirty men.

Stanza 6. *Padre.* Literally the Portuguese for 'father.' Applied by the Portuguese to their priests, it has been adopted into the slang of the British army for a clergyman of any denomination. While cholera

THE SEVEN SEAS

or other epidemic disease is about, it is the duty of the officers to do their utmost to keep the men in good spirits by organising camp concerts and other entertainments (cf. 'Only a Subaltern' (*Under the Deodars*), in which Bobby Wick devoted himself to 'comforting the panic stricken with rude speech, and more than once tending the dying who had no friends . . . organising, with banjos and burnt cork, sing-songs which should allow the talent of the regiment full play').

Stanza 8. *'Cause we've found it doesn't pay.* It is a recognised fact that the mind can influence the body in resisting or giving way to disease. As an Irish army doctor once said, 'If you tell a man what's wrong with him he'll get it for a certainty.'

Last stanza. *Flies.* Parts of a tent that form a second roof and thus increase its efficiency.

THE MOTHER–LODGE

The term 'Lodge' in freemasonry means the meeting-place of a branch of the craft. Modern freemasons are said to derive their organisation from the craftsmen that raised English cathedrals and other great buildings during the Middle Ages. When a building was in course of erection a small temporary structure was built close by in which stones, the method of cutting which it was desirable to keep secret, were prepared. In this structure, also, the craftsmen had their midday meals and discussed matters of interest to their guild. This building—the name first occurs in 1370—was called *the loge*. And the term has thus in the course of generations been amplified to mean not only the meeting-place of a branch of the craft, but also the members of the craft who assemble there.

Originally a freemason was taught that 'he must love wel God and holy Church algate and hys master also that he ys wythe.' Adherence to the Christian Church is not now demanded, and membership of the craft is open to men of every creed, caste, or colour. Belief in the Great Architect of the Universe is, however, essential. The Lodge in which a freemason is first initiated is called his 'mother-lodge.'

Stanza 1. *Conductor-Sargent*. A warrant officer in the Commissariat Department.

Europe-shop. A shop in which European products of a miscellaneous kind, from sofas to patent medicines, are sold. Such shops in India are usually kept by Parsees.

Chorus. The *Level* and the *Square* are two of the six jewels in a Lodge's regalia. The Level symbolises the equality of all freemasons, and the Square symbolises the honourable conduct required of them. Hence the colloquial expression 'to act on the square.' The other jewels are the rough ashlar, the perfect ashlar, the trestle, and the plumb-line.

Junior Deacon. The fourth and fifth officers of a Lodge are called deacons. It is their duty to receive

THE SEVEN SEAS

at the Lodge visitors as to whose standing as freemasons no doubt arises.

Stanza 2. The principal races and creeds of India as disclosed by their names are represented here. Framjee Eduljee is a Parsee name; Bola Nath, that of a Hindoo from the United Provinces; Din Mohammed, that of a Mohammedan; Baby Chuckerbutty, that of a Bengali; and Castro, an Eurasian who inherits his name, his religion, and the white element in his blood from a remote Portuguese ancestor.

Stanza 3. *The Ancient Landmarks* are the twenty-five leading principles of freemasonry. One of these is a sincere belief in the Great Architect of the Universe. Another is the recognition of the equality of all freemasons.

Stanza 4. *Labour.* The solemn ceremonials, such as initiations, which take place when a Lodge meets.

We dursn't give no banquits. Mohammedans and Jews cannot eat meat the slaughter of which has not been accompanied by certain ceremonies. A Hindoo cannot eat meat that has been cooked by a man of a lower caste than himself, and would feel insulted if cooked beef were brought into his presence. Sikhs will not eat meat or drink wine.

Stanza 5. *Shiva.* The third god in the Hindu supreme trinity. He is The Destroyer, and as, according to Hindu belief, death is admission to a new form of life, he is styled the Bright or Happy One.

Stanza 7. *Trichies*. Coarse cheap cigars made in Trichinopoly in southern India.

Master. The highest of the three degrees in freemasonry.

'FOLLOW ME 'OME'

Chorus. *Swipes*. Beer.

Note that the chorus runs roughly to the tune of the 'Dead March in Saul.'

Stanza 3. *Bombardier*. An artillery non-commissioned officer ranking below a corporal.

Stanza 5. *Stripe*. The chevron awarded for good conduct during two years' service, worn on the left arm by private soldiers. The right to wear it is accompanied by extra pay daily of 1d. for each stripe. A quarter of a century ago the general conduct of British soldiers was less good than to-day. Then it was exceptional for a man to be able to keep his stripe, now it is seldom forfeited for misconduct.

Last two stanzas. A soldier who dies when with the colours is entitled to a military funeral. His coffin is carried on a gun-carriage and the band plays slow music. Soldiers line the approach to the grave leaning on their arms reversed, *i. e.* the muzzles of their rifles pointed downwards. After the service three rounds of blank cartridge are fired over the grave and the bugler plays the beautiful long wailing notes of the 'Last Post.'

THE SEVEN SEAS

THE SERGEANT'S WEDDIN'

Stanza 2.   *'E's a bloomin' robber,*
                    An' 'e keeps canteen.

The canteen is the regimental beer-shop, open at stated hours. It is part of the regimental institute, and is run at a small profit, which is devoted to regimental sports, purchases of newspapers for the reading-room, etc. It is managed by a committee of officers, but the actual care of it is entrusted to a sergeant. Thanks in a great measure to the efforts of Lord Roberts, canteens are now better conducted, but it was formerly possible for sergeants to make extraordinary profits for themselves by giving short measure and charging exorbitant prices for liquor sold at unauthorised hours, practices which the soldiers' code of honour did not allow them to report.

Stanza 4. *Side arms.* Bayonets worn in sheaths in the belts.

Dressin' (see note 'Back to the Army Again,' stanza 3, p. 174).

Stanza 5. *Voice that breathed o'er Eden.* The first line of a well-known hymn frequently sung during the marriage service.

THE JACKET

The incident recorded in this poem occurred in the war against Arabi. It was not the first time that a battery had charged. During the Peninsular War a

THE SEVEN SEAS

battery charged French cavalry and carried off the French 'Eagles.' Since then it has been known as the 'Eagle' troop, and carries an eagle on the metal work of its harness.

Stanza 1. *Arabi.* Ahmad Arabi, War Minister and practically Dictator of Egypt in 1882, defeated by Sir Garnet Wolseley at Tel-el-Kebir.

The Captain 'ad 'is jacket. Officers in the Royal Horse Artillery are promoted from the Field Artillery. An officer thus promoted will wear a very gorgeous gold-laced tight-fitting jacket in place of the comparatively unadorned tunic that he wore in the Field Artillery. When he is promoted, therefore, he is said to 'get his jacket.'

The wettin' of the jacket. The celebration of his promotion by providing liquor to be drunk by those under him.

Stanza 2. *A sand redoubt.* An earthwork erected to serve the purpose of a temporary fort.

Axle-arms. The lockers on the gun itself, in which a supply of emergency ammunition is kept. The main supply is carried in ammunition waggons, and that for immediate use in the limbers.

Case. Case-shot, a projectile used for firing at close quarters. It consists of a thin metal case containing a large number of bullets which scatter when the envelope bursts. It is now rarely employed, its place being usually taken by *shrapnel* with the fuse set at zero. Shrapnel is similar to case but with this

THE SEVEN SEAS

distinction: case-shot is not provided with a fuse, it explodes on leaving the gun and is not therefore effective at any but short range (four hundred yards in the case of field-guns); shrapnel, on the other hand, is provided with a fuse by means of which the gunner can burst his shells at any desired point from close quarters up to three thousand yards.

Crackers. Ammunition.

Stanza 5. *Loosin' 'igh an' wide.* Firing wildly and without aim.

Glassy. Glacis, the long mound of earth thrown up to offer cover to those in the redoubt. To get a vehicle over such an obstacle it would be necessary to drive it sideways up its face—hence the command 'right incline.'

Limberful. The two parts of a gun-carriage are the gun itself and the limber in which ammunition for the gun is carried.

Brut. The soldiers probably saw the last word on the label of the champagne bottle and applied it to the liquor generally.

THE 'EATHEN

Stanza 2. *'E draf's from Gawd knows where.* Recruits are enlisted at the regimental depots in England which are situated within the area from which the recruits are supposed to be drawn. After a period of training they are 'drafted' to wherever the battalion of the regiment to which they have been assigned may be.

THE SEVEN SEAS

'E calls it bloomin' nonsense. Part of a private soldier's duties is to submit his kit periodically to inspection, so that any deficiencies may be noted and replaced—at the soldier's expense. When laid out for inspection, every article must be placed in a particular position, his clothes-brush in one place, his needle and thread case in another. The reason for this particularity is partly to teach the soldier to be methodical—among the most important of the lessons he must learn—and partly because kits may be inspected much more quickly and efficiently if arranged according to a definite plan than if the arrangement of each is left to the taste and fancy of its individual owner. Nevertheless a recruit too inexperienced to understand the reasons that underlie the regulations he has to obey is apt to feel injured if he is reprimanded for placing his boots in the particular spot that should have been occupied by his razor. Because much of the education of a recruit can best be instilled by his comrades, a whole room full of men will be blamed if the kit of one of their number is carelessly arranged. Should this occur the men will probably find some fairly effective way of reprimanding the delinquent as soon as the inspection is over.

Stanza 3. *'E'll swing for.* For murdering whom he will be hanged.

Stanza 5. *You 'ear 'im slap 'is boot.* That is with the swagger-cane which he is taught by regimental etiquette to carry. It is wonderful how much self-confidence may be imparted to a shambling, bashful man who does not know what to do with his hands by giving him a cane to play with.

Bars and rings. The paraphernalia of the gymnasium in which the recruit has to exercise. Gymnasium exercise is as important as drill in making an efficient soldier; a man who proves to be a poor shot often improves after undergoing an additional course of gymnastics.

Stanza 6. '*Lance.*' Lance-Corporal. As such the soldier still has the pay of a private only, but the acting rank of a non-commissioned officer. During his probation as lance-corporal he will show whether he is fit to have his promotion confirmed.

Stanza 8. *Colour-Sergeant.* The senior sergeant of a company of about one hundred and twenty men. He is responsible for a good deal of administrative work in connection with his company and on parade. He escorts the regimental colour when this is carried.

Core. Corps.

Stanza 10. *He'll see their socks are right.* A colour-sergeant, adequately to fill his position, should have somewhat of the feelings of a mother towards those under him. He should keep the cooks up to their work, so that the men do not have to march on an empty stomach in the morning. If his company is mounted he should keep a look-out for sore backs among the horses. No detail that makes for efficiency is too trivial to receive the attention of a good colour-

THE SEVEN SEAS

sergeant. It was to a large extent the absence of this maternal spirit in officers of all ranks that made France so easy a prey to Germany in 1870.

Sight. Aim.

Stanza 11. *Squad.* Half a section of a company of thirty men.

Stanza 14. *Doolies.* The canvas litters in which the wounded are carried off the battlefield.

THE SHUT-EYE SENTRY

Stanza 1. *Orderly Orf'cer.* An officer is appointed every twenty-four hours to be orderly officer for the day. It is his duty at intervals during the night to visit the various sentry posts in order to see that the sentries are awake and alert, and to inspect the guard in the guard-room or guard-tent. The men in the guard-room, who take it in turn to mount guard, are allowed to sleep, but must remain fully dressed so as to turn out immediately the sentry on duty calls them to do so. The orderly officer's rounds are called 'visiting rounds.' An officer of higher rank to the orderly officer is appointed to be field officer for the week. While on duty he does not leave barracks, and takes command in any emergency until the arrival of an officer senior to himself. His rounds of inspection are called 'grand-rounds.'

Hokee-mut. Very drunk.

For the wine was old and the night is cold. The effect of cold fresh air on a man who has been drinking incautiously in a warm room is often disastrous—immediately he comes into the open he is liable to be overcome by liquor the effect of which he has till then hardly felt.

Rounds! What Rounds? When the orderly officer and his attendants come within earshot of a sentry the latter challenges 'Who goes there?' The orderly officer replies 'Rounds.' The sentry inquires 'What rounds?' The reply is 'Visiting rounds' or 'Grand rounds.' The sentry, if no password for the night has been ordered, then replies 'Pass, visiting rounds; all's well!' unless he is the sentry stationed at the guard-room. In this case he will call 'Guard, turn out,' and the guard will turn out for inspection.

Stanza 4. *But 'is sergeant pulled him through.* Probably the sergeant prompted him as to the proper words of command to issue, took care that the men did not obey any improper order that he gave, and shepherded his officer into his correct position of the parade.

Marker. The markers are the soldiers who give the alignment to the others.

The Five Nations

BEFORE A MIDNIGHT BREAKS IN STORM

Stanza 3. According to the late Andrew Lang, of those who use the crystal-ball for purposes of divination, few have quite the same experience. In the case of almost every one, the ball gradually assumes a milky or misty appearance. Many people can go no further than this. In the case of others the mistiness gives place to blackness, followed by blankness, after which pictures appear in the glass. In rare cases the ball seems to disappear, and the gazer finds himself apparently witnessing an actual scene.

THE SEA AND THE HILLS

Stanza 1. *Comber.* A 'breaker' is a wave that breaks on a rock or beach. A 'comber' is a long, curling wave that breaks out at sea.

The sleek-barrelled swell before storm. The influence of a distant storm is felt long before it arrives. When the air is still quite calm the water begins to heave. The waves in this case are not jagged or foam-crested, as are wind-driven waves, but have a smooth oily surface from trough to crest.

Stark calm on the lap of the Line. A belt of almost

THE FIVE NATIONS

constant calm extends from the equator to 3° north.

Stanza 2. *The shudder, the stumble, the swerve as the star-stabbing bowsprit emerges.* The bowsprit is a spar projecting from the ship's bows to carry the forestay. No one unfamiliar with the sea can fully appreciate the appropriateness of the words here used. When a ship is struck by a wave it quivers under the blow. Then the bow drops into the trough behind the wave so suddenly that the ship seems to stumble forwards. As the wave passes and the bow rises to the next, the ship swerves from her true course (unless the line of the waves is exactly at right angles to the ship), because the weight of water on the one side is greater than on the other.

The orderly clouds of the Trades. The Trade Winds blow continuously towards the equator from each side of it. The North-east Trade from 35° N. to 3° N.; the South-east Trade from 28° S. to the equator. A ship approaching the region of the Trade Winds can see on the horizon masses of cloud that are collected and driven by them.

Unheralded cliff-haunting flaws. Light wind that blows off high land is very irregular, as its direction and force is modified by the contour of the cliffs. It comes in sudden gusts, seldom twice from exactly the same quarter. The 'low volleying thunder' of the sails occurs when an unexpected gust striking them at the wrong angle shakes them violently against the masts and sets the braces rattling.

THE FIVE NATIONS

Stanza 3. The unstable mined berg going South, and the calvings and groans that declare it. An iceberg drifting southward melts more rapidly below the water-line than above it. Its centre of gravity is thus constantly changing, and at intervals the huge mass of ice rolls over in a welter of foam. Sometimes a large mass breaks off the parent berg, which is then said to 'calve.' The rending growling noise that it makes in so doing can be heard for a long distance. In foggy weather—the vicinity of ice is usually foggy—the noise sometimes gives timely warning to approaching ships.

White water half guessed overside. White water is the seaman's word for the foam caused by waves breaking on a reef. (The patches of foam made by waves breaking in deep water are called 'white horses.') On a thick night, cloudy, dark, and rainy, white water shows so dimly that those on watch are often not sure whether they see it or only imagine it.

So and no otherwise—hillmen desire their hills. The charm of the hills—their silence, their space, their peace—'the charm that in the end draws all who have the least touch of hill-blood in their veins,' is the theme of 'The Miracle of Purun Bhagat' (*The Second Jungle Book*).

THE BELL BUOY

Stanza 4. Could I speak or be still at the Church's will? In the mediæval Church the Pope had the

THE FIVE NATIONS

power of laying a country under an interdict, the effect of which was to suspend all public worship, the administration of the principal sacraments, the ecclesiastical burial of the dead, and, of course, to silence all church bells.

Stanza 7. *From bitt to trees.* The bitts are posts on the deck of a ship to which cables, ropes, etc., are made fast. The trees (cross-trees) are horizontal timbers at the head of the lower mast that support the top-mast.

CRUISERS

Stanza 1. *Our mother the frigate.* During the Napoleonic Wars the frigate was a three-masted, fully rigged vessel built for speed. Her duty was to scout rather than fight, and also to attempt to decoy the enemy's ships towards the heavier and slower and more fully armed 'ships of the line' on her own side. When iron took the place of wood in shipbuilding, the frigate disappeared and the modern cruiser took her place, a vessel very differently built but having the same duty—to scout, and lure the enemy towards her own supporting battleships. When this poem was written (1899) cruisers had attained a speed of 20 knots and battleships 18. Since then cruisers of the Dreadnought type have attained 28 and Dreadnought battleships 22 knots.

Stanza 4. Merchant vessels are compelled by international law to carry a headlight at the masthead and a coloured light on each side, but warships on

THE FIVE NATIONS

active service steam without lights. The term potbellied is justified by the fact that the designer of a merchant vessel, other than passenger liners, makes cargo-carrying capacity his main object.

Stanza 8. *Spindrift.* Spray blown from the crests of waves.

Cross-surges. Waves set up by conflicting currents or by a swift current at a different angle to the wind.

Stanza 9. *Widdershins.* (See note, 'Rhyme of the Three Sealers,' line 142, p. 130.)

Fleereth. Jeers at. So military heliograph signallers while waiting instructions sometimes pass the weary hours by flashing chaff from hilltop to hilltop.

Stanza 10. *Levin.* Lightning.

Their lights, or the Daystar. A star rising above the horizon may easily be mistaken for a ship's light.

DESTROYERS

A destroyer is a torpedo-boat destroyer. It is larger and faster than a torpedo-boat, can carry more guns, and can stay longer at sea without putting back to port for a fresh supply of coal. Soon after destroyers came into use it was realised that, in addition to their intended work of destroying torpedo-boats, they were more suited to do the work of torpedo-boats than those boats themselves. They thus tended to supplant the type of boat they were designed to destroy. The speed of British torpedo-boat destroyers varies. The *Cobra* (350 tons), launched in

THE FIVE NATIONS

1899, had a speed of 34 knots; the *Swift* (1800 tons), launched in 1907, a speed of 35 knots; the *Beagle* (860 tons), launched in 1909, a speed of 27 knots.

Stanza 1. *Stripped hulls.* When a ship is cleared for action everything that it is possible to remove from the decks, such as boats, ventilators, etc., are sent below and awning stanchions are laid flat on the deck.

The Choosers of the Slain. In northern mythology spirits of the air named Valkyries hovered over a battle, choosing those who were to die and go to Valhalla. In Hindoo mythology the same function is performed by spirits called Upsaras (see note, 'With Scindia to Delhi,' stanza 6, p. 92).

Stanza 2. *Adown the stricken capes no flare—*
No mark on spit or bar.
During war time a country that fears invasion removes all buoys from the channels that lead to its ports and extinguishes the lights of its lighthouses and lightships. The destroyers must therefore do their work blindfold.

Stanza 3. *The up-flung beams that spell*
The council of our foes.
Among the methods of signalling at sea practised by warships is the flashing of light on to the clouds. By covering and uncovering a searchlight long or short flashes are made, and thus, by means of the Morse code, messages are spelt out. The development of wireless telegraphy tends to supersede this method.

THE FIVE NATIONS

Stanza 4. *Hooded eyne.* The searchlights which the enemy is flashing on to the sea on the look out for destroyers that may be approaching.

Stanza 5. *Crackling tops.* Battleships carry at their mastheads platforms called 'tops' on which quick-firing guns are placed. The noise made by a quick-firing gun is very much like the crackle of a newly-lit fire.

Stanza 7. *Panic that shells the drifting spar.* A floating spar, suddenly seen in bad light, may well be mistaken for a submarine emerging from the water.

Stanza 8. *Lance them to the quick.* A metaphor borrowed from whale-fishing. When a harpooned whale rises to the surface exhausted, the whalers dash in and spear it with long lances.

Stanza 9. *Shut down!* Shut down stokehold and engine-room hatches preparatory to going into action with forced draught.

WHITE HORSES

White horses. The name given to the patches of white foam that are made by waves breaking out at sea, as distinct from foam caused by waves breaking on a beach or reef.

Stanza 1. *Sargasso weed.* In the West Central Atlantic, at a point where there is an eddy among the great Atlantic currents, the surface of the sea is covered by large patches of floating weed, called

THE FIVE NATIONS

Sargasso weed, from the name of the sea in which it is found.

Stanza 4. *Ere yet the deep is stirred.* (See note on 'The Sea and the Hills,' stanza 1, p. 196.)

Stanza 5. *That rope us where we run.* In the early days of the settlement of the American prairies, cowboys used to ride down herds or 'mobs' of wild horses and catch the most valuable with the lasso.

Stanza 10. *The moaning groundswell.* The swell set up by an approaching storm.

Bray. Crush to atoms as rock is crushed in a mortar.

THE SECOND VOYAGE

This poem is an allegory of settled matrimony.

Stanza 2. *The sea has shorn our galleries away.* Ships of the Tudor and early Stuart period had galleries running round their sterns. Until a later date sterns and bows were ornately carved and gilded. All such unpractical additions and ornaments are now obsolete.

Petrels. Mother Carey's chickens (see note, 'Anchor Song,' stanza 2, p. 141). Petrels fly close to ships in bad weather or when bad weather is brooding, but are seldom seen in fine weather. Hence they are usually called 'stormy petrels.'

Stanza 3. *Quartermasters* on board ship are experienced seamen to whom responsible work is entrusted.

THE FIVE NATIONS

Port o' Paphos mutineer. Some unlicensed little cupid sailing from Venus's own port, Paphos.

Stanza 5. *Brace and trim.* Alter the position of the sails so as to get the fullest advantage of the wind as it changes its direction.

The watch. A ship's company is divided into two watches. At night-time one watch keeps the deck while the other goes below to rest. Those whose watch it is below are called up only when an emergency requires all hands.

Stanza 6. *Warp.* Sailing vessels that have been moored against wharves or quays are warped (or hauled out into deep water), before their sails can be used, by means of hawsers attached to anchored buoys.

Hesperides. Islands of delight in Greek mythology, situated where the sun sets in the ocean, in which grew golden apples symbolising love and fruitfulness.

Saffroned. Saffron was used by the ancient Greeks both as a dye and a perfume.

THE DYKES

This poem deals with the fate of those who have forgotten how to hold the land that the toil of their fathers won for them from the sea. The meaning of the parable, intended to arouse a nation too well satisfied with a sense of national security, is obvious.

Stanza 2. *Sea-gate.* The dykes that protect the outer margin of land below high-water mark have

THE FIVE NATIONS

to be provided with gates to let off the constantly accumulating water from inland as the tide falls, and to shut out the sea as the tide rises.

Stanza 6. *Saltings.* Land behind a dyke where brackish water sometimes stands; a term often applied to pastures by the seaside.

Stanza 7. *Ninefold deep . . . the galloping breakers stride.* An allusion to the popular and not wholly unfounded belief that each ninth wave is bigger than its eight predecessors.

Till the bents and the furze and the sand are dragged out, and the old-time hurdles beneath. The first step in the construction of a dyke is to lay down bents (bundles of any stiff wiry grass), furze, etc., on a foundation of hurdles. Wind-blown sand will bank up against the furze, and gradually the dyke will become firm enough to allow of its being more elaborately strengthened. At last it will become so strong that, so long as it is kept in repair, roads and even railways may be laid along its top.

THE SONG OF THE DIEGO VALDEZ

Stanza 4. *Careen.* Ships need to be periodically cleansed of the barnacles and weed that gather on their sides and bottoms. In the old days crews of ships far from port, or unable by reason of their crimes to visit a port, used to find some natural harbour, and there, by placing their guns, ballast, etc., on one side of the ship, cause it to heel over so that the other side was lifted sufficiently clear of the water to be cleaned. This process was called 'careening.'

Stanza 5. *Breaming-fagots*. Fire was sometimes applied to a ship's bottom to assist in the work of cleaning it. This was called 'breaming.'

THE BROKEN MEN

Stanza 2. Until recently Callao, a port on the Peruvian coast, afforded a haven to fraudulent bankrupts, those who had embezzled trust funds, and others who were 'wanted' by the English police. Some other South American republics, and some islands in the Pacific that did not belong to any of the Great Powers, were equally hospitable to men who would have been sent to penal servitude at Dartmoor if they had remained at home. The extension of extradition treaties, however, has greatly restricted the area in which criminals can escape the long arm of British Law.

Stanza 5. The daily life of the average Peruvian consists of work, not too strenuous, till noon, then siesta, then, when the cool of the evening comes, recreation.

Yuccas. Plants with bayonet-shaped leaves common in tropical America.

Jalousies. Sun-blinds made of split cane or wood.

Stanza 9. *Lord Warden*. The Lord Warden Hotel, named after the ancient office of Lord Warden of the Cinque Ports, stands near the pier and railway

THE FIVE NATIONS

station at Dover. It is therefore the first hotel that offers refreshment, liquid or otherwise, to the returning exile.

THE FEET OF THE YOUNG MEN

INTRODUCTORY STANZAS

Lodge. A Red Indian's wigwam or tent.
The Smokes of Spring. Cf. the account of the time in the Indian jungle when 'all the smells are new and delightful' in 'The Spring Running' (*Second Jungle Book*).

II

Lee-boarded luggers. Lee-boards are boards fitted to the sides of a flat-bottomed craft that on being let down check her drift to leeward. They are hauled up when the vessel is running before the wind.
Threshing. Beating to windward.

III

A gentle, yellow pirate. Though the Malays of the East Indies were till recently pirates, they are no more naturally blood-thirsty than a butcher is necessarily brutal. They are in fact notably courteous, and so gentle by temperament that they have a horror even of sky-larking. They were pirates because piracy was their profession, just as the Sea Dyaks, another very gentle people, were, until they came under the rule of Rajah Brooke of Borneo, head-hunters, not because they loved bloodshed, but because none of them could marry or enjoy the full privileges of manhood until he had a skull of his own providing to venerate, and because he believed that the health and welfare of a new-born child necessitated the presentation to its mother of a newly acquired skull.

IV

Ovis Poli. The magnificent wild sheep of the Pamir plateau, whose home is 16,000 feet above sea-level. It is named after Marco Polo, who met with it in the thirteenth century. Its horns, which are very large and stand well out from the head instead of curling round as in most sheep, are much coveted by big-game hunters.

Spoor. A Dutch word adopted by African hunters for an animal's footprints. Hunters read many *signs* which the untrained eye might see without understanding. Thus if vultures are seen circling in the sky it is an indication of lions round a carcass down below. They would not be circling if they had not seen a carcass, and they would not be wasting time in the air if they were not afraid to descend.

THE TRUCE OF THE BEAR

This poem is held to have a political significance. The bear is the totem of Russia, India's most powerful neighbour.

THE FIVE NATIONS

Stanza 1. *The pass called Muttianee.* In 'The Miracle of Purun Bhagat' (*Second Jungle Book*), Sir Purun Dass, after becoming a mendicant, passed through Simla and mounted the Himalaya-Thibet road till 'he had put the Muttianee Pass behind him.'

Stanza 2. *Adam-zad.* Owing to the resemblance between the anatomy of a man and that of a bear, shikarris of Kashmir call the latter Adam-zad—the son of Adam.

THE OLD MEN

Stanza 3. *Plough the sands.* The originator of this futile performance was Ulysses. He had pledged his word to join in protecting Helen if need should ever arise. When he was called upon to redeem his promise he did not wish to leave his wife. In the hope that he would be regarded as insane, and therefore released from his obligation, he yoked a horse and a bull together, ploughed the seashore, and sowed salt instead of grain.

THE EXPLORER

As the scene of this poem might be laid in almost any unexplored land in a temperate climate, the colloquial expressions used are not those of any one country. Some of them are primarily Australian, such as 'station,' 'blazed,' 'ringed,' and 'Never-never country.' 'Foothills,' 'trail,' and 'Norther' are American expressions.

THE FIVE NATIONS

Stanza 1. *Tucked away below the foothills where the trails run out and stop.* Foothills are the comparatively low hills that lie on the flanks of great mountain ranges. A feature of such country, if it is grazed by game or cattle, is that well-defined trails lead from the drinking-places on the plains to the bases of the hills, where they fade away. The explanation of this is that pasture is better and sweeter on the well-drained hillside than on the level alluvial plains, where it is coarse and rank. Cattle therefore graze for choice among the hills, and only come down on to the plains to drink. As cattle naturally take the shortest cut to water, moving in small herds in single file and without spreading to feed, they make well-defined paths from the grazing-grounds to the drinking-places and back again. As they spread out on returning to the grazing-ground these tracks do not continue for any considerable distance beyond the level, but become faint and shortly disappear.

Stanza 3. *Pack.* Gear such as blankets, cooking utensils, food, etc., carried on a pack-horse.

The faith that moveth mountains. Cf. Matthew xxi. 21: 'If ye have faith, and doubt not . . . if ye shall say unto this mountain, Be thou removed, and be thou cast into the sea; it shall be done.'

Whipping up and leading down. A good horseman does not ride up and down steep pinches unless he is in a great hurry. A horse cannot be easily led up a steep place, as he hangs back and strains at the bridle.

THE FIVE NATIONS

It is better therefore to drive him from behind, urging him when necessary. (A horse cannot kick when he is on a steep slope, as he would lose his balance if he tried to do so.) He will go down hill more willingly and should therefore be led, lest on reaching level ground he should take it into his head to gallop away.

Stanza 4. *Headed back for lack of grass.* A traveller who takes horses for any considerable distance must depend for their food on whatever pasture he can find, as a horse will soon eat as much forage as it can carry. If he finds himself on a long barren stretch he will turn back to the nearest grass and give his horses a long rest and time to lay up a store of energy before facing it again. Where water is scarce, however, he is sometimes in such a position that, knowing how long it is since he last found water, to go back would be certain death. He must then go on at all costs, however slender may be his chances of finding water on ahead.

Stanza 5. *Norther.* An American term for a strong wind off the snows and accompanied by intense cold. Sometimes it reduces the temperature 50° F. in twenty-four hours. Originally used in Texas, where it is a true north wind, it has been misapplied to cold winds generally. (Cf. the use of the word in 'The Merchantmen,' stanza 5, for the wind off the Andes.)

Stanza 7. Flowers stand cold better than almost any kind of vegetation except moss and lichens.

THE FIVE NATIONS

They grow in profusion in the Arctic as well as at high altitudes. Aloes need a higher temperature. Thorn-bearing plants abound in dry or exposed windy places, because as the giving off of water is one of the chief functions of leaves, desert plants economise their strength by producing thorns instead. Desert plants, moreover, being slow of growth would quickly be eaten down if their thorns did not protect them.

Stanza 10. *White Man's Country.* A country in which white men can live, do manual labour and rear families without physical degeneration. Countries where this is impossible—such as the East Indies, the Philippine Islands, India, etc., where the white man is an aristocrat and directs the labour of coloured men—have been called in contradistinction 'Sahibs' country.'

Stanza 11. *Chose my trees and blazed and ringed 'em.* An explorer's easiest way of making rough landmarks is to 'blaze' trees by cutting large, easily noticeable squares in their bark. Where there is no timber he makes cairns of stones (see stanza 15). Trees are 'ringed' (or ring-barked) by cutting a ring in the bark right round the trunk. This stops the circulation of the sap and kills the tree. Incidentally it greatly improves the pasture below it.

Saul he went to look for donkeys, and by God he found a kingdom. Cf. 1 Samuel ix. 3-27, x. 1-24.

Stanza 13. *Head.* The unit of water-power.

Stanza 14. *Tracked me by the camps I'd quitted,*

THE FIVE NATIONS

used the water-holes I'd hollowed. The marks of an abandoned camp are principally the ashes of the camp fire, dry grass or leaves that have been pulled for bedding, and possibly firewood that has been gathered but not used. A camp that has been used for several days will also probably have the ruins of a bough-shelter, and a framework of saplings erected to support the billycan or kettle above the fire. Water may often be obtained where none is visible by digging in the beds of apparently dry watercourses.

Stanza 18. *Never-never country.* A term applied to the desolate wastes of central and northern Australia, possibly because so many of the explorers and prospectors who penetrated it in the early days never came back.

THE BURIAL

Stanza 2. *So brief the term allowed.* Some years before his death Rhodes, knowing that he had at best but a few years to live (constitutional weakness had driven him at the age of seventeen to seek relief in the Natal climate) said, 'There are so many things I want to do in South Africa, and I have got only so many years to do them in.' His dying words were, 'So little done: so much to do! Good-bye. God bless you.' So little done! Rhodes extended British dominions from southern Bechuanaland to the shores of Lake Tanganyika and was the determining factor in retaining Uganda for the British Empire.

THE FIVE NATIONS

Stanza 3. *Great spaces washed with sun.* Rhodes was buried at a spot chosen by himself in the Matoppo Hills, and commanding a view—a valley set within an amphitheatre of hills—which he declared to be the finest view in the world. The majestic, silent rock-crowned hills standing up above vast rolling downs make a fit resting-place for the dreamer of great dreams.

The Death he dared. Four months after the outbreak of the second Matabele War the natives withdrew to a practically impregnable position in the Matoppo Hills. Realising that they could be subdued only at an immense cost to the lives both of themselves and the British forces, Rhodes determined to attempt to pacify them without further bloodshed. He pitched his tent between the Matabele and the British camp, sent a message to the former that he wished to negotiate peace with them, and for six weeks waited unguarded for a reply. The Matabele invited him to attend a council in the depths of the hills where no armed force could touch them. Rhodes, accompanied by Dr. Hans Sauer and Mr. J. Colenbrander, immediately rode unarmed to the appointed place and successfully laid down the terms on which he would agree to peace. So greatly did the personality of Rhodes impress the Matabele, that when a bare-headed statue of him was erected in Buluwayo they earnestly petitioned that it should be provided with headgear, for they believed that until this was done a drought would be caused by the heavens refusing to rain on his image.

GENERAL JOUBERT

Petrus Jacobus Joubert, commandant-general of the South African Republic from 1880-1890, was, in the words of Sir George White, the defender of Ladysmith, 'a soldier and a gentleman, and a brave and honourable opponent.' Lord Roberts, writing to condole with Kruger on the death of Joubert, said, 'His personal gallantry was only surpassed by his humane conduct and chivalrous bearing under all circumstances.' In his public life Joubert was free from corruption. On several occasions he urged the futility of war against Britain, and had his counsels been followed there would have been no war, for he advocated the redressing of the Uitlander's grievances. Nevertheless he took command of the Boer forces on the outbreak of hostilities. Before very long, however, his health failed him, and a month after the relief of Ladysmith he died. In the words of President Kruger, his political opponent, 'he died as he had lived, on the path of puty and honour.'

THE PALACE

In countries that were once the seats of ancient civilisations excavators often find that one town has been built upon, and to some extent with, the ruins of another, which in its day was built on the site of a

THE FIVE NATIONS

still older town. In excavating the ruins of ancient Babylon, for instance, Professor Koldeway had first to clear away modern Arab dwellings. Beneath these were Parthian habitations. The opening of the next stratum revealed remains of Greek settlements. At last, beneath a huge mound, Professor Koldeway discovered the remains of a vast building, constructed of large square tiles, cemented with asphalt, each of which was stamped with the name of Nebuchadnezzar.

Stanza 2. *Footings*. Foundations.

Stanza 3. *Quoins*. Stones placed at the angle made by two walls.

Ashlars. Dressed stones used in the facings of walls.

Stanza 6. *Sheers*. Appliances used for the mechanical lifting of heavy weights.

SUSSEX

The wonderful charm of Sussex colours much of Mr. Rudyard Kipling's later work. In 'The Knife and the Naked Chalk' (*Rewards and Fairies*) are some admirable pen-pictures of the Downs. The scenes of 'They' and 'Below the Mill Dam' in *Traffics and Discoveries*, of 'An Habitation Enforced' in *Actions and Reactions*, of many of the stories in *Rewards and Fairies*, and of most of those in *Puck of Pook's Hill*, are laid in Sussex.

Stanza 1. *And see that it is good*. Cf. Genesis i. 31: 'And God saw every thing that He had made, and, behold, it was very good.'

THE FIVE NATIONS

Stanza 2. *Levuka's Trade.* The trade-wind that sweeps the Fiji Islands. Levuka is on a small island between Viti Levu and Vanua Levu. Until 1882 it was the capital of the archipelago.

The lot has fallen to me. Cf. Psalm xvi. 7 (Prayer-Book version): 'The lot is fallen unto me in a fair ground: yea, I have a goodly heritage.'

Stanza 3 (see note to 'A Three-part Song,' p. 277).

Stanza 4. *The barrow and the camp.* Barrows or funeral mounds of the Stone, Bronze, and Iron Ages have been found at Bow Hill, Bury Hill, Bignor Hill, Steyning, and other parts of Sussex. There are ancient British and Roman camps at the Devil's Dyke, Ditchling Beacon, Hollingsbury Castle, Whitehawk Hill, Mount Caburn, Rook's Hill, Cissbury, and Chanctonbury. In several places the Romans occupied camps that had been made many centuries before the Roman invasion by men of the Neolithic or 'new stone age' (see note 'Puck's Song,' stanzas 9 and 10, p. 275).

Stanza 6. *Only the dewpond on the height*
Unfed, that never fails.

At various points on the Downs are remarkable reservoirs made by men of the Neolithic or later Stone Age. These are called 'dewponds,' because the water they contain is the product not of springs but of condensed dew. The making of a dewpond necessitated much labour and care. An excavation was made in the chalk on the hilltop and lined with dry straw, on top of which was laid a layer of finely puddled clay. The reservoir thus made rapidly filled with water even when no rain fell. The explanation of this phenomenon is as follows: During the heat of the day the chalk becomes hot, but the clay, kept from contact with the chalk by the layer of non-conducting material, is chilled by evaporation from its surface. The consequence is that during the night the moisture of the comparatively warm air is condensed on the surface of the colder clay. As condensation during the night is greater than the evaporation during the day, the pond gradually fills (see a fascinating book, *Neolithic Dewponds and Cattleways*, by A. J. and G. Hubbard). If a stream finds its way into the pond, the latter loses its power of condensing dew owing to the straw becoming damp and ceasing to act as a non-conductor. In the driest weather the ponds are fullest. Thus 'unfed, they never fail.'

The following suggestion as to how our remote ancestors stumbled on a principle in thermo-dynamics is put forward by the writer of these notes for what it is worth. Primitive man, knowing nothing of the potter's wheel, moulded his pots on plaited straw. Perhaps the makers of the dewponds, whose camps on the heights were far from the natural water-supply of the valleys, conceived the idea of making on the hilltop a gigantic reservoir by the same method, though on a far larger scale, as that by which they made their pots, intending subsequently to fill it by hand or leave it to be filled by rain. If this is what they did, no doubt Nature intervened, when the process was nearly complete, and filled the pond for them. The authors of *Neolithic Dewponds and Cattleways* believe these ponds, and the camps which adjoin them, to be from 4000 to 6000 years old. The ponds are protected by earthworks.

For a reconstruction of the life of those who made the ponds, see 'The Knife and the Naked Chalk' in *Rewards and Fairies*.

Stanza 7. *Little lost Down churches.* One of the Down churches, that of Lullington under Winddoor Hill, is probably the smallest in England. It stands in a hollow a few yards from, but out of sight of, the road. The inside area is about sixteen feet square, and if crowded to its utmost it can hold about thirty people. Traces of ruins in the churchyard show that the church was formerly larger than it is at present.

The heathen kingdom Wilfrid found. In the seventh century the kingdom of the South Saxons was to a great extent cut off from neighbouring English kingdoms—on east and west by marshes, and on the north by the forest of the Weald (Celtic *Andredsweald*, *i. e.* the uninhabited forest). The sloping beaches of the coast made it also particularly liable to invasion by pirates. It is natural, therefore, that heathenism should have lingered longer in Sussex than in other parts of England. A ship in which Wilfrid, Archbishop of York, was sailing homeward from France was driven ashore on the Sussex coast. The inhabitants gathered to loot whatever might be washed ashore, and one of their number began to practise magical arts, designed to hasten the wrecking of the ship. One of Wilfrid's men slung a stone at the wizard and killed him, whereupon a fight began. Wilfrid's men, one hundred and twenty in number, held their ground so well that only five of them were killed. The Saxons were preparing to attack the third time when the tide, rising before its time, floated the ship, and Wilfrid and his men escaped. About twenty years later, Wilfrid, having been driven from York, came as a missionary to the South Saxons. According to Bede, no rain had fallen for three years. Wilfrid relieved the famine that resulted by teaching the people to fish. In gratitude for this they consented to be baptized. On the day fixed for the ceremony rain fell in torrents, and the famine was ended. St. Wilfrid established a monastery and cathedral at Selsey, on a spot now covered by the sea. (See 'The Conversion of St. Wilfrid' in *Rewards and Fairies*.)

Stanza 9. *Scarp*. The steepest side of a hill. On the Sussex Downs this is always the north side.

The long man of Wilmington. A giant figure, 240 feet long, cut in the turf on the northern slope of Winddoor Hill. One tradition says that it is a work with which a shepherd lad amused his idle hours. Another says that it was made for some unstated purpose by the monks of the neighbouring Benedic-

THE FIVE NATIONS

tine Priory of Wilmington. It has been suggested that it is a representation of an ancient British deity.

Sea-forgotten walls. Since Plantagenet times the sea has receded a mile and more from the old ports of Rye and Winchelsea. Pevensey Castle, the walls of which were formerly lapped by the sea, is now nearly a mile from the nearest beach.

Stanza 10. *Shaws.* Thickets or small groves on a steep hillside.

Ghylls. Rocky clefts in the hillside forming the course of a stream.

Sussex steers. Sussex has a breed of cattle of its own. They resemble the better known Devon cattle, but are larger, coarser, and of a deeper red colour.

SONG OF THE WISE CHILDREN

Stanza 1. *The darkened Fifties.* The United Kingdom lies between latitudes 50° and 60° North.

And the day is dead at his breaking forth. Compare this with the description of daybreak in the Bay of Bengal, where 'the dawn comes up like thunder' (*Mandalay*).

The Bear. The constellation that dominates the northern skies.

Stanza 4. *We have forfeited our birthright*, i. e. by leaving the land of sunshine.

Stanza 8. *The wayside magic, the threshold spells.* One may sometimes see by the side of the road in India an image that has been emblematically married to a well. Sometimes a saucer containing sand, grain, yellow cloth, and other things has been placed there by some one who is ill, in the hope that a passer-by by meddling with its contents will take the disease on himself. If the saucer contain wine or cooked food a ghost is to be propitiated. Sometimes one may see a heap of earth, to which each passer-by contributes a clod in honour of the god who protects wayfarers.

Once a year Hindoo women mark their houses with lines of cow-dung and worship the serpent, the symbol of eternity, with milk and parched grain. Every morning in a Hindoo household the ceremony of the Salutation of the Threshold is performed. A pattern is drawn on the threshold in lines of powdered rice, decorated at intervals with flowers. In many houses, especially where there are young children or animals liable to the evil-eye, the wall beside the doorpost is marked with a representation of the sign of Ganésa, the Swastika, or mystic cross, which is supposed to represent the sun in its journey through the heavens. A Swastika beside an elephant's head is stamped on the covers of many of Rudyard Kipling's books.

BUDDHA AT KAMAKURA

An additional stanza to this poem appears as a heading to Chapter III. of KIM *(see note, p. 357).*

Buddha is the name neither of a man nor a god. The word is generally translated 'enlightened,' and is a title applied to any one who, 'by self-denying efforts,

THE FIVE NATIONS

continued through many hundreds of different births, has acquired the ten cardinal virtues in such perfection that he is able, when sin and ignorance have gained the upper hand throughout the world, to save the human race from impending ruin.'

There have been over a million Buddhas in former worlds. In this world there have been four, and there is one yet to come.

The title Buddha is specifically applied to Gautama, the son of a Hindoo rajah of the military caste, who renounced the world, became a prophet, and taught the essentials of the creed that is now called Buddhism, a creed based on Hinduism, but far nobler and more enlightened. He lived in the fifth or sixth century B. C. Gautama is believed to have had five hundred and ten previous existences. Brahmans declare him to have been the ninth incarnation of their god Vishnu.

Kamakura, formerly one of the most populous and powerful cities of Japan, the seat of the Shogunate, is now a mouldering hamlet. It contains many Buddhist shrines, but there is in particular one giant figure of the Buddha that is a masterpiece of statuary. The following is from Lafcadio Hearne's *Glimpses of Unfamiliar Japan*, published in 1894:—

'Here still dwell the ancient gods in the great silence of their decaying temples, without worshippers, without revenues, surrounded by desolations of rice-fields, where the chanting of frogs replaces the sea-like murmur of the city that was and is not . . . The nearer you approach the giant Buddha, the greater this charm becomes. You look up into the solemnly beautiful face, and you feel that the image typifies all that is tender and calm in the Soul of the East.'

Stanza 1. *The Narrow way.* Western theology recognises two spiritual paths: 'broad is the way that leadeth to destruction; narrow is the way which leadeth unto eternal life.' Eastern theology, both Buddhist and Brahman, recognises one path which the spirit must follow through many successive lives, and perhaps through many hells. In Buddhism the goal is Nirvana—literally the 'dying out' in the heart of the three cardinal sins, sensuality, ill-will, and stupidity, which frees the soul from the necessity for rebirth.

Stanza 2. *The Way.* The following definition of 'The Way' is ascribed to Gautama Buddha himself:—

'There is a path which opens the eyes and bestows understanding, which leads to peace, to insight, to the higher wisdom, to Nirvana. Verily, it is this Noble Eightfold Path: that is to say, Right Views, Right Aspirations, Right Speech, Right Conduct, Right Mode of Livelihood, Right Effort, Right Mindedness, and Right Rapture.'

The Law. The dogma set forth in the Four Noble Truths: (1) that existence in any form involves Suffering and Sorrow; (2) that the cause of suffering is Desire and Lust of Life; (3) that the cessation of suffering is effected by the complete conquest over and destruction of Desire and Lust of Life; (4) that the path leading to the Cessation of Suffering is the Noble Eightfold Path.

Maya. The mother of Gautama.

Ananda. A cousin of Gautama. He has been called the 'beloved disciple' of the Buddhist story. He was born at the same moment as Buddha, at which moment also the sacred Bo-tree (see 'Buddh-Gaya,' stanza 10, p. 228) sprang from the ground.

Bodhisat. A being destined eventually to become a Buddha. Gautama was a Bodhisat until he attained enlightenment. The Grand Lama of Thibet is a Bodhisat who refuses to attain Buddhahood, in order that he may continue to be born again and again for the benefit of mankind.

Stanza 4. *Joss-sticks.* The Japanese reverence Buddha by burning sticks of incense before his images. These sticks are popularly called by Europeans 'joss-sticks.' Joss is the pidgin-English word for a heathen god. It is a corruption of the Portuguese word *deus*, god.

Stanza 6. *Contemning neither creed nor priest.* Buddhism enjoins Love, Sorrow for the Sorrows of others, Joy in the Joy of others, and equanimity as regards one's own joys and sorrows. 'Our minds should not waver. No evil speech will we utter. Tender and compassionate will we abide, loving in heart, void of malice within.'

THE FIVE NATIONS

Stanza 7. *Every tale Ananda heard*. This is a reference to the Jatakas, the five hundred and forty-seven tales of the successive lives lived by Gautama. Most of them deal with occasions in which Gautama was born as some form of animal. In *Kim* the Lama tells a jataka in which Gautama is an elephant. Planudes, who compiled the stories miscalled *Æsop's Fables*, is supposed to have obtained much of his material from such of the Jatakas as had reached Europe in the fourteenth century. The story of Sindbad the Sailor is based on the Jatakas. Boccacio and Chaucer unconsciously borrowed from them, and the ideas of the three caskets and the pound of flesh in the *Merchant of Venice* are to be found in them.

Stanza 8. *Htee*. The golden top of a Buddhist temple in Burma.

Shwe-Dagon. A Buddhist pagoda at Rangoon, the centre of Burmese religious life. It stands on a hill, and is in itself loftier than St. Paul's Cathedral. It is covered from base to summit with pure gold, which is renewed once in every generation. Ralph Fitch, the first Englishman to see this wonder (in 1586), wrote of it, 'It is the fairest place, as I suppose, that is in the world.' In *From Sea to Sea* it is described as 'a golden mystery, a beautiful winking wonder.'

Stanza 9. *The thunder of Thibetan drums*. The beating of drums forms part of the worship of the priests in Thibet, although anything in the way of ritual was expressly discountenanced by Gautama.

THE FIVE NATIONS

Om mane padme om is an invocation in Thibetan Sanskrit. It is the prayer that is written or printed on the Thibetan prayer-wheels; on some it is printed one hundred million times. It is the first prayer that a child learns and the last that a dying man utters. It is, in fact, the only prayer known to the average Thibetan. It is addressed to the Bodhisat Padmapani, the patron saint of Thibet, and contains the essence of all happiness, prosperity, and knowledge, and the great means of deliverance. Each syllable has its own special power in safeguarding the utterer from rebirth. *Om* saves him from rebirth among gods, *ma* among Titans, *ni* from rebirth as a man, *pad* from rebirth as a beast, and *me* from rebirth in hell. The meaning seems to be lost, but 'Hail to the Jewel in the Lotus' or 'God the Jewel in the Lotus' have been suggested as translations.

To an Oriental the incessant repetition of a formula is not the futile performance that it appears to the western mind. In 'The Miracle of Purun Bhagat' (*The Second Jungle Book*), Purun Bhagat in his last resting-place among the silence and the space of the hills, 'would repeat a Name softly to himself a hundred, hundred times, till, at each repetition, he seemed to move more and more out of his body, sweeping up to the doors of some tremendous discovery.'

Stanza 10. *Brahmans rule Benares still.* Brahmans are Hindoos of the highest caste; though they may follow various trades and professions, they are fundamentally and hereditarily priests. Benares is the great centre of that form of Hinduism which is devoted to the worship of Siva, and it is there that the lowest forms of Hinduism, grossest superstition and inexpressible obscenities, are most apparent to-day; forms of religion as opposed to the pure and enlightened teachings of Gautama as any creed could be. One of the four chief events in the life of Gautama Buddha occurred at Benares—his first expounding of his doctrines. As late as the seventh century A. D. the city contained thirty Buddhist monasteries. But Buddhism is now practically extinct not only in Benares, but, except where it survives in the form of Jainism, almost throughout India. It has become, however, the religion of thirty-five per cent. of the world's inhabitants, and is the sole or principal religion of Japan, China, Korea, Thibet, Burma, and Ceylon.

Buddh-Gaya, a few miles south of Gaya in Bengal, is one of the most holy places of Buddhism. Here grew the sacred Bo-tree under which Gautama sat in meditation for forty-nine days, during which time he did not bathe nor take any food yet did not experience the least want. Powers of evil and good warred around him, and he was tempted in turn by a demon in the shape of a young girl, one in the shape of a young woman, and one in the shape of a middle-aged woman. At the end of his meditation he came to a perfect knowledge of the Law and thus became Buddha ('Enlightened').

THE FIVE NATIONS

THE WHITE MAN'S BURDEN

This poem was published in *M'Clures' Magazine* (New York) shortly after the signing of the Treaty of Paris (December 10, 1898), by which peace was made between the United States of America and Spain.

After her war with Spain the United States found herself in a position such as had not arisen during the course of her history. She had made war with Spain with the object of freeing Cuba from the Spanish yoke and without any intention of annexing that island to herself. Her constitution was precise and made no provision for imperial responsibilities. Yet to have abandoned Cuba and the Philippines would have placed these islands in a worse position than before the war. Both on selfish and unselfish grounds it was imperative that, in spite of her Constitution, the United States should 'take up the White man's burden' of imperial responsibility and charge herself with the care of the semi-civilised islands that she had wrested from Spain. One splendid result of her assumption of this responsibility is that yellow-fever, which had been the curse of Cuba for centuries, has been eradicated throughout that island.

Stanza 4. *The ports ye shall not enter.* By the Treaty of Paris the United States undertook to hand back Cuba, the Philippines, and Puerto Rico to their own inhabitants after the expiration of ten years.

THE FIVE NATIONS

Stanza 5.   *Why brought ye us from bondage,*
            Our loved Egyptian night?

When the Israelites were hungry in the wilderness they murmured against Moses and Aaron, saying, 'Would to God we had died by the hand of the Lord in the land of Egypt, when we sat by the flesh pots, and when we did eat bread to the full' (Exodus xvi. 2 and 3).

PHARAOH AND THE SERGEANT

Stanza 1.   In January, 1883, the year after armed British occupation of Egypt, Sir Evelyn Wood was given £200,000, and directed to spend it on raising a force of six thousand soldiers from the native peasantry for the protection of Egypt. Though the Egyptian fellah is unwarlike by nature, he has, when trained and led by British officers, developed soldierly qualities of an exceptionally high character.

Stanza 3.   *Coptics.*   Before the Mohammedan invasion of Egypt the inhabitants who were Christians spoke Coptic. Though their descendants have held to their religion, they long since abandoned Coptic speech and adopted the language of their Arab conquerors.

Stanza 4.   *Cautions.*   To ensure that orders on parade shall be carried out smartly by all the soldiers in unison, the actual words of command are reduced to monosyllables. Before the word is given the sergeant will give warning by uttering the 'caution.'

Thus he may say, pausing between the two words, 'Quick'—'march.' The 'caution' in this case is the word 'Quick.' 'March' is the actual word of command, for which the men will wait before moving. A sergeant wishing to call his men to attention will say 'Squad—'shun.' 'Squad' is the caution and ''shun' (the word 'attention' concentrated) the word of command.

Combed old Pharaoh out. A slang expression equivalent to 'made him sit up.'

Gordon. The British Government delayed five months after the siege of Khartum began before deciding to take steps to relieve General Gordon. The relieving force reached Khartum two days after the garrison had fallen and Gordon had been killed.

Stanza 5. *And he mended it again in a little more than ten.* The first severe test to which the re-organised Egyptian army was put was in the Dongola campaign of 1896, when it did magnificent work against the Sudanese dervishes.

Stanza 6. *'Tween a cloud of dust and fire.* Cf. Exodus xiii. 21: 'And the Lord went before them by day in a pillar of a cloud, to lead them the way; and by night in a pillar of fire, to give them light.'

OUR LADY OF THE SNOWS

On a most appropriate day, St. George's Day, in 1897, the year of Queen Victoria's Diamond Jubilee, the Canadian House of Commons gave a preference to imports from the mother-country. Immediately after the passing of the Bill a member of the House struck up 'God Save the Queen.' The other members joined in singing the hymn, after which the House was adjourned.

Stanza 2. *Not for the Gentiles' clamour*. The question was raised during the debate on the revision of the tariff as to whether Germany and Belgium would protest against Canada's giving a preference to Great Britain. The reply of Mr. Fielding, the Finance Minister, amounted to a statement that he neither knew nor cared whether they would or not.

Stanza 4. *A troubled year*. The year 1896, in which Sir Wilfrid Laurier inaugurated his proposal of a preferential tariff in favour of the mother-country, was marked by friction between the United States and Great Britain over the Venezuela Boundary question.

'ET DONA FERENTES'

The title is a quotation from Virgil's *Aeneid*, ii. 49. The full line is 'Quidquid id est, timeo Danaos et dona ferentes' (whatever it may be, I fear the Greeks even when they bring gifts), and is spoken by Laocoon with reference to the wooden horse which the Greeks left outside the walls of Troy.

Stanza 1. *The Four-mile radius* is that part of London which lies within four miles of Charing Cross station.

THE FIVE NATIONS

Stanza 2. *Pentecostal crew.* On the day of the Pentecost (Acts ii. 4) the apostles 'began to speak with other tongues.'

Stanza 3. *St. Lawrence*, while being burnt alive on a gridiron, joked with his executioners, saying, 'I am roasted enough on this side; turn me round and eat.'

Stanza 6. *Nous sommes allong à notre batteau, nous ne voulong pas un row.* This is French (not of the purest Parisian variety!) for 'We are going to our boat, we don't want a row.'

Stanza 10. *Aas-vogels.* Afrikander-Dutch for vultures.

KITCHENER'S SCHOOL

Stanza 1. *Hubshee.* A corruption of the Arabic *Habashi.* The word originally meant an Abyssinian, but is now applied in India to any African or to any one with woolly hair. It is also applied to a woolly-haired horse, generally esteemed unlucky.

Carry your shoes in your hand. In British India a visitor to a temple, mosque, or friend's house always leaves his shoes at the door. Cf. Exodus iii. 5. The Lord commanded Moses, saying, 'Put off thy shoes from off thy feet.'

Emirs. Commanders or governors of provinces. The Emirs of the Sudanese Provinces revolted from the authority of the Khedive of Egypt and gave their allegiance to the Mahdi in 1883. After the Mahdi's

THE FIVE NATIONS

death they were commanded by the Khalifa until defeated by British and Egyptian troops under Sir Herbert (afterwards Lord) Kitchener in September, 1898.

Stanza 2. *The tomb ye knew.* The tomb of Mahommed Ahmed ibn Seyyid Abdullah, who had claimed to be the Mahdi (lit. 'he who is guided aright'), and who had been recognised by his followers as divinely appointed to regenerate Islam. On September 1, 1898, Kitchener's troops were within reach of Omdurman, and the Mahdi's tomb was shelled by howitzers at 2,300 yards range. The tomb was regarded as a sacred shrine, and its destruction was intended to have, and had, a moral effect, as the Sudanese dervishes held that its safety was necessary to theirs. On the following day the dervishes, about 35,000 in number, streamed out of Omdurman and advanced to the attack. Though they fought magnificently they were routed by noon, and soon afterwards the Anglo-Egyptian army entered the town.

Stanza 4. *Letter by letter, from Kaf to Kaf.* A pun of the favourite Oriental kind is contained in the expression from *Kaf to Kaf.* The phrase means 'from world's end to world's end.' (Kaf is the name of a mythical girdle of mountains that surrounds the world and keeps the earth's carpet from being blown off by the winds.) Kaf is also the letter of the Arabic alphabet which corresponds to the English K, the initial letter of Kitchener and of Khartoum.

Openly asking the English for money to buy you

THE FIVE NATIONS

Hakims and scribes. Hakims are teachers of medicine or philosophy. On November 30, 1898, Lord Kitchener made an appeal to the public to found and maintain with British money a college bearing the name of the Gordon Memorial College, 'to be a pledge that the memory of Gordon is still alive among us, and that his aspirations are at length to be realised.' The College was founded at Khartoum, and young men from all parts of the Sudan are now being educated there. In the Wellcome Tropical Research Laboratory, which is attached to the Gordon Memorial College, dervishes who fought against us at Omdurman have actually been trained to use the microscope and join in the war, waged for the benefit of mankind, against tropical disease.

THE YOUNG QUEEN

Stanza 1. *Bright-eyed out of the battle.* The Commonwealth of Australia was inaugurated during the progress of the South African war, in which the Imperial Forces received very material assistance from Australian troops.

Stanza 2. *The Hall of Our Thousand Years.* Almost exactly one thousand years before New Year's Day, 1901, died Alfred, King of the English, who laid the first stone of the structure that was destined to become the British Empire.

The Five Free Nations—England, Canada, Australia, New Zealand, South Africa.

THE FIVE NATIONS

Stanza 3. *The Leeuwin*. The cape of southwestern Australia that catches the full force of the swell from the great Southern Ocean. The other side of Australia, the north-east, is protected for a thousand miles by a coral reef, the Great Barrier Reef.

Stanza 5. *The pearls of the Northland*. Thursday Island, to the north of Cape York, is the centre of the Australian pearl-fishery.

Gold of the West. Australia produces about one quarter of the world's supply of gold, and of this more than half comes from Western Australia.

Her lands own opals. A large proportion of the world's supply of opals are found in Queensland and New South Wales.

Levin. Lightning.

Stanza 7. *Child of the child I bore*. Federated Australia as a whole was the result of the union of all Australia, which was planted and settled by England.

RIMMON

After Naaman, the Syrian, was healed of his leprosy he promised Elisha that he would henceforth 'offer neither burnt offering nor sacrifice to other gods, but unto the Lord,' but asked pardon in advance for bowing in the house of Rimmon when he had to attend the king in his worship of the idol (2 Kings v. 17 and 18).

Stanza 6. Cf. 1 Kings xviii., in which Elisha mocks the priests of Baal and suggests that the reason their god does not hear them may be that he is talking or hunting, or asleep or on a journey.

THE OLD ISSUE

October 9, 1899, was the day on which the South African Republic presented its ultimatum to Great Britain.

Stanza 1. *Trumpets in the marshes—in the eyot at Runnymede.* It was on an eyot or small island in the Thames, between Staines and Windsor, that King John very reluctantly signed the Great Charter, one of the provisions of which was 'to none will we *sell or deny or delay* right or justice.' The barons who thus brought him to his knees had their camp on Runnymede, a marshy flat opposite the island.

Stanza 2. *Trumpets round the scaffold at the dawning by Whitehall.* Charles I., another king who never could learn, reiterated his conviction a moment before his execution on the scaffold before the Banqueting House at Whitehall, that the people had no right to a share in the government. 'A sovereign and a subject are clean different things.'

Stanza 3. *He hath veiled the Crown and hid the Sceptre.* Paul Kruger, though nominally President of a Republic, was an autocrat by instinct, and, so far as intrigue against either the British or against Thomas Burgers and Piet Joubert, his own fellow-countrymen, could make him so, an autocrat in actual fact. 'This is my country,' he said to a deputation of Uitlanders who petitioned that the English language should be legalised in the Transvaal. 'These are my laws. Those who do not like to obey my laws can leave my country.'

Stanza 7. *Grey-goose wing.* Goose-feathers were used by the English archers for their arrows.

Stanza 8. *How our King is one with us, first among his peers.* Monarchy in England has always been limited in theory, if not in practice. A Plantagenet king was not an absolute monarch, but the chief and leader of the peers of the realm ('peers' strictly means 'equals'). In those days none but the nobility were of any importance so far as government was concerned. During the Wars of the Roses the barons broke each other's power so effectively that when peace was re-established the Tudor kings were able to make themselves practically absolute, and as they combined tact with their despotism few resented the change. When the Stuarts tried to rule despotically without tact, the English, this time the commoners, established for all time the principle that the king is the servant and not the master of his subjects.

Stanza 19. *He shall rule above the Law calling on the Lord.* President Kruger professed, and quite possibly sincerely believed himself, to be the object of special Divine guidance. When he set aside the laws of the land, he persuaded himself that he had Divine sanction for so doing.

THE FIVE NATIONS

BRIDGE-GUARD IN THE KARROO

Stanza 1. *Oudtshoorn ranges.* Mountains in the Little Karroo Desert in Cape Colony.

Stanza 4. *Picket.* A body of men placed at a short distance from camp to protect points of importance or to detach sentries to posts of observation.

Stanza 5. *Details.* Small miscellaneous bodies of men detached from their corps. Men charged with the duty of guarding a bridge on the line of communication, but far from the actual war area, undergo all the discomforts of active service added to the tedium of deadly monotony. If the unexpected happens they may be called upon to fight at any time —otherwise they would not be there—but the chances of fighting are remote. They have therefore the very hard task of performing a duty from which every element of interest and every chance of distinction seem to be eliminated.

Stanza 10. *Ties.* The wooden 'sleepers' that hold the railway lines in their places.

Stanza 13. During the South African War some of those whose business led them to travel by train in the war areas, remembering the loneliness of those who guarded communications, carried with them bundles of newspapers for distribution along the line. Such newspapers, and the few occasional moments' chat with passengers on the trains, were the only

THE FIVE NATIONS

means of contact with the outside world enjoyed by those who guarded the lines of communication.

THE LESSON

Stanza 1. *Knocked higher than Gilderoy's kite.* There is no evidence that the original Gilderoy ever had a kite. He was a sturdy law-breaker, hanged long ago at Edinburgh—on higher gallows than those of other criminals, as a sign that his crimes were greater. He was hanged so high that he *looked like a kite* in the air.

> 'Of Gilderoy sae fraid they were
> They bound him mickle strong,
> Till Edenburrow they led him thair
> And on a gallows hong;
> They hong him high above the rest.'

To be hanged higher than Gilderoy's kite has come to mean to be punished with exceptional severity.

Stanza 2. *From Lamberts to Delagoa Bay, and from Pietersburg to Sutherland.* These places mark respectively the westernmost, easternmost, northernmost, and southernmost limits of the South African War area.

Stanza 4. *That horses are quicker than men afoot.* One of the first and most important mistakes made on the British side was the pitting of foot-soldiers against riflemen who were without exception mounted; and one of the most valuable lessons that the British

THE FIVE NATIONS

learned from the war was the value of mounted infantry.

THE FILES

One of the most wearisome of a journalist's duties is to grub for information as to some past and half-forgotten event through the masses of newspapers that accumulate month by month and year by year in a newspaper office. If he is uncertain of the date of the occurrence to which he wishes to refer, he must hunt through one dusty file after another, backwards and forwards, till he finds what he seeks. The tedium of the task is occasionally relieved by the interest of lighting upon records of occurrences long since forgotten, that were obviously considered of tremendous importance when they took place.

Line 12. *Faenza.* An Italian town that has had many masters. The reference is to Browning's 'Soul's Tragedy,' the scene of which is laid in Faenza. Ogniben, the Papal Legate, says, 'I have known four and twenty leaders of revolts' (in Faenza). There is a pun on the word 'leader,' which in journalistic language means the principal article in each issue of a paper.

Lines 18 and 19. *Kensall Green* and *Père-la-Chaise* are two huge cemeteries, the former in London, and the latter in Paris.

Lines 32-34. *Long primer, brevier,* and *minion* are the names of three different sizes of type used in printing a newspaper. A prominent man who outlives his importance in the public eye will have his actions chronicled at first in *long primer*, the type used for the most important pages of the newspaper; later they will be noticed on one of the less important pages for which *brevier*, a somewhat smaller type, is used. At last he will be honoured only by a short '*para*,' *i. e.* paragraph, printed *solid* — that is, the lines close together instead of 'leaded' or spaced out as in the more important parts of the paper—in *minion*, the smallest type in general use and at the bottom of a column.

Line 36. *Leaded.* The opposite of solid (see preceding note).

Line 37. *Triple-headed.* Recorded in a column prefaced by three headlines. Even the most sensational English newspapers seldom have more than this number of headlines to a column, but three would be quite a moderate number for many American newspapers.

Line 43. *Bomba.* The nickname given to Ferdinand II., King of the Two Sicilies, after he authorised the bombardment of the chief cities of Sicily in 1849.

Line 44. *Saffi.* An Italian patriot, and a colleague of Mazzini in the triumvirate to which the government of Rome was entrusted during a few weeks of 1849.

Line 67. *Samuel Smiles.* The author of *Self-*

THE FIVE NATIONS

Help—his most popular work—and books entitled *Character*, *Thrift*, and *Duty*, as well as biographies of various successful men, the purpose of each of which was to teach the reader how to get on in the world.

Lines 73 and 74. These two lines are taken bodily from the works of Dr. Thomas Holley Chivers of Georgia, author of *The Lost Pleiad*. *Circa* 1840.

Conchimarian horns. Conches, trumpets made of sea-shells.

Reboantic. Bellowing.

Norns. In northern mythology divine prophetesses who foretold the destiny of new-born children.

Line 79. *Brocken-spectres.* Shadows of men enormously magnified cast on banks of clouds. The phenomenon, first noticed on the Brocken, may be seen under certain atmospheric conditions in high mountain regions when the sun is low.

Lines 84 and 85.   '*Quod ubique*, *Quod ab omnibus* means *semper!*' These words are part of what is called the motto of St. Vincent, an ecclesiastical writer of the fifth century, who defines the Catholic faith as '*quod ubique, quod semper, quod ab omnibus, creditum est*' (that which everywhere, that which always, and that which by all men must be believed). The lesson taught by the files is that that which is believed everywhere (*ubique*) and by all (*ab omnibus*) is not necessarily believed for all time (*semper*).

THE FIVE NATIONS

THE REFORMERS

This poem was published in the *Times* on October 12th, 1901. Two days earlier Sir Redvers Buller, at a public luncheon, had made a spirited reply to the Press criticisms on his conduct of the earlier part of the war in South Africa.

DIRGE OF DEAD SISTERS

Stanza 2. *Let us now remember many Honourable Women.* Cf. Ecclesiasticus xliv. 1, 3: 'Let us now praise famous men . . . such as did bear rule in their kingdoms.'

Stanza 7. *Blanket-hidden bodies, flagless.* At the height of the typhoid epidemic in Bloemfontein it was not always possible to secure one or other of the regimental funeral flags to put over the corpse, which was therefore carried to its grave wrapped in a blanket only.

Stanza 9. *Them that died at Uitvlugt when the plague was on the city.* Cape Town was visited by epidemic plague in 1901-2. The hospital and isolation camps were at Uitvlugt, on the Cape Flats, some five or six miles out of the city. Two of the nurses on plague duty contracted the disease and died there.

Her that fell at Simon's Town in service on our foes. This is a tribute to the memory of Mary Kingsley, niece of Charles and Henry Kingsley, and herself distinguished as an intrepid explorer, a scientist of parts,

THE FIVE NATIONS

an acute observer, and a writer of peculiar charm. At the age of thirty-two she made her second journey to West Africa to collect scientific data on fresh-water fishes, as well as information with regard to native law and customs. During this tour she explored the country of the cannibal Fans, being the first European to enter their country, suffering much hardship, and running considerable risk of losing her life. Her books on West Africa are remarkable in that though they deal ably and authoritatively with scientific subjects, the information they contain is presented in so light and humorous a style that the dullest reader could not fail to enjoy them. She was preparing for a third journey to West Africa when the South African War broke out, and she went to the Cape as a hospital nurse. While tending Boer prisoners at Simon's Town she died of enteric fever (according to one account—other accounts say that she died of blackwater fever, a little understood disease, the seeds of which may have entered her system when she was in West Africa). Throughout her life she set a high example of sound sense, chivalry, and courage. Her funeral was in accordance with her own wishes. Her body was carried on a gun-carriage to a torpedo-boat, which took it out to sea and committed it to the deep.

THE ISLANDERS

Line 1. *No doubt but ye are the People.* In these words Job sarcastically answered his critics. 'No

THE FIVE NATIONS

doubt but ye are the people, and wisdom shall die with you' (Job xii. 2).

Line 12. *Ye grudged . . . your fields for their camping-place.* A serious difficulty which hampers the training of troops in England arises from the limitations of the space over which troops may manœuvre. Private landowners, especially those who preserve game, will not allow their land to be used for the purpose. Troops on manœuvres are therefore obliged to keep very largely to roads. All land over which they are not allowed to pass is, for the purposes of the manœuvre, supposed to be swamp land or some other impassable obstacle. Under these conditions it is impossible to handle troops as they would be handled in actual warfare, and the efficiency of both men and officers is impaired in consequence. There are districts, such as Salisbury Plain, where troops can manœuvre unrestricted, but as officers get to know these districts by heart, the educational value of training there is not what it would otherwise be.

Line 21. *Sons of the sheltered city.* (See note on 'Two Kopjes,' stanza 3, p. 260.)

Line 28. *And ye sent them comfits and pictures.* The late Queen Victoria sent in December, 1899, a Christmas present consisting of a box of chocolate to every British soldier in the field. The gift was most highly appreciated, partly on sentimental grounds, partly because of the excellent sense shown

THE FIVE NATIONS

in choosing the gift. Men living on such food as is issued under active service conditions have a craving, caused by abstention from fresh vegetables, for sweet food. Chocolate not only satisfies this craving but is a concentrated food of high value. Since it suited the taste of all, chocolate was more suitable as a gift than tobacco or anything else that could have been sent. The Queen's example set a fashion, and for a while the troops received a bewildering succession of presents—pipes, cigarettes, Balaklava caps, etc. In some cases it seemed obvious that those who paid for these presents exercised no supervision over the contractors who supplied them, for some of the goods presented to the soldiers were so poor in quality as to be practically useless, and certainly not worth carriage from England to the front.

Line 30. *The men who could shoot and ride.* Very soon after the war had begun, the authorities recognised the need of the assistance of frontiersmen, such as the Boers themselves. The offers of the different colonies to send troops were therefore accepted, and the towns of Cape Colony and Natal were placarded with advertisements inviting those who could 'shoot and ride' to join one or other of the irregular corps (The Imperial Light Horse, Thornycroft's Mounted Infantry, and many others) that were raised to meet the emergency.

Line 59. *Ye say, 'It will minish our trade.'* Nevertheless the following theories prevalent in Ger-

THE FIVE NATIONS

many with regard to conscription bear on the British National Service problem: Conscription increases the earning power of the community because the security ensured by a strong army attracts capital: it increases the earning power of the individual, because men who have undergone training are stronger in body and more intelligent than untrained men of the same class: it has been estimated that the life of a trained man is on the average five years longer than that of one who has not been trained.

Line 77. *Teraphs*—idols. *Sept*—a subdivision of a tribe.

THE PEACE OF DIVES

The name Dives does not occur in the English Bible, but is taken from the Vulgate translation of the Gospels, where the word is used, not as a proper name, but for the 'certain rich man' (*quidam dives*) who, being in hell, pleaded that Lazarus might be allowed to bring him water. Luke xvi. 19-31. The theme of this poem—that those who control the world's money markets 'decide between themselves how, and when, and for how long king should draw sword against king, and people rise up against people'—is also the theme of 'The Treasure and the Law' (*Puck of Pook's Hill*).

Stanza 3. *Goshen*. That part of Egypt which was inhabited by the Israelites when they lived in Egypt.

THE FIVE NATIONS

Gadire. The country of the Gadarenes, near the Sea of Galilee.

Stanza 7. *Habergeon.* A coat of mail.

Stanza 16. *Ancient Akkad.* One of the cities of Nimrod (Genesis x. 10), and the principal city of Sargon I., King of Babylon (3800 B. C.), who carried his conquests from the Euphrates to the shore of the Mediterranean.

Islands of the Seas. Cf. Isaiah xi. 11: 'From Assyria, and from Egypt, and from Pathros, and from Cush, and from Elam, and from Shinar, and from Hamath, and from the islands of the sea.'

Stanza 17. *Ashdod.* A city of the Philistines (1 Samuel v. 1), situated on the military route between Syria and Egypt. It was captured by the Assyrians in 711 B. C. (Isaiah xx. 1) under a later *Sargon*, who assumed the name of his famous predecessor on seizing the throne of Babylon.

Stanza 18. *Is not Calno like Carchemish?* Cf. Isaiah x. 7, 8, 9: 'It is in his heart to destroy and cut off nations not a few. For he saith, Are not my princes altogether kings? Is not Calno as Carchemish?' *Calno* is supposed to be Calneh (Genesis x. 10 and Amos vi. 2), one of Nimrod's cities on the east bank of the Tigris, a place of considerable commercial importance. *Carchemish* was a town on the Euphrates. It was the Hittite capital in the Bronze Age, but was lost to the Hittite Empire before the periods at which it was mentioned in the Bible. Necho, King of

THE FIVE NATIONS

Egypt, took it from the Assyrians (2 Chron. xxxv. 20), and Nebuchadnezzar, King of Babylon, took it from Egypt (Jeremiah xlvi. 2).

Stanza 19. *Hast thou seen the pride of Moab?* Cf. Jeremiah xlviii 29 and Isaiah xvi. 6.

Gaza was the chief stronghold of the Philistines. *Askalon* and *Gath* were respectively the westernmost and easternmost towns of Philistia.

THE SETTLER

Stanza 3. *Here will we join against our foes.* In no country is economic organisation, such as irrigation and the provision on a large scale of the means of combating the diseases that attack crops and herds, more necessary than in South Africa. Under the Boer rule little was done in this direction. Irrigation on a small scale was practised by some of the Boer farmers, but South Africa needs irrigation on a larger scale than can be undertaken by private individuals. The Boer governments did little to promote irrigation, and were backward also in taking measures to check diseases among cattle and sheep and to kill off the swarms of locusts that periodically ravage the country, many Boers, members of the Legislature, considering that to do so would be an unrighteous attempt to interfere with Providence. One of the results of the South African War was that the establishment of a progressive government made possible economic organisation on a large scale.

THE FIVE NATIONS

CHANT PAGAN

Chant pagan. The original meaning of the Latin *paganus* was a 'villager' or 'rustic,' but it came to mean a light armed irregular soldier, enrolled for temporary service, as opposed to *miles*, a fully enrolled soldier.

Stanza 2. *Kopje on kop.* *Kop* is Afrikander-Dutch for a mountain, and *kopje* for a hill.

'Elios (see note, 'A Code of Morals,' stanza 1, p. 9).

Stanza 3. *Ma'ollisberg.* Magaliesberg Mountains, west of Pretoria. General De la Rey used the range as a hiding-place from which to make sudden attacks on the British.

Stanza 4. *Barberton.* A town in the eastern Transvaal enclosed by precipitous mountains. When General French took it he crossed these mountains by means of a goat track so steep that he had to put sixteen horses instead of six to each field-gun. He surprised the Boers by arriving at Barberton two days before they expected him.

Di'mond 'Ill. Diamond Hill was an indecisive battle lasting two days (June 11th and 12th, 1900), in which a large number of troops on both sides were engaged. Its effect was to save Pretoria from the danger of an attack from General Botha. The total forces engaged numbered twenty thousand men.

Pieters. The capture of Pieter's Hill (27th February 1900) was the last of the series of engagements

THE FIVE NATIONS

on the Tugela River by means of which Ladysmith was relieved.

Springs. A village east of Johannesburg, where General Dartnell had an engagement with the Boers on the first day of General French's organised 'drive.'

Belfast. An action fought on 26th and 27th August, 1900, in which Lord Roberts defeated General Botha, whose troops dispersed in the bushveld to the north of the Middleburg railway.

Dundee. Here the first action of the Boer War in Natal was fought, on 20th October, 1899. The Boer army surprised a small British force and compelled it to retreat towards Ladysmith.

Vereeniging. Here the Articles of Peace were signed on 31st May, 1902.

Five bloomin' bars on my chest. The speaker would have both the King's and the Queen's medals for the Boer War. With the latter medal he would have the following clasps: *Talana*, for the action at Dundee; *Tugela Heights*, for the action at Pieter's Hill; *Relief of Ladysmith*, for the general series of actions of which Pieter's Hill was one; *Diamond Hill*, and *Belfast*.

'Ands up. A captured man holds up his hands in token of surrender.

That state of life to which it shall please God to call me. A quotation from the Church of England catechism.

Stanza 5. *The place where the Lightnin's are made.*

Sudden and very violent thunderstorms are a feature of the South African climate.

Brandwater Basin. A horseshoe shaped valley in the Drakensberg Mountains. Here over four thousand Boers were surrounded and captured by General Sir A. Hunter, from whom, however, Generals de Wet and Steyn cleverly escaped.

Stanza 6. *Trek.* An Afrikander-Dutch word meaning 'draw.' Hence the word is the starting signal given to his oxen by a Boer waggon-driver. To 'trek' thus comes to mean in particular to travel by waggons, and in general to travel by any method.

Where there's neither a road nor a tree. A description which fits a great part of South Africa.

M. I.

Stanza 1. *A fence post under my arm.* As there is very little or no timber in many districts of South Africa, those who fought in the Boer War were often hard put to it to find fuel with which to cook their food. A soldier who when out on patrol came across a fence post would therefore regard it as a valuable find, and he would carry it away even though he were several miles from his camp or next halting-place.

A sore-backed Argentine. Many of the horses imported for the South African War came from the Argentine Republic.

Stanza 2. *Chronic ikonas.* A mixture of Cockney and Afrikander slang. The word 'chronic' among

Cockneys has many uses. A soldier may describe the weather, or his commanding officer, or his food as 'bloody chronic,' and in such cases the interpretation is left to the choice of the hearer. In this case the word is used to give emphasis to the word that follows. 'Ikona' (pronounced *aikorner*) is an Afrikander word which means anything from simple 'no' to 'no you don't, my boy.' The language is 'Kitchen-Kafir,' a manufactured dialect which enables Englishmen and South African Kafirs to meet each other half-way, each party thinking that it is speaking the other's language. The word is in general use in South Africa, even between English-speaking people. An M. I. trooper who strolled into a neighbour's horse-lines on the lookout for a remount (see stanza 6) would probably be greeted by a shout of 'ikona' from any one who saw him and suspected his motives. As the M. I. learned 'to steal for themselves' as efficiently as marines (see 'Soldier and Sailor too,' *The Seven Seas*), the word would often be shouted at them. Hence the nickname.

Stanza 3. *Veldt-sores.* A kind of sore that in various parts of Africa, from the Cape to the Soudan, attacks men whose blood has been made thin by lack of proper food. The sore is liable to break out wherever the skin is broken. In a mounted man it occurs most frequently on the bridle hand, as a horse, worried by flies, constantly jerks the rein forward and knocks its rider's left hand against the pommel of the saddle.

THE FIVE NATIONS

The things I've used my bay'nit for. The bayonet is a most useful tool. It may be used for chopping wood, digging drains to carry off rain-water from the ground around a tent, opening tins of meat or sardines, or cutting up a sheep. It may be used to take the place of a tent-peg, and it makes an admirable candle-stick.

From the Vaal to the Orange, etc. The Vaal River separates the Transvaal from the Orange Free State. The Orange River forms the southern boundary of the latter State, and the Pongola is in the east of the former State. The Mounted Infantryman of this poem is quite under a false impression in believing that his duties ever took him anywhere near the Zambesi River, which lies far to the north of the Boer War area.

Stanza 4. *Push.* Gang.

Stanza 5. *Our Adjutant's 'late of Somebody's 'Orse,' an' a Melbourne auctioneer.* Troops became very mixed during the latter part of the South African War. An officer who returned from hospital or from some special duty, to find that his regiment was scattered in detachments over a large area, that no one could tell him the precise whereabouts of any one detachment, and that there was no one in particular for him to report himself to, often attached himself to the first available column that seemed in need of his services. In the story 'A Sahib's War' (*Traffics and Discoveries*), an officer in the Indian army, who had been attached to a remount depot in Cape Colony, is

THE FIVE NATIONS

sent up to the front, and forgetting to return is 'stolen' by an Australian irregular corps.

Stanza 6. *Beggin' the loan of an 'ead-stall an' makin' a mount to the same.* A dismounted man in a mounted corps is not only useless but a nuisance. Until he can get another horse to replace the one he has lost through illness or otherwise, he has to march on foot with the waggons of his corps, and misses anything that may be going. Naturally, whenever he falls in with another mounted corps he endeavours to take steps to render himself a useful soldier again. The Mounted Infantryman would deny that it was stealing to take a horse from the horse-lines of another corps. If asked whence he had got a horse found in his possession he would say that he had 'made' it—a very common euphemism among those who are not punctilious as to methods of acquiring property.

Footsack. Afrikander slang for 'Go away.'

Stanza 8. *Cow guns.* Heavy guns drawn by teams of bullocks.

Convoys. Trains of waggons loaded with supplies for the front and guarded by men both on foot and on horseback.

Mister de Wet. A Boer general who displayed an extraordinary genius for guerilla warfare. On many occasions the British troops surrounded him, closed round him, and found at the last that he had somehow contrived to escape. He remained at large until the conclusion of the war.

THE FIVE NATIONS

Stanza 12. *Mausered.* The Boer forces were armed with the Mauser rifle; the British with the Lee-Metford.

Five-bob colonials. Five shillings a day was the pay of a trooper or private in the various colonial corps that were raised for the South African War.

COLUMNS

Stanza 1. *Trekkin'.* (See note, 'Chant Pagan,' stanza 6, p. 253.)

Detail supply. A store established at the war end of the line of communications to which mobile columns resort when necessary for the replenishing of their stores.

A section. A section of an artillery battery consisting of two guns and four ammunition waggons.

A pompom. A Maxim automatic quick-firing gun, firing a 1 lb. shell, used for the first time by the Boers in the South African War, and subsequently adopted by the British. Its name—at first merely a nickname, but afterwards seriously adopted—arose from the noise of its report: pompompompompom, etc.

Stanza 3. *Where do we lay?* Troops have to make their beds on ground assigned to them. It may be on ploughed land, which is soft and dirty, especially in rainy weather.

Stanza 4. *The tin street.* In South Africa the roofs of almost all houses, and even the walls of many, are made of sheets of galvanised iron, commonly known as 'tin.'

Stanza 5. *The outspan.* In every South African village an area of land is reserved on which visitors to the village may 'outspan' (*i. e.* unyoke) their oxen. The owner of the waggon usually sleeps in it during his stay in the village instead of putting up at an hotel.

Stanza 8. *'Untin' for shade as the long hours pass.* The mobile columns of the later South African War had to dispense with such luxuries as tents. When one was halted during the middle of the day the men used to seek relief from the burning sun by making tents with rifles for poles, blankets for canvas, and bayonets and jack-knives for tent-pegs. It was always hard to decide whether the stuffiness of the improvised tent was more or less bearable than the full glare and heat of the breezier open.

Stanza 9. *Dossin'.* Sleeping.

Beatin' a shirt. Among the hardships of the war was the unavoidable prevalence of vermin in the clothing of men of every rank. Whenever opportunity offered, men turned their shirts inside out and endeavoured to get rid of the lice and their eggs that infested the seams.

Stanza 12. *'Orse-guard.* The men who during the halt have been herding the grazing horses.

Stanza 13. *Alpha Centauri.* A star of the first magnitude in the southern hemisphere. It is the nearest star to the earth.

THE FIVE NATIONS

Somethin' Orion. The constellation Orion consists of three stars of the first magnitude, four of the second, and many of inferior magnitude. They are distinguished by letters of the Greek alphabet: alpha Orionis, beta Orionis, etc.

Stanza 21. *Stoep.* Veranda of a house.

Kraal. The word is applied in South Africa both to an enclosure for sheep, cattle, etc., and also to a group of native huts. It is often supposed to be a native word, but as a matter of fact comes from the Portuguese *corral.*

THE PARTING OF THE COLUMNS

Stanza 2. *Doubled out.* Came out 'at the double,' a military expression for 'at the run.'

Stanza 4. *Bloeming-typhoidtein.* A portmanteau word of which the ingredients are 'Blooming,' 'Typhoid,' and 'Bloemfontein,' where the British forces suffered severely from typhoid fever. Some Cockneys have a genius for the construction of such portmanteau words. A word, particularly the universal adjective, is often sandwiched between the beginning and the end of another word to give it emphasis, *e. g.* 'absobloodylutely.'

Stanza 6. *Mouse* and *caribou* (reindeer) are Canadian. The parrot that peeks lambs to death is the Kea parrot of New Zealand. *Ranch* is a Canadian word for a stock farm; *run* is its Australian equivalent. The towns mentioned are in Eastern

THE FIVE NATIONS

and Western Canada, New Zealand, and New South Wales.

Trek. (See note, 'Chant Pagan,' stanza 6, p. 253.)

Stanza 8. *Dorps*—towns. *Dawson* is the capital of the Yukon territory in Canada. *Galle* is a port in Ceylon from which many tea-planters went to serve in South Africa. *Port Darwin* is in the Northern Territory of Australia. *Timaru* is a little seaport town in New Zealand.

Stanza 9 *Drift*. Ford of a river.

Kraal. (See note, 'Columns,' stanza 21, p. 259.)

TWO KOPJES

Stanza 1. *Kopjes*. Hills.

Stanza 3. *Only baboons—at the bottom,*
Only some buck on the move.

Baboons do not come down from the kopjes to the flats below except at early morning and at late evening unless frightened by some one moving among their usual haunts. Nor do buck move during the heat of the day unless disturbed. Baboons at the bottom of a hill and buck on the move at mid-day are therefore signs that mean a lot to a scout.

Only a Kensington draper. London civilians were represented in the South African War by the C. I. V.'s —the City Imperial Volunteers. As they had had very little military training and no previous war experience, and being town-bred men had no bushcraft whatever, they had practically no knowledge of the

THE FIVE NATIONS

art of scouting. They therefore made many mistakes, anecdotes of which afforded much amusement for those who stayed comfortably at home. An unkind story which went the round of the newspapers may be quoted as an example. The commander of a Boer column captured a member of the C. I. V. whom he had captured several times before. He communicated with the officer commanding the column to which his prisoner belonged, offering to exchange him for a bale of forage. This offer was refused on the ground that the terms demanded were exorbitant!

Knock-out. A defeat. In boxing the term is used for a blow that renders the man who receives it unable to continue the fight.

Stanza 4. *Simmering.* Appearing to quiver owing to the motion of the heated air.

The kopje beloved by the guide. Many of the guides locally picked up by the British columns often endeavoured to lead them into traps.

Stanza 5. *A bolted commando.* The Boer forces were divided into groups named commandos. The art of drawing an enemy on by a feigned retreat was brought to perfection by the Boers in their wars with the Kaffirs.

By sections retire. If a force were to retire all together the result might be disastrous. Panic might spread and in any case the enemy, having no one to face them, could afford to discard all precautions, leave their cover and stand up to fire on the retreating

THE FIVE NATIONS

body. An orderly retreat should therefore be conducted 'by sections': a portion only of the company retires for a short distance (the others remaining to cover its retreat), and then takes cover and opens fire on the enemy in order to cover the retreat of the other sections. The sections thus take it in turns to retreat or stand their ground until all have withdrawn.

Stanza 7. *Voorloopers.* A voorlooper is a man or boy who leads the leading pair of oxen in a waggon-team.

Stanza 8. *The Staff.* A set of officers to whom general (*i. e.* non-regimental) duties are entrusted. In the field these include the planning of operations, the collection of information, etc.

BOOTS

The first four words in each line of this poem should be read slowly, at the rate of two words to a second. This will give the time at which a foot soldier normally marches.

There's no discharge in the war. Cf. Ecclesiastes viii. 8: 'There is no man that hath power over the spirit to retain the spirit; neither hath he power in the day of death: and there is no discharge in that war.'

THE MARRIED MAN

After service with the army private soldiers are transferred to the Reserve, that is to say they are free to follow any civilian occupation they choose, but must return to their regiment when called upon for active service. The great majority of the rank and file have to wait until they are in the Reserve before they can marry. During the South African War all the reservists were called out.

LICHTENBERG

Lichtenberg is a pretty little village in the Western Transvaal, built round a market square. Little streams flow down the streets, and until General De la Rey's attack on the place on March 2nd, 1901, a profusion of trees shaded the houses. These were cut down in order to make the place more easy to defend.

Some time after the war a group of men in a New Zealand club were discussing Rudyard Kipling's accuracy. One man referred to this poem, and declared positively that there was no wattle in Lichtenberg. An argument followed, and the point was referred to a man present, an Australian, who had been to Lichtenberg. The Australian declared the first speaker to be wrong. He said that on a rainy day in Lichtenberg he had smelt wattle though he could not at first see any. Later, when opportunity offered, he had searched for it and found one small wattle-bush in full flower.

The wattle of Australia, the doorn-boom of South Africa, the babul of India, and the acacia (which by masonic ritual is thrown into a Brother's grave) are all of the Mimosa family.

Stanza 2. *Sold-out-shops*. The shops in most small towns in the war area sooner or later became empty, as it was impossible to get fresh stocks of goods up from the coast owing to the railways being fully occupied with the carriage of war materials.

STELLENBOSH

Stellenbosh is a town near Cape Town. During the early part of the South African War it was used as a remount camp, as horses and mules thrive there. Officers who attracted the unfavourable notice of the Commander-in-Chief were sent there to perform the safe and uninteresting duties associated with a base camp. In consequence the expression 'to be stellenboshed' came into use, and was applied to any officer who was relieved of responsible duty at the front and given a less onerous task beyond the war area.

Stanza 1. *Told 'im off*. Reprimanded him.
The Staff. (See note on 'Two Kopjes,' p. 262.)
Stanza 2. *The drift*. Ford.
The last survivin' bandolier an' boot. During the last stage of the South African War the Boers, having little enough food for their own use, did not care to embarrass themselves with prisoners. To supply their own deficiencies, however, before releasing their prisoners they took away their arms, ammunition, and clothes, sometimes giving them in return a handful of tobacco, to show that there was no personal ill-feeling.

THE FIVE NATIONS

Stanza 3. *Stoep.* Veranda.

The Boer commandos in the later part of the war, knowing the country intimately and not being tied to supply-bases, were exceedingly mobile, and again and again slipped through the lines of columns that were closing upon them.

Stanza 4. *'Elios.* Heliographs, signalling instruments that catch and flash sunlight (see note 'A Code of Morals,' stanza 1, p. 9).

Pompom. A quick-firing automatic gun, or in this case the projectiles discharged from it (see note, 'Columns,' stanza 1, p. 257).

Krantzes. Steep hillsides.

K. C. B. The order of a Knight Commander of the Bath. The honour is given as a reward for military and (more seldom) civil service.

Stanza 5. *D. S. O.s.* Distinguished Service Orders given in recognition of military merit. Some critics, who considered that these orders were not distributed with proper impartiality, suggested that they were awarded to Duke's Sons Only.

HALF-BALLAD OF WATERVAL

Waterval is a village fifteen miles north of Pretoria. There the Boers imprisoned a large number of the soldiers whom they captured during the earlier part of the South African War. The prisoners were placed in compounds surrounded by tall fences of barbed wire, strongly guarded, and lit at night by electricity.

THE FIVE NATIONS

There were over four thousand British prisoners there when Lord Roberts entered Pretoria on June 5th, 1900. The Boers had intended to carry them farther east, but were so hurried by Lord Roberts's rapid movements that they were only able to take one thousand. On the morning of the 5th June a number of the British prisoners overcame their guards and escaped. The Boers shelled them as they ran and shelled a train sent to pick them up, but only one casualty occurred.

Boer prisoners captured by the British were sent to Ceylon or to St. Helena.

PIET

Stanza 1. *All that foreign lot.* At the outbreak of the South African War a number of men of European or American nationality offered their services to the Boers. Of these from three to four hundred were German, four hundred were Dutch, two hundred were Irish—mostly Irish-American—three hundred were French, and one hundred Scandinavian. There were also some American, Swiss, Italian, and Russian. In all, the Boers' foreign allies numbered about two thousand five hundred. The Boer attitude towards them was not very cordial. Kruger, when welcoming a party of German volunteers, said, 'Thank you for coming. Don't imagine that we had need of you. But as you wish to fight for us you are welcome.' The foreign allies received no pay, but expected a reward after the war was over. Some had offered themselves out of sympathy with the Boer cause; others joined from love of adventure, desire for military experience, or greed for plunder. An American who joined the Boers in order to test a gun that he had invented is the chief character in 'The Captive.' (*Traffics and Discoveries*).

'Is coat-tails lyin' level. The Boers did not adopt any uniform but wore their usual civilian dress—in many cases frock coats of the fashion of half a century ago. In the latter part of the war, being unable to replenish their wardrobes in the normal way, many of them wore uniforms taken from British prisoners. This was a violation of the rules of civilised warfare as laid down by the Hague War Regulations, which enact that combatants must wear 'a distinctive emblem recognisable at a distance'; but in the circumstances it would have been exceedingly difficult for them to have obeyed this regulation.

Stanza 3. *Camp and cattle guards.* When a column is not on the march pickets are thrown out to guard the camp, and men are sent to herd and guard the horses and oxen as they graze. If opportunity offers, these guards will wile away the time by sniping at the enemy.

Boer bread. The bread used by the Boers in the field was very much like what is known as 'pulled bread.' They made bread in the ordinary way, then broke up the loaves into small lumps and baked these again. In this form the bread kept its freshness much longer than it would otherwise have done. Being crisper and more palatable than British army biscuit, it was much appreciated by British soldiers who had the luck to raid a Boer camp.

Biltong. Meat that has been cut into strips and dried in the sun. It will keep thus for a long period. It is eaten without any further preparation.

Dop. Coarse kind of brandy made by Afrikander farmers.

Stanza 4. *An' borrowed all my Sunday clo'es.* (See note, 'Stellenbosh,' stanza 2, p. 264.)

Spoored. Spoor is Afrikander-Dutch for footprints. The verb therefore means to track a man or a beast by following its footprints.

You've sold me many a pup. Often tricked me.

''Ands up!' The sign of surrender.

Stanza 5. *From Plewman's to Marabastad.* Plewman's is just to the south of Colesberg in Cape Colony, and Marabastad is in the northern Transvaal. The two places are connected by railway; the line between them formed the longest stretch of railway line in the war area.

From Ookeip to De Aar. Ookeip is a village in Namaqualand, which was besieged by Smuts in April, 1902. De Aar is the junction of the Cape Town and Port Elizabeth railways. Between Ookeip and De Aar lies the longest stretch of war area unserved by any railway line.

THE FIVE NATIONS

The drive. At the beginning of 1902, though the main Boer forces were broken, there were still 25,000 Boers in the field. These had dispersed into small bands and were carrying on guerilla warfare. To suppress these bands Lord Kitchener organised a series of 'drives,' in which small British forces moving in line with each other, and in communication with each other, swept across the country, capturing or driving before them such Boer commandos as they encountered.

Stanza 6. *Block'ouse fence.* Before the system of 'drives' was initiated, long lines of blockhouses, within range of each other and connected by barbed wire fences, were built across and across the war area. The effect of these blockhouses was two-fold. Before the system was adopted the British mobile columns could not operate far away from the railways, on which they were dependent for supplies: when the lines of blockhouses were built they served to protect convoys that, by keeping close to them, could advance far into the war area to feed the mobile columns, which were thus freed from the necessity of returning periodically to the railways. The lines also served to check the movements of the Boer commandos, which could not cross them without coming under the fire of those who garrisoned the blockhouses.

Gifts and loans. After the declaration of peace the British Government issued the sum of £3,000,000, to be spent on giving the Boer farmers a new start in life.

THE FIVE NATIONS

They were supplied with stock, seed-corn, etc., and allowed to borrow money free of interest. The Government ploughed the land of those to whom it could not immediately issue draught-oxen.

Frow. Wife.

'WILFUL MISSING'

Stanza 4. *Name, number, record.* Each British soldier carried sewn into a pocket of his tunic a parchment—colloquially known as his photograph—on which was written his name, regimental number, address of his nearest relative, etc. A man who died on the field could thus be identified. A man who deserted could cover his tracks by putting his tunic, with his identification card in its pocket, on to the body of a dead Boer.

Stanza 9. *Domino.* In the game of dominoes a player who has played all his 'cards' says 'Domino' to his opponent.

UBIQUE

The Royal Regiment of Artillery is divided into Horse Artillery, Field Artillery, and Garrison Artillery. Each branch bears the motto *Ubique* ('everywhere').

Stanza 2. *You've caught the flash and timed it by the sound.* Light travels faster than sound. If the time that elapses between the flash of a gun's discharge and the sound of its report reaching the ob-

THE FIVE NATIONS

server is carefully noted, it will be possible to ascertain how far away the gun is situated.

Stanza 3. *Ubique means Blue Fuse, an' make the 'ole to sink the trail.* The trail is that part of a gun which is connected to the limber when the gun-carriage is in motion. When the gun is detached from the limber the trail rests on the ground. As the trail is on one side of the axle, and the muzzle of the gun on the other, the trail must be sunk into a hole in the ground when, in order to give the gun its greatest possible range, it is desired to elevate the muzzle. The fuses used in shells that are to burst at extreme range are painted blue.

Stanza 4. *Bank, 'Olborn, Bank.* Many of the horses used by the Field Artillery in the South African War had been purchased from the London Omnibus Companies. It therefore became a standing joke in the columns to greet Field Artillery on the march with the cries of London 'bus conductors.

De Wet. The Boer general who became famous for his success in evading capture.

Stanza 5. *Drift.* Ford.

Khaki muzzles. The guns were painted khaki (mud coloured) to make them inconspicuous.

Stanza 6. *R. A. M. R. Infantillery Corps.* Royal Artillery Mounted Rifles was the official title of the gunners who were used for duty during the South African War as mounted infantry.

Stanza 7. *Linesman.* Foot soldier. Artillery

and infantry are of mutual advantage to each other. Artillery can help infantry by supplementing its fire, and by firing bursting shells can compel the enemy to keep close cover. Infantry, on the other hand, help artillery by protecting the flanks of the guns. When the two arms are co-operating artillery usually fires over the heads of its own infantry.

Stanza 8. *Colesberg Kop.* A precipitous isolated hill, 800 feet high, near Colesberg, in Cape Colony. The 4th Battery dragged two fifteen-pounders to the top, from which, by sinking the trails, they were able to obtain a range of nearly 9000 yards.

Quagga's Poort. On the west of Cape Colony, near Sutherland.

Ninety-nine. The South African War began on October 11th, 1899.

RECESSIONAL

A recessional is a hymn sung when clergy and choir leave the church at the end of a service.

This poem was published on the 17th July, 1897, towards the close of the celebration of Queen Victoria's Diamond Jubilee. The Prime Ministers of all the self-governing colonies, troops from these colonies, Imperial Service Troops sent by native Indian princes, Hausas from the West Coast of Africa, Negroes from the West Indies, Zaptiehs from Cyprus, Chinamen from Hong Kong, even Dyaks from Borneo, took part in ceremonies of unparalleled splendour. One hundred and sixty-five vessels of the Royal Navy assembled for review. The poem was an appropriate monition at a time when the British people might well have been dazzled by the pomp that typified the 'might, majesty, dominion, and power' of the greatest empire in the world's history.

There are in this poem, with one exception, no literal quotations from the Bible such as are found in many of Rudyard Kipling's other poems, but the following references show that in his choice of words he has been considerably under the influence of the Authorised Version.

> Deuteronomy vi. 12: 'Then beware lest thou forget the Lord, which brought thee forth out of the land of Egypt.'
>
> Job xxxix. 25: 'The thunder of the captains, and the shouting.'
>
> Psalm li. 17: 'The sacrifices of God are a broken spirit: a broken and a contrite heart, O God, Thou wilt not despise.'
>
> Psalm xc. 4: 'For a thousand years in Thy sight are but as yesterday.'
>
> Nahum iii. 7: 'Nineveh is laid waste: who will bemoan her?'
>
> Romans ii. 14: 'The Gentiles, which have not the law.'

Songs from Books

The order of the following notes on the songs and chapter headings in Mr. Kipling's prose works follows the order of the collected volume of these poems published in the autumn of 1913 under the title *Songs from Books*. In several cases the collected edition of these contains portions of poems that did not appear in the prose works.

PUCK'S SONG

This song as published in Songs from Books *contains more stanzas than the version which appears in* Puck of Pook's Hill. *The numbers given in parentheses refer to the order of the stanzas as they appear in* Puck of Pook's Hill.

In this song Puck sings of the history of the county of Sussex.

Stanza 1. *Trafalgar.* This word is usually mispronounced in English. The accent should be on the last syllable.

Stanza 2. *Bayham's mouldering walls.* Bayham Abbey is in the Weald, five miles to the south-east of Tunbridge Wells, and on the border between Kent and Sussex. It belonged to the White Canons. A Tudor mansion took the place of the abbey at the Reformation, but ruins of the church and a gateway are still standing.

SONGS FROM BOOKS

Stanzas 3 and 4 (1). From the earliest days down to the end of the eighteenth century iron was worked in Sussex, timber from the Weald being used to smelt it. The decline of the industry was due to the gradual disappearance of the timber and to the discovery of the process of smelting with coal instead of charcoal, a discovery which made it possible to smelt iron more cheaply in the north of England, where coal and iron are found side by side, than in Sussex. A Roman forge in the parish of Burwash is mentioned by Parnesius in the story 'A Centurion of the Twentieth,' and the allied trades of cannon-founding and gun-running are the subject of the story 'Hal o' the Draft.' All the guns used in the Tudor navy were forged in Sussex.

Stanza 5 (2). The story 'Below the Mill Dam,' in *Traffics and Discoveries*, has for its subject a water-mill older than Domesday Book.

Stanza 7 (4). The pasture-land to the south of the town of Rye was covered by sea in the days when Alfred the Great built a navy with which to drive off the Norse pirates. The Norsemen sailed up the Rother, the river which makes the port of Rye, in 893 A. D., and left one of their galleys behind them. This galley was found in the year 1822 buried under 10 feet of sand and mud in a field at Northiam, near the present channel of the Rother, but several miles from the sea.

Stanzas 9 and 10 (6 and 7). There are a number of

ancient camps—Roman, British, and Neolithic—on the Sussex Downs. Two of these, known as Cissbury Ring and Chanctonbury Ring, are believed to be from four to six thousand years old. Cissbury, inside of which are the remains of a number of flint-quarries, must have been for the south of England what Sheffield is to-day. The flint-workings are far more extensive than local needs could have required, and tools made there probably passed from tribe to tribe over a wide area at a time when London, if it existed at all, was only a pile-built fishing village. When the Romans came they made camps of their own, but also made use of the fortifications constructed by Neolithic men many centuries before Cæsar landed in Britain.

As some of the embankments of these prehistoric towns are still as much as 30 feet high they are easily seen. Others, lower and more worn, are difficult to trace. Standing actually on them, it is not obvious that the rise of the ground is artificial, and one must go some distance away and get something of a bird's-eye view in order to realise that what seemed at first a chance hillock is really part of a definite scheme of fortification. Even then one can only detect the lines of the earthworks under favourable atmospheric conditions. On a warm day there is too much heat shimmer in the air. Camps can most easily be seen after rain, when the air is cool and clear. After rain, too, surface accumulations of dust are washed away

SONGS FROM BOOKS

and the permanent outlines of what lies below it are revealed. (See also 'Sussex,' stanza 6, p. 217.)

Stanza 11 (8). *Salt marsh where now is corn.* The coast-line of Sussex has altered considerably within historical times. Wilfrid's cathedral and monastery (see note, 'Sussex,' stanza 7, p. 219) long ago disappeared below the sea, but, on the other hand, the sea has receded a mile and more from the old ports of Rye, Winchelsea, and Pevensey, and cattle now graze where Norse, Norman, and Plantagenet ships once sailed.

A THREE-PART SONG

Weald, marsh, and chalk down are the three characteristics of Sussex. On the south 'levels,' formerly undrained marshes, alternate with lofty chalk downs running east and west, roughly parallel with the coast. To the north of the Downs stretches the Weald, which was all forest land until the growth of the iron industry, which needed charcoal for smelting, caused the destruction of the timber.

Stanza 3. *Brenzett* is a low-lying village between Romney Marsh and Wayland Marsh.

Stanza 4. *Firle* and *Ditchling* Beacons are the two highest points in the county.

THE RUN OF THE DOWNS

The places mentioned in this poem are the most prominent points of the South Downs westwards from

SONGS FROM BOOKS

Beachy Head. Near Mount Harry, Henry III. defeated the Barons under Simon de Montfort. A large cross cut in the turf on the west side of it, now overgrown, is supposed to have been made to invoke prayers for the souls of those who died in the battle. Truleigh, Duncton, Linch, and Treyford are mentioned in Domesday Book under the names Traigli, Donechitone, Lince, and Treverde. King Alfred had a park near Ditchling Beacon. The Long Man of Wilmington (see note, 'Sussex,' stanza 9, p. 220) was cut on the side of Winddoor Hill. The Roman road from Chichester to London passed over Bignor Hill, and traces of Roman occupation have been found near Ditchling Beacon. Chanctonbury Ring became a Roman camp, but it was made by Neolithic men many centuries before Rome was built (see notes on 'Puck's Song,' stanzas 9 and 10, p. 275, and on 'Sussex,' stanza 4, p. 217).

BROOKLAND ROAD

Stanza 3. *Duntin'*. Dunting, literally 'striking with a dull-sounding blow.'

Stanza 6. *Goodman's Farm*. The Goodwin Sands, six miles from the east coast of Kent. There is a tradition to the effect that they are all that is left of an island called Lomea, which belonged to Earl Godwin. This island passed into the hands of the Abbot of St. Augustine, Canterbury, who devoted the money which he should have spent in keeping its

SONGS FROM BOOKS

sea-wall in repair to the building of Tenterden steeple. In 1099 the island was swamped by the sea. Hence there is a cryptic saying in Kent, 'Tenterden steeple was the cause of Goodwin Sands.'

Stanza 7. *Fairfield Church* stands in a lonely part of Romney Marsh between Brookland and Appledore. Though about five miles from the nearest coast it is only fifteen feet above sea-level. Built of old red brick and roofed with shingles, the tiny church is interesting rather than beautiful. It is one of the churches that were formerly used by smugglers.

SIR RICHARD'S SONG

Stanza 1. *Fief and fee.* Land granted by a feudal lord in return for military and other services. The duke referred to is William the Conqueror, Duke of Normandy. In the story 'Young Men at the Manor' (*Puck of Pook's Hill*), Sir Richard Dalynridge holds his land from de Aquila on condition of supplying him, when required to do so, with six mounted men or twelve archers, three bags of seed-corn yearly, and of giving him entertainment for two days in each year in the Great Hall of the Manor.

A TREE SONG

The date attached to this poem in *Songs from Books*, 1200 A.D., is the year in which Layamon, the early English poet, wrote his chronicle *Brut*, which con-

SONGS FROM BOOKS

tained an account of Brutus, the Trojan, and of his more or less mythical kingly descendants, Bladud, Lear, Lud, Cymbeline, Vortigern, Uther, Arthur, and others.

Stanza 2. *Brut*, Brute, or Brutus was grandson of Aeneas of Troy. Having killed his father by accident, he fled to Britain and became the first king of the Britons. He founded *New Troy* (Troy Novant) where London now stands. This legend was invented by mediæval etymologists to explain why London was called Troy Novant. The word is really a corruption of Trinovantes, the name of a British tribe conquered by the Romans in 43 A. D. The similarity between the names Bryt, a Briton, and Brutus supplies the source of the rest of the legend.

Stanza 5. *A-conjuring Summer in!* It was the custom throughout Europe in pre-Christian days (and still is the custom in Italy) to dance round bonfires on the hilltops on Midsummer Eve. Christian priests objected first to the custom, but later gave it a Christian significance by dedicating Midsummer Day to St. John the Baptist.

A CHARM

Stanza 3. *Candelmas*—2nd February. An ancient Church festival to commemorate the presentation of the infant Christ in the Temple. It is so called because since the eleventh century it has been the custom of the Roman Catholic Church to consecrate

SONGS FROM BOOKS

on that day all the candles that will be needed for church use throughout the year.

Simples. Herbalists used to apply this name to plants that they used medicinally.

CHAPTER HEADINGS

PLAIN TALES FROM THE HILLS
IN THE HOUSE OF SUDDHOO

'A STONE'S THROW OUT ON EITHER HAND'

Churel and ghoul and Djinn and sprite. A churel is 'the ghost of a woman who has died in childbed. She haunts lonely roads, her feet are turned backwards on the ankles, and she leads men to torment.' When *Kim* overheard the conspiracy to murder Mahbub Ali at Umballa station, in order to have an excuse for leaving his sleeping-place, he pretended to have a nightmare and rose screaming out that he had seen the churel.

Djinn. (See note, 'The Captive,' line 7, p. 290.)

CUPID'S ARROWS

'PIT WHERE THE BUFFALO COOLED HIS HIDE'

Log in the reh-grass, hidden and lone;
Bund where the earth-rat's mounds are strown.
The version of this poem that appears in *Plain Tales from the Hills* has 'plume-grass' for 'reh-grass' and 'dam' for 'bund.'

SONGS FROM BOOKS

COLD IRON

In European folklore iron is held to have power to drive away witches, fairies, or any supernatural beings. Iron horseshoes nailed to stable-doors protect the horses from being ridden by witches. The superstition probably comes down from prehistoric days, when those tribes who knew how to make weapons of iron had an immense advantage over those whose weapons were made of nothing better than wood and stone. It has been shown elsewhere (see note, 'A Pict Song,' p. 296) that, so far as Great Britain is concerned, the aboriginal Picts were probably the ancestors of the more modern fairies. In Scotland, if a man blasphemes, it sometimes happens that those who hear him will call out 'Cauld airn,' and all present will touch the nails in their boots or the nearest piece of iron. When the passage of the Bible about devils entering into the Gadarene swine is being read in a Scotch church, the fishermen in the congregation have been known to whisper 'cauld airn.'

A SONG OF KABIR

Kabir was a religious reformer of northern India who lived and preached in the earlier part of the fifteenth century. Both Hindoos and Mohammedans claim him to have been born within their fold. He taught the Unity of the Godhead, the vanity of idols, the powerlessness of both Brahmans (Hindoo priests) and mullahs (Mohammedan priests) to guide or help, and the divine origin of the human soul. He proclaimed that distinctions of creed have no importance in the eyes of God, that all men are brothers, and that it is a crime to take the life of any living creature. 'No act of devotion can equal truth,' he said, 'no crime is so bad as falsehood.' Kabir's followers have been compared to Quakers on account of their hatred of bloodshed and their unobtrusive piety. The religion of the Sikhs was at first largely based on the teachings of Kabir.

Stanza 1. *Guddee*. (See note, 'Shiva and the Grasshopper,' stanza 1, p. 285.)

Bairagi. A mendicant member of the sect founded by Ramananda, to which Kabir belonged. Though most members of this sect are of the sudra or lowest caste, it is open to men of all castes. Ramananda's chief disciples included a weaver, a currier, a Rajput, a Jat, a barber, and several Brahmans.

Stanza 2. *The sal and the kikar* are two shade trees, bastard teak and acacia. The former is grown in the Central Provinces of India; the latter is found in the Punjab.

He is seeking the Way. (See note on 'Buddha at Kamakura,' stanza 2, p. 224.) Kabir was in no sense a Buddhist, but his definition of the Way, had he left one, would probably have been very similar to that of Gautama.

SONGS FROM BOOKS

'MY NEW-CUT ASHLAR'

This poem appeared originally as an envoy to the volume *Life's Handicap*.

Ashlar is a word used by builders and architects for a hewn or squared stone used in facing a wall. In freemasonry the word has a symbolic meaning. Rough stone as it comes from the quarry symbolises man unregenerate and ignorant, whereas the ashlar, the stone that is properly cut and fit for a place in the temple, symbolises a man whose mind is freed from earthly taints.

EDDI'S SERVICE

Eddi (Aeddi or Eddius) was a Kentishman who was choirmaster (and later biographer) of Wilfrid, Archbishop of York (see note on 'Sussex,' stanza 7, p. 219).

Manhood was the name of the 'hundred' or district granted to Wilfrid by Ethelwalch, King of the South Saxons. It was among the 'levels' which now terminate in Selsey Bill.

The date attached to this poem, 687 A. D., was the year following Wilfrid's return to York. Possibly Eddi found the newly converted Sussex men less tractable when his master's dominating personality was withdrawn.

SHIV AND THE GRASSHOPPER

Shiva, the third god in the Hindoo Trinity, is the Destroyer (Brahma is the Creator and Vishnu the

SONGS FROM BOOKS

Preserver). As, however, Death, in Hindoo belief, is merely a transition to a new form of life, Shiva is really a re-creator, and is therefore styled the Bright or Happy One.

Stanza 1. *Guddee.* Cushion of state, throne—thus any seat of office or power.

Mahadeo. The 'Great' God.

THE FAIRIES' SIEGE

Stanza 3. *To the Triple Crown I would not bow down.* The Triple Crown is the triregnum or tiara of the Popes. It has no sacred character, being solely the ensign of sovereign power. It is therefore never worn at liturgical functions, when the Pope always wears the mitre.

A SONG TO MITHRAS

Mithras was the god of light and identified with the sun. Though originally a minor Persian deity, his worship began to be adopted by the Romans during the first century B. C. It did not become popular till the second century A. D., by the end of which it was well established, especially among Roman soldiers.

He was the giver of victory, the protector of armies, and the champion of heroes. His worshippers had to be truthful, loyal, pure, and brave in fight, both against human foes and the forces of evil.

He was worshipped at sunrise, noon, and sunset, his worshippers facing east, south, and west in turn,

SONGS FROM BOOKS

but the most ceremonial form of worship was enacted at night-time in underground temples.

The 30th Legion was stationed at the Roman Wall at the date assigned to this poem (*circa* 350 A. D.). See 'A Centurion of the Thirtieth,' 'On the Great Wall,' and 'Winged Hats' in *Puck of Pook's Hill*. In 360 the Scots and Picts, to withstand whom the wall (see below) was built, invaded Britain.

Stanza 1. *The Wall.* Hadrian's Wall, stretching from Solway Firth to Tyne. Septimus Severus rebuilt it in 208 A. D., from which time till the departure of the Romans it was the northern frontier in Britain of the Roman Empire. The more northern wall, built by Antoninus Pius, was abandoned in 185 A. D.

Stanza 4. *Here where the great bull dies.* Bulls were sacrificed to Mithras because one of the most important acts of mythical Mithras, before he was received among the immortals, was the sacrifice of a bull, by means of which sacrifice life was created.

THE NEW KNIGHTHOOD

For the various ceremonies connected with the conferring of knighthood—the Bath, the laying on of the sword, the buckling of the belt and spurs, etc.—see note on 'The last Rhyme of True Thomas,' stanzas 4 and 5, p. 156.

SONGS FROM BOOKS

OUTSONG IN THE JUNGLE

In the *Jungle Books* (to which this poem forms an envoy) Mowgli, called the 'wise Frog,' is a child who has been reared from infancy by wolves, and has become intimate with, and learned the speech of, all the inhabitants of the jungle. Baloo is the Bear that taught him the Jungle-law. Tabaqui is the jackal, the attendant of Shere Khan, the tiger whom Mowgli slew. Kaa is the big rock-python that saved Mowgli from the Bandar-log, the monkey-folk. Bagheera is the panther, who always swears 'by the Broken-Lock' that freed him from captivity among men in the King's Palace at Oodeypore; he paid for Mowgli's admission to the Wolf-pack. The Flower is fire, the special possession of menfolk.

A ST. HELENA LULLABY

The rioting in Paris streets which brought about primarily the fall of the Bastille and ultimately the downfall of the French monarchy gave Napoleon Bonaparte his opportunity. At Austerlitz, by defeating the combined Austrian and Russian armies, he made himself master of the Continent of Europe. He was crowned Emperor of the French 'to complete his work by rendering it, like his glory, immortal.' At Trafalgar he lost his naval power. At the Beresina his magnificent army, retreating from Moscow, be-

SONGS FROM BOOKS

came a terror-stricken rabble, and Waterloo completed his downfall.

Stanza 8. *Trapesings.* Gaddings about.

CHIL'S SONG

Chil, the Indian kite, is one of the characters in the *Jungle Books*. He marked the way the Bandar-log went when they carried off Mowgli (see note on 'Out-song in the Jungle,' p. 287), and thus enabled Mowgli's friends, Baloo, Bagheera, and Kaa, to recover him. Chil is described as 'a cold-blooded kind of creature at heart,' because he knows that almost everybody in the jungle comes to him in the long run.

Stanza 2. *They that bade the sambhur wheel.* The sambhur is the Indian elk. Wolves hunting in packs make a division of labour. While some keep the game on the run others lie in ambush in places it is likely to pass, and by showing themselves at the right moment make it wheel. The game is thus driven backwards and forwards and becomes exhausted more quickly than the wolves that are hunting it.

They that shunned the level horn. When a deer is at bay it holds its head low down between its forefeet and its horns advanced parallel with the ground in a position to gore the first wolf that springs at it.

THE CAPTIVE

The poem here noticed is entitled 'The Captive' in Songs from Books *and 'From the Masjid-al-aqsa of Sayyid Ahmed (Wahabi)' in* Traffics and Discoveries.

SONGS FROM BOOKS

The Masjid-al-aqsa literally means 'the most distant mosque,' and is a common name among Indian Mohammedans for the Temple at Jerusalem. It owes special sanctity to the fact that from there, according to Mohammedan belief, Mahomet was translated to heaven. A Turkish mosque built in 691 A. D. now bears the name, and is the 'most distant' mosque to which pilgrimages from India are made.

Sayyid Ahmed was a learned Mussalman of the Wahabi sect, which endeavours to restore Mohammedanism to the primitive simplicity of conduct and worship taught by Mahomet. After preaching his doctrines with much success in India, Sayyid Ahmed in 1822 made the pilgrimage to Mecca. He then travelled in Turkey and Arabia, propagating the tenets of the Wahabi sect. He returned to India and began what might be called a revival mission, denouncing the superstitions which the Indian Mohammedans had borrowed from the Hindoos. The official Mohammedan leaders opposed him, and the dispute led to the reformers being interdicted by the British Government in 1827. Sayyid Ahmed then went to the Punjab accompanied by a hundred thousand disciples. In 1829 he declared a holy war against the Sikhs and made himself master of Peshawur. Soon afterwards, however, his Afghan allies deserted him, finding his austerities too rigorous for their tastes. Sayyid Ahmed fled across the Indus, and in 1831 encountered a body of Sikhs under Sher Singh, by whom he was put to death. Sayyid Ahmed's chief literary work was entitled *Tambihu-l-ghafilin*, or 'Awakener of the Heedless.' The poem here attributed to him was, however, written by Rudyard Kipling.

Embroidered with names of the Djinns. The Djinns, according to Mohammedan mythology, are spirits midway in rank between men and angels. Whoever knows the name of a Djinn and uses it with proper precautions has power to command its owner to perform wonderful things. A carpet embroidered with the names of Djinns, therefore, could only be possessed by a great magician. Mohammedans believe that the Djinns built the Pyramids and used formerly to spy on the secrets of heaven.

HADRAMAUTI

The sixth stanza only of this poem, as it appears in Songs from Books, *is to be found in* Plain Tales from the Hills. *It introduces the story 'A Friend's Friend.'*

Hadramaut is a district on the south coast of Arabia. Its inhabitants are of the most aristocratic and conservative type of Arab. A large proportion of them are Seyyids (descendants of Hosain, grandson of Mahomet).

Stanza 2. *Booted, bareheaded he enters*. An Arab on entering a building removes his shoes but keeps on his headgear.

SONGS FROM BOOKS

He asks of us news of the household. Although woman's position in Arabia is higher than it is in Mohammedan India—in tribal wars a woman riding in a camel-litter often accompanies her tribesmen singing songs in praise of her own people and of insult to the enemy—they are as rigidly secluded. No man mentions his own wife in conversation or speaks of another's. The utmost that politeness allows among intimate friends is a casual inquiry as to the health of a man's 'household.'

Stanza 3.   *I refreshed him, I fed him
   As he were even a brother.*
Hospitality is a sacred duty among the Arabs. The wealthier members of a community will dispute among themselves for the privilege of receiving a guest, and a host will defend his guest at peril of his own life.

Eblis. The chief of the fallen angels. He was cast out of heaven for refusing to worship Adam.

Stanza 4. *He talked with his head, hands, and feet. I endured him with loathing.* According to Burckhardt, one of the few Europeans who have succeeded in visiting Mecca, the Arab is studiously calm, and rarely so much as raises his voice in a dispute. But his outward tranquillity conceals a passionate and revengeful nature. A rash jest may be revenged years after it has been uttered.

Stanza 6.   *I gave him rice and goat's flesh.* Rice

and meat of any kind are luxuries among the Arabs. Their staple food is bread made of roughly-ground wheat, beans, lentils, and dates.

CHAPTER HEADINGS

THE NAULAHKA

'BEAT OFF IN OUR LAST FIGHT WERE WE'?

Caravel and Picaroon. A *caravel* was a light trading vessel of the fifteenth and sixteenth centuries, usually armed to resist attack. A *picaroon* was a pirate ship.

> *Every sun-dried buccaneer*
> *Must hand and reef and watch and steer.*

The qualifications of an A. B. (able seaman) as distinct from an ordinary seaman are that he must know how to *hand* (furl sails), *reef* (reduce the area of a sail), and *steer*. To *watch* in this sense is to keep a look-out at night.

'WE BE GODS OF THE EAST'

> *To the life that he knows where the altar-flame*
> *glows and the tulsi is trimmed in the*
> *urns.*

The *tulsi plant* (holy basil) is consecrated to Vishnu and Krishna and is worshipped by the women-folk of every Hindoo household. It grows on the altar before the house or in a pot placed in one of the front windows.

SONGS FROM BOOKS

THE LIGHT THAT FAILED

'THE LARK WILL MAKE HER HYMN TO GOD'

Stanza 2. *'Tis dule to know not night from morn.* 'Dule' is a Scottish word for misery. It appears in the better known word 'doleful.'

'YET AT THE LAST, ERE OUR SPEARMEN HAD FOUND HIM'

Though the Kafirs had maimed him. Kafirs in this context means 'unbelievers,' men who do not accept Mahomet as a Prophet of God.

He called upon Allah, and died a believer! Mohammedans believe it necessary for a man's salvation that he should at least once in a lifetime declare that *'there is no God but God; Mahomet is the apostle of God'* ('la ilaha illa-llahu; Muhammad rasul allahi'). Mungo Park relates that he saw drivers of Arab slave caravans, though utterly callous to the bodily welfare of their victims, endeavour to ensure that none of them should die pagan. If a slave fell dying on the march they would urge him to utter the profession of Faith before they abandoned him to the vultures.

GALLIO'S SONG

'And when Gallio was the deputy of Achaia, the Jews made insurrection with one accord against Paul, and brought him to the judgment seat. . . . **And when Paul was now about to open his mouth, Gallio said unto the Jews, "If it were a matter of wrong or wicked lewdness, O ye Jews, reason would that I should bear with you: but if it be a question of words and names, and of your law, look ye to it; for I will be no judge of such matters." And he drave them from the judgment seat. Then all the Greeks took Sosthenes, the chief ruler of the synagogue, and beat him before the judgment seat. And Gallio cared for none of those things'** (Acts xviii. 12-17).

Stanza 2. *This maker of tents.* 'And because he (Paul) was of the same craft, he abode with them, and wrought: for by their occupation they were tent-makers' (Acts xviii. 3).

Lictor. The officer who attended a Roman magistrate and kept order in his presence.

Stanza 4. *Claudius Cæsar hath set me here.* In the second verse of the chapter quoted above it appears indirectly that Claudius was Emperor when Gallio was deputy of Achaia. Aquila, the tentmaker with whom Paul lodged, had lately come from Italy, 'because that Claudius had lately commanded all Jews to depart from Rome.'

Stanza 5. *This stanza is not included in the version of the poem that appears in* Actions and Reactions.

Whether ye follow Priapus or Paul. Priapus was the most obscene of the Greek gods. Originally the personification of the fruitfulness of nature, he came to be regarded as the god of sensuality. His symbol was the phallus.

THE BEES AND THE FLIES

Aristaeus, son of Apollo and Cyrene, possessed some swarms of bees which the gods destroyed. To learn why they had robbed him, Aristaeus surprised Proteus and bound him with chains. Proteus, after making vigorous but futile efforts to escape—such as turning himself in turn into a fire, a fierce savage, and a running river—revealed the secret that the gods had destroyed the bees of Aristaeus to punish him for his conduct to Eurydice. Cyrene then tells her son that he must appease the nymphs by sacrificing four choice bulls of beauteous form and four heifers who had never felt the yoke. He does so, and nine days afterwards visits the carcasses of the cattle he had sacrificed. He finds them full of bees which promptly swarm on a neighbouring tree.

In the fourth book of the *Georgics*, which is devoted to hints, many of them eminently practical, on the keeping of bees, Virgil recounts this tale and gives the following instructions for the replacing of lost swarms: —Build a shed with four windows towards the four winds; drive a two-year-old steer into it and there suffocate it; then cover the carcass with boughs of trees, thyme, and cassia. A swarm of bees will soon emerge from the carrion.'

SONGS FROM BOOKS

Bees, as a matter of fact, have been known to hive in a decaying carcass, but the method here advocated of obtaining new swarms has not met with general favour among bee-keepers!

ROAD SONG OF THE BANDAR-LOG

The Bandar-log are the monkey-people. According to the story 'Kaa's Hunting' in *The Jungle Book*, they are known in the jungle as 'the people without a Law.' Baloo, the Bear, told Mowgli, the Man-cub, that 'They are outcaste. They are without leaders. They have no remembrance. They boast and chatter and pretend that they are a great people about to do great affairs in the jungle, but the falling of a nut turns their minds to laughter and all is forgotten.'

A BRITISH ROMAN SONG

The withdrawal of Roman troops from Britain began in 401 A. D. In 406 A. D., the date ascribed to this poem, the remaining Roman troops in Britain elected their own emperor.

The Seven Hills are the seven hills on which Rome was built.

A PICT SONG

We are the Little Folk. That the Picts were a 'little folk' physically as well as numerically is evident from the remains that exist of their beehive-shaped underground inhabitations, in which it is impossible for a modern average-sized man to stand erect (see David MacRitchie's *Fians, Fairies, and Picts*). It is quite possible that vague traditions about the Picts gave rise to many of the popular beliefs about fairies. As what was known about them became more and more vague with the lapse of time, their smallness may well have been exaggerated, until we get the conventional idea of a fairy small enough to lie in a cowslip bell and fly on a bat's back.

RIMINI

Only the first stanza of this song appears in Puck of Pook's Hill.

In the story 'On the Great Wall' (*Puck of Pook's Hill*), Parnesius said that this song was 'one of the tunes that are always being born somewhere in the Empire. They run like a pestilence for six months or a year, till another one pleases the Legions, and then they march to *that*.'

Stanza 1. *Rimini* is the Roman Ariminum on the Adriatic coast. The *Pontic shore* is the shore of the Black Sea.

Stanza 2. *Via Aurelia*. This road ran along the Italian coast from Rome to Genoa.

Stanza 4. *Narbo*. Narbo or Narbo Martius is the modern Narbonne in France. It was there that the Romans founded their first colony in Gaul. When Rome was tottering to her fall it was occupied in turn by Alans, Suevi, and Vandals. Finally it was captured in 413 by the Visigoths, who eventually made it their capital.

The Eagles. The insignia carried by the Roman legions. In this context it means the troops that followed the Eagles.

'POOR HONEST MEN'

Stanza 1. *Virginny.* Virginia tobacco.

Churchwarden. A clay pipe with a long slender stem; the most popular form of pipe in the eighteenth century.

Stanza 2. *The Capes of the Delaware.* The last American land sighted by ships bound from Philadelphia to Europe.

They press half a score of us. During the Napoleonic wars all British seamen, between the ages of eighteen and fifty-five, with some privileged exceptions, were liable to be compelled to serve in the Navy. British men-of-war often stopped vessels on the high seas and impressed their crews. They were supposed to leave on board enough men to work the ship, but they were not over-generous in the matter. On one occasion a homeward bound East Indiaman had so many men taken out of her that immediately afterwards she had to surrender to a small French privateer.

Stanza 4. *New canvas to bend.* New sails to set in place of those damaged by the cruiser's guns.

Off the Azores. Before the introduction of steam the Islands of the Azores—as the Spaniards found to their cost when Sir Richard Grenville cruised there—were of immense strategic importance in maritime warfare. Standing as they do almost in the centre of the North Atlantic, all ships bound to Europe from North or South America, or from eastwards of the Cape of Good Hope, had to pass near them. They therefore afforded an excellent base for privateers.

Stanza 5. *Roll, twist, and leaf.* The three forms into which Virginia tobacco was made up.

Stanza 6. A '*stern-chaser*' is a gun directed over the stern of a vessel that carries it, in which position it can be used against a pursuing vessel. A ship's fore braces keep her yards in position, and if these are cut by a cannon shot the ship's squaresails, which depend from the yards, become temporarily useless. A ship fighting another to the death would pound away at her hull with the intention of sinking her. A ship whose chief object was to escape would, on the other hand, gain more advantage by cutting up her pursuer's rigging, thus compelling her to stop and renew it.

Stanza 7. *'Twix the Forties and Fifties.*
South-Eastward the drift is.

The Capes of the Delaware are in 39° N. The Land's End is just north of 50°. The course of a vessel bound from the Delaware River to the English Channel is therefore almost entirely between latitudes 40° N. and 50° N. When thick weather makes it difficult to take observations with which to correct her course, she is liable to make her first landfall at Ushant, the southern gatepost of the English Channel (in 48° N.), as the outer rim of the Gulf Stream from mid-Atlantic eastwards has a southerly tendency.

Stanza 8. *Nor'ard.* Northward.

A homeward-bound convoy. During the Napoleonic wars British merchant vessels sailed in fleets protected by warships. Those bound for the East and West Indies, for example, would sail together under the escort of men-of-war until they reached the neighbourhood of Madeira, where they would separate and proceed independently. The men-of-war would then cruise at a rendezvous in the Atlantic until a number of homeward-bound vessels had collected, which they would then escort to the English Channel. The British Newfoundland fishing-fleet had a permanent escort that accompanied it to the Banks, stayed with it during the fishing season, and brought it home again.

Stanza 10. *Handspike.* An iron-bound wooden lever used in handling a muzzle-loading cannon.

PROPHETS AT HOME

Stanza 2. Jonah, the prophet, predicted the downfall of Nineveh. The city did not fall, which 'displeased Jonah exceedingly, and he was very angry' (Jonah iv. 1).

JUBAL AND TUBAL-CAIN

Jubal and Tubal-cain. Jubal and Tubal-cain were the sons of Lamech (Genesis iv. 21 and 22). Jubal

SONGS FROM BOOKS

was 'the father of all such as handle the harp and the organ'; Tubal-cain was 'an instructor of every artificer in brass and iron.' The two thus typify respectively the artistic and the practical temperaments.

Stanza 3. *New as the Nine point Two, Older than Lamech's slain.*

The Nine point Two is a naval gun, the bore of which is 9·2 inches in diameter.

In Genesis iv. 23 (Authorised Version) Lamech confesses, 'I have slain a man to my wounding, and a young man to my hurt,' or according to the Revised Version, 'I have slain a man for wounding me, and a young man for bruising me.' The words occur in a poem, the first that appears in the Bible. Commentators suggest that the poem expresses Lamech's exultation at the power, enabling him to take vengeance for the slightest injury, which Tubal-cain's new invention will give him.

THE VOORTREKKER

Voortrekker. An Afrikander word for a pioneer, one who 'treks' or travels before or ahead of others (see note on the word '*trek*,' 'Chant Pagan,' stanza 6, p. 253).

Line 12. *Stamp.* Ore-crushing battery.

Line 13. *Blaze.* (See note, 'The Explorer,' stanza 11, p. 212.)

SONGS FROM BOOKS

A SCHOOL SONG

Stalky and Co., in which this poem first appeared, is dedicated to Cornell Price, Headmaster of the United Service College, Westward Ho, Mr. Rudyard Kipling's old school. In many parts of the book the author pays affectionate tribute to the shrewdness, the wisdom, and the kindliness of his old headmaster. One passage is particularly interesting as showing how, under the wise guidance of 'the Head,' he laid the foundations of his extraordinarily broad and varied knowledge.

'He gave Beetle' (Kipling's nickname at Westward Ho) 'the run of his brown-bound, tobacco-scented library. . . . There were scores and scores of ancient dramatists; there were Hakluyt, his voyages; French translations of Muscovite authors called Pushkin and Lermontoff; little tales of a heady and bewildering nature, interspersed with unusual songs—Peacock was that writer's name; there was Borrow's *Lavengro;* an odd theme, purporting to be a translation of something called a "Rubaiyat," which the Head said was a poem not yet come to its own; there were hundreds of volumes of verse—Crashaw, Dryden, Alexander Smith, L. E. L., Lydia Sigourney, Fletcher and a purple island, Donne, Marlowe's *Faust*, and—this made M'Turk (to whom Beetle conveyed it) sheer drunk for three days—Ossian, The Earthly Paradise, Atalanta in Calydon, and Rossetti—to name but a few.'

SONGS FROM BOOKS

Stanza 1. *Let us now praise famous men.* Cf. Ecclesiasticus xliv. 1, 3, 4: 'Let us now praise famous men . . . Such as did bear rule in their kingdoms . . . Giving counsel by their understanding . . . Wise were their words in their instruction.'

Stanza 2. *Flung us on a naked shore.* Westward Ho is on the east side of Barnstaple Bay, North Devon.

Stanza 4. *Far and sure our bands have gone—*
Hy-Brasil or Babylon.
Islands of the Southern Run,
And cities of Cathaia.

Hy-Brasil was one of the islands—such as St. Brandan's Island, the Fortunate Islands, Avalon, Lyonesse, etc.—that the geographers of the Middle Ages placed somewhere in the Atlantic Ocean. A Venetian map marks 'I. de Brazi' in the Azores, and in Purdy's Chart of the Atlantic, 'corrected to 1830,' it is marked in 51° 10′ N. and 15° 50′ W. as 'Brazil Rock (high).' Cathaia, down till Tudor times, was the western name for China.

Stanza 6. *Each degree of Latitude*
Strung above Creation
Seeth one (or more) of us.

As boys educated at the United Service College were principally sons of men in the services, it was natural that on growing to manhood they, in turn, should disperse over the globe.

SONGS FROM BOOKS

OUR FATHERS OF OLD

The story which precedes this poem ('A Doctor of Medicine,' in *Rewards and Fairies*) has for its central character Nicholas Culpeper (1616-1654), astrologer, physician, and herbalist, who got into serious trouble with the College of Physicians in 1649 for translating their Pharmacopœia from Latin into a language that all could understand, thus jeopardising the profits of medical men. He practised as an astrologer and physician in Red Lion Street, Spitalfields, and wrote among other works *Semeiotica Uranica, or an Astronomical Judgement*. Quotations below from his book, '*The British Herbal and Family Physician for the use of Private Families*,' show the great extent to which he believed the sciences of astrology and medicine to be related.

Stanza 1. *Alexander* (wild parsley), according to Culpeper, is 'an herb of Jupiter and therefore friendly to nature, for it warmeth a cold stomach.' *Marigold* is a herb of the sun and under Leo. It strengthens the heart exceedingly. *Eyebright*, of course, strengthens the eyesight. 'If the herb was but as much used as it is neglected, it would half spoil the spectacle-maker's trade. . . . It also helpeth a weak brain or memory. . . . It is under the sign of the Lion, and Sol claims dominion over it.' *Elecampane* is under Mercury and good for coughs, stitch in the side, the teeth, etc. Of *Basil* Culpeper writes, 'This is the herb which all authors are together by the ears about; and rail at one another like lawyers. Galen and Dioscorides hold it not fitting to be taken inwardly, and Chrysipus rails at it with downright Billingsgate rhetoric. Pliny and the Arabian physicians defend it. To Dr. Reason went I, who told me it was an herb of Mars, and under the Scorpion, and therefore called basillicon, and it is no marvel if it carry a kind of virulent quality with it. Being applied to the place bitten by venomous beasts, or stung by a wasp or a hornet, it speedily draws the poison to it. EVERY LIKE DRAWS ITS LIKE. Hilarius, a French physician, affirms upon his own knowledge, that an acquaintance of his by common smelling to it, had a scorpion bred in his brain.' The seed of the *rocket* is useful against the bitings of the shrew mouse, but it must be used with caution, 'for angry Mars rules it, and he will sometimes be rusty when he meets with fools.' *Rue* sharpens the wits. *Vervain* is an herb of Venus. Worn as an amulet by itself, it used to be considered a safeguard against ague, or, together with a baked toad, against scrofula. *Cowslip*. 'Venus lays claim to this herb as her own, and it is under the sign of Aries, and our city dames know well enough the ointment or distilled water of it adds to beauty.' *Rose of the Sun* (or Sun-Dew). 'The sun rules it, and it is under the sign of Cancer. There is an usual drink made thereof with Aqua Vitae and spices, to good purpose used in qualms and passions of the heart.'

Stanza 4. From the fourteenth to the end of the seventeenth centuries England was scarcely ever entirely free from plague. Sometimes an epidemic, visiting a town or village, killed as many as two-thirds of the inhabitants. During the reign of Charles I., if not earlier, the law came into force compelling the inhabitants of a plague-stricken house to indicate that it was infected by chalking a cross on the door and writing underneath 'God have mercy upon us.' When the mortality was so great as to dislocate the usual arrangements for the disposal of the dead, corpses were carried away in carts, the drivers of which patrolled the streets ringing a bell and crying, 'Bring out your dead.'

Stanza 5. *Hippocrates*, the Father of Medicine, lived in the fifth century B. C. *Galen*, who lived six centuries later, wrote fifteen separate treatises on the writings of Hippocrates. Both men were daring thinkers, and notable for comparative freedom from the superstitions and blind traditions of their age.

CHAPTER HEADINGS

BEAST AND MAN IN INDIA

'DARK CHILDREN OF THE MERE AND MARSH'

In his chapter on 'Indian Buffaloes and Pigs,' John Lockwood Kipling quotes a native proverb. 'Yoke a buffalo and a bullock together and the buffalo will head towards the pool, the ox to the upland,' and says, 'The buffalo bears the sun badly, and to thrive prop-

SONGS FROM BOOKS

erly should have free access to a pool or mud swamp.' In 'Tiger-Tiger' (*The Jungle Book*) Rudyard Kipling describes how buffaloes 'get down into muddy pools one after another, and work their way into the mud till only their noses and staring china-blue eyes show above the surface, and then they lie like logs.'

Their food the cattle's scorn. John Lockwood Kipling says that 'one of many unpleasing features in the practice of keeping milch buffaloes in great cities is the usage of feeding them on stable refuse.'

Woe to those who dare
To rouse the herd bull from his keep,
The wild-boar from his lair.

In 'Tiger-Tiger' Rudyard Kipling describes the killing of Shere Khan, the tiger, by a herd of tame buffaloes under Mowgli's directions. In the same story he says that the buffaloes, though allowing themselves to be bullied by the herd-children, would trample a white man to death. John Lockwood Kipling says 'there is something ignominious in a party of stalwart British sportsmen being treed by a herd of angry buffaloes, and obliged to wait for a rescue at the hands of a tiny naked herdsman's child, but this has happened.' In the same chapter he says that the wild boar has been known to face and defeat a tiger.

SONG OF THE FIFTH RIVER

This poem has for its text a saying of Kadmiel, the Jew, in 'The Treasure and the Law' (*Puck of Pook's*

Hill). 'There can be no war without gold, and we Jews know how the earth's gold moves with the seasons, and the crops and the winds; circling and looping and rising and sinking away like a river—a wonderful underground river.'

A devout Jew, in conversation with the writer of these notes, once declared that the prosperity of every European country has risen and waned according to whether its treatment of the Jews was generous or the reverse, and that no country could prosper without Jewish inhabitants. He further declared his conviction that the millennium would come when the Jews returned to Palestine and became a united people. Asked how, considering their relatively small numbers, they would impose universal peace upon the world, and whether they would employ non-Jewish armies, he replied that the employment of armies would become unnecessary, since they would control the world through the money market. No war from the Crusades onwards, he said, had ever been waged without Jewish consent, and war would have ceased long since if the Jews had been able to agree among themselves.

PARADE SONG OF THE CAMP ANIMALS

Stanza 1. *We lent to Alexander the strength of Hercules.* Alexander the Great, after the invasion of the Punjab in 328 B.C., retreated westwards, taking with him elephants which were used by his successors in their wars. In 302 B.C. Seleucus sent to India for a fresh supply, and thenceforward elephants, either brought from India or bred in the royal stables, were constantly used in the Seleucid armies. It appears, however, that the Greeks, instead of attempting to drive the elephants themselves, employed natives of India for the purpose. 1 Maccabees vi. 37: 'And towers of wood were upon them, strong and covered, one upon each beast, girt fast upon him with cunning contrivances; and upon each beast were two and thirty valiant men, that fought upon them, *beside his Indian.*'

THE TWO-SIDED MAN

Stanza 3.   *Shaman, Ju-ju,* or *Angekok*
              Minister, Mukamuk, Bonze.

Shaman. The word is loosely applied to the priests of many low types of religions. In its correcter and more restricted sense it means a priest of the Tunguses, inhabitants of the Yenesei Valley in Asiatic Russia. A Shaman's duty is to control good and evil spirits, to perform sacrifices, and deliver oracles. A Shaman is by no means necessarily a conscious fraud. Doubtless much of his magic seems to miss its intended effect, but probably a good half of it seems to succeed enough to preserve his reputation and his own self-esteem.

Ju-ju. The word has wandered far from its original meaning. It is derived from the French *joujou*, a doll or toy, and with this meaning was applied by early French navigator-explorers to the idols venerated by the negroes of the West Coast of Africa. It has come to mean the religion of the people who worship these idols. The average European who now uses the word supposes it to be an African word, but the negro who uses it firmly believes it to be English.

Angekok. An Eskimo priest or medicine man. Any Eskimo who believes that when in a state of trance he can visit Sedna, the Queen of the Underworld (see 'Quiquern' in *The Second Jungle Book*), can declare himself to be an angekok. The darkness and intense silence of the long Arctic night tend to produce in the Eskimo the abnormal state of mind in which a man believes that he sees visions and holds intercourse with supernatural beings. The extent of credit that a self-constituted angekok can obtain among his fellows depends largely on the intensity of his own belief in his own powers. An angekok is supposed to be able to kill by a mere wish, by the glance of his eye, or by the terror inspired by his appearance; he is able also to divine people's thoughts, to know the whereabouts of game, to prevent the fire-drill from producing fire, to visit the moon (which is believed to be a man), and to find lost objects. He can see the sins of men, and the dark colour of objects that have come into contact with something tabooed, and are thus to be avoided. An angekok cannot, however—practical experience has probably taught them this—see through falling snow or fog any better than an ordinary man. An angekok's chief duties are to heal the sick and to propitiate Sedna and animals that, being offended by the violation of taboos connected with them, will not allow themselves to be killed. Angekoks have a special language of their own.

Mukamuk. A medicine man or sorcerer among the Red Indians. Unlike the angekok, he is not self-appointed. He must be selected from a family in which priesthood is hereditary, and he must be very carefully educated for and initiated into his duties.

Bonze. The European name for any member of a Buddhist religious order.

LUKANNON

Lukannon is one of the seal-rookeries on the Island of St. Paul in the Pribilof Group in the Bering Sea, an island from which nearly half the world's supply of sealskin is obtained. From May till August every year about three million seals come there for the breeding season, but only the young males (Russian *holluschickie*, 'bachelors') are killed for their skins. The adult males with their cows stay on the rocky shores, but the young play about the sand-dunes and among the salt lagoons inland. When the seals arrive the island is covered with vegetation—grass, moss, lichen, etc.—but this is quickly worn away by the seals, who, moving about in their thousands, wear down even the sand hummucks. The right to kill seals on St. Paul's is farmed out by the United States Government.

SONGS FROM BOOKS

(See also notes on the envoy to 'The Rhyme of the Three Sealers,' p. 132.)

Stanza 6. *Wheel down, wheel down to Southward—oh, Gooverooska go!* Gooverooska is Russian for a sea-gull (*Larus brevirostris*) of the same species as the kittiwake. Russian is the language of the Pribilof Islands, because they belonged to Russia before they were ceded, together with Alaska, to the United States.

AN ASTROLOGER'S SONG

Stanza 1. *While the Stars in their courses
Do fight on our side.*
Cf. Judges v. 20: 'The stars in their courses fought against Sisera.'

Stanza 5. *The Sign that commands 'em.* The heavens are dominated in turn by each of the twelve signs of the Zodiac—the Ram, the Bull, etc. These constellations, according to astrologers, have a powerful influence over what happens on the earth. The fate of a man, they believe, depends greatly upon the stars that are rising at the moment of his birth, and the relation between these stars and the signs of the Zodiac.

THE BEE BOY'S SONG

The common superstition that bees must be told every item of news is easy to explain. They seem to be overwhelmed with curiosity as they fly into one flower after another. As they are so valuable, and apparently liable to fly away at a moment's notice, it is worth while to keep on good terms with them by telling them the news.

Stanza 2. *Where the fanners fan.* Among the many duties of worker-bees is that of keeping the hive cool and ventilated by standing in the passages and ceaselessly moving their wings. Much bee-lore is to be found in the allegorical story 'The Mother Hive' (*Actions and Reactions*).

MERROW DOWN

There runs a road by Merrow Down
A grassy track to-day it is.

And a wonderful road it is! One of the oldest in Europe, and much older than the Roman roads that run straight as arrows across and across England. It is part of what is called the Pilgrim's Way, because long ago pilgrims from the west of England and from the west of France and Spain used to travel along it to visit the shrine of Thomas Becket at Canterbury. But the road was there long before Becket was born, and even long before Canterbury was built. In fact, so far from the road owing its existence to Canterbury, Canterbury owes its existence to the road. It used to be the main road between the west of England and the Straits of Dover, and is thus probably the end of an old trade route that ran from Cornwall across the Straits of Dover through France and Switzerland to Greece, Italy, Troy, Crete, Egypt, and beyond. At Farnham, a few miles to the west of Merrow Down, the road divides; the newer part of it runs to Winchester and Southampton Water — along that part of it the pilgrims from the west of Europe came to Canterbury; the older part runs to Stonehenge (Stonehenge is where it is because of the road, so you may judge how old the road is) and right through Devonshire and Cornwall to the tidal island now called St. Michael's Mount, where the Phœnicians made their camp when they traded with the ancient Britons. This older part is still called the Harrow Road (that is the 'hoary' or very old road). The road is not straight like a Roman road, but follows wherever possible the line of the chalk downs, and runs just below the crest of the downs on their southern sides. There are several reasons for this. Down in the valley travellers from or to the west of England would have had to pass through the thick forests, where they could not see far and were therefore liable to be attacked by the warlike tribes through whose territory they passed. Up near the top of the downs above the forest they could not be attacked without having time to get ready to fight. On the well-drained chalk downs, too, the ground was drier than in the clay valleys and so easier to walk on, and the south side of the downs along which the old road runs is drier than the north side because it gets more sun. Why did not the travellers who made the road walk along the *top* of the downs?

Because had they done so all the people from the valleys below could have seen them against the skyline and could have had ample time to gather a large force to attack them. There are so many interesting things to say about this wonderful old road—such as why it stops short at Canterbury instead of running on to one or other of the harbours in the Straits of Dover—that whole books have been written about it. One of the best is *The Old Road*, by Hilaire Belloc.

Looking southwards from Merrow Down you see one of the prettiest valleys in England. You see Broadstonebrook and Bramley (where the beavers built their dams), and Shere that is now inhabited by artists instead of bears, because it is one of the prettiest villages in England. And on a hilltop near by you can see St. Martha's church, which was built for the pilgrims. (People think it was then called St. Martyr's in honour of the martyr, Thomas Becket.) John Bunyan is supposed to have had the whole scene in his mind when he wrote *The Pilgrim's Progress*.

The Phœnicians carried their goods on packhorses because the old road was not good enough for carts. Their horses had bells on their necks so that they could easily be found in the mornings after they had been turned out to graze at night. The moccasins that Taffy wore were shoes made of soft skin. They fitted the foot like a glove, and so never made blisters on her heels. They were much better than boots, too, because she could walk up a steep rock much more easily in soft moccasins than in hard-soled boots. Red Indians still wear them and so do South African Boers, but Boers call them 'veldtschoen.' When Taffy wanted to send a message to her daddy she made a fire by rubbing two sticks together, then she put damp wood on to it so that it would make plenty of smoke for him to see. Then she kept on covering and uncovering it so as to make long and short smokes. Australian blacks send messages to each other in the same way. In the story that accompanies this poem, 'How the First Letter was Written,' Rudyard Kipling says that Taffy is short for Taffimai Metallumai, and that this means 'Small-person-without-any-manners-who-ought-to-be-spanked.' I wonder if he really knows!

OLD MOTHER LAIDINWOOL

Stanza 1. This song is sung by Puck as, in the form of Tom Shoesmith, he comes to the oast-house in which Hobden is drying hops ('Dymchurch Flit' in *Puck of Pook's Hill*). As soon as Hobden sees his friend he exclaims, 'They do say hoppin 'll draw the very deadest, and now I belieft 'em.' The first two lines are a quotation from an old song.

Stanza 3. *With stockin's on their hands*. The juice of the hop stains the hands almost as effectively as walnut juice, and hops are prickly. The better class hoppers, therefore, wear old gloves or some other covering for the hands when at work.

SONGS FROM BOOKS

An' none of 'em was foreigners. In the agricultural districts of Sussex and Kent the villagers of each little community speak of any kind of stranger as a 'foreigner.' In many districts local labour suffices to gather the hop-harvest. In others labour is imported temporarily from the London slums. The local labourers consider themselves, with reason, to be socially superior to the imported foreigners, and endeavour to avoid mingling with them. In fields that are picked by both local and imported labour, the local people will take one side of the field and leave the other to the 'foreigners.' In 'Dymchurch Flit' (*Puck of Pook's Hill*) Puck, masquerading as Tom Shoesmith, in order to show that he is a fit and proper person to be with Dan and Una, assures the maidservant he is no 'foreigner.'

Stanza 4. *An' she moved among the babies an' she stilled 'em when they cried.* In the hop-districts hopping time is regarded as a profitable annual holiday. Many of the small trades people and mechanics shut up their shops, and with their whole families go to work in the fields. Maidservants from large houses spend their 'afternoons off' in the field, working a little and flirting a lot. Old women come out of the almshouses to help their daughters pick, and five-year-old children work for a while in the intervals between picking blackberries and sleeping in the sun. The smallest children of all, who must necessarily be brought to the field, as the houses are all shut up, are left in their perambulators in charge of some aged volunteer nurse.

CHAPTER HEADINGS

JUST-SO STORIES

'WHEN THE CABIN PORT-HOLES ARE DARK AND GREEN'

. . . .

*Why, then you will know (if you haven't guessed)
You're 'fifty north and forty west!'*

Strictly speaking, the part of the world's surface that is known as 50° N. and 40° W. (fifty degrees north of the equator and forty west of Greenwich) is a little more than half-way from London to New York on the course that the great liners take, but it is an old sea expression for any part of the mid-Atlantic that is rough and unpleasant. If you complained, in the hearing of a seasoned traveller, that the passage between Dover and Calais was not exactly smooth, the latter would almost certainly put on a superior air and say, 'You wait till you've been Fifty North and Forty West!'

'THIS IS THE MOUTH-FILLING SONG OF THE RACE THAT WAS RUN BY A BOOMER'

A Boomer is the same as an Old-Man-Kangaroo, that is the biggest kind of kangaroo. You will not find Warrigaborrigarooma on the map of Australia, because the race between the kangaroo and the Yellow-Dog Dingo happened so long ago. All the names of Australian places are shorter now; such as Warragamba, Burrangong, Cumbooglecumbong, Goondiwindi, Ringarooma, etc. The dingo is the wild Australian dog. It is generally all yellow, but sometimes it has a white tip to its tail like a fox. It is the only Australian mammal except the bat that has not got a pocket in which to put its young ones.

> 'CHINA GOING P. AND O'S
> PASS PAU AMMA'S PLAYGROUND CLOSE.'

Pau Amma is the giant king-crab that ranges from Singapore to Torres Straits. Learned people call him *Tachypleus gigas moluccanus*. The Malays believe that there is a huge hole in the bottom of the sea, and that Pau Amma sits on the top of it. When he comes out for food the water pours through this hole into the underworld, and that makes the tide go down. When he goes back to it again the water cannot flow through the hole, and as plenty of rivers are all the time pouring water into the sea it fills up. That makes the tide rise. The hole is called Pusat Tasek. You can read about it in a book called *Malay Magic*, by W. W. Skeat.

P. and O.'s means Peninsula and Oriental ships that go from London to India, China, and Australia.

SONGS FROM BOOKS

B. I.'s are British India boats. Some of them go past Pusat Tasek to China, the Philippine Islands, and Queensland, but some don't go near it, as they have to go to the Persian Gulf or East Africa instead. N. Y. K.'s are Nippon Yusen Kaisha; they are Japanese steamers running to Europe. N. D. L.'s are German Nord-deutscher-Lloyd boats. They run to Eastern Asia and Australia as well as to America. M. M.'s are the French Messageries Maritimes steamers. They go to China, Australia, and New Caledonia. Rubattinos are Italian steamers, running from Genoa to Hong-Kong. The A. T. L. (Atlantic Transport Line) only goes from London to New York. The D. O. A. is the German East African line (Deutsche-Ost-Afrika). Their ships go right round Africa, outwards by the east coast and homewards by the west coast, or *vice versa*. The Orient liners go round the south of Australia, so they do not go near the Malay Peninsula. The Anchor boats stop short at the Indian ports; those of the Bibby line get no farther than Burma. The U. C. L. is the Union-Castle Line running round Africa. The Beavers go to West Africa. The Shaw Savill steamers go round the world, touching at the Cape and New Zealand, then home round the Horn. The White Star boats go to America, to the Mediterranean, to South Africa and Australia, but do not go near the East Indies.

There is not really any such person as Mr. Lloyds.

SONGS FROM BOOKS

Over two hundred years ago shipping merchants used to meet to discuss business at a coffee-house kept by Edward Lloyd in London, who also published a newspaper about shipping matters called *Lloyds' News*. The present great association of merchants and ship-owners called Lloyds takes its name from the coffee-house where it originated.

Mangosteens are considered by many people to be the most delicious fruit in the world. You cut through a thick reddish brown rind and find inside a soft, very juicy, snow-white pulp that looks like a water-ice and tastes rather like red-currants, and a little bit like acid drops. You cannot taste mangosteens unless you go to Ceylon or the East Indies, because they will not grow anywhere else, and the fruit cannot be sent all over the world as bananas and oranges can, because they are too delicate.

'THERE WAS NEVER A QUEEN LIKE BALKIS'

Balkis was the name of the Queen of Sheba who came to see Solomon because she heard how wonderfully wise he was. She is said to have married Solomon and to have had a son called Menelek, who was the first king of Abyssinia, but you will not find that in the Bible. You will find stories about Solomon and the Queen of Sheba in the Koran, which is the Sacred Book of the Mohammedans. Sabaea is that part of Arabia that is now called Yemen, at the back of Aden.

SONGS FROM BOOKS

THE QUEEN'S MEN

This poem, which precedes the story 'Gloriana' (Rewards and Fairies), is there entitled 'The Two Cousins.'

Stanza 3. *Belphœbe* is a character in Spenser's *Faerie Queen* intended to portray Queen Elizabeth.

GOW'S WATCH

Tiercel. A name applied to the male of various kinds of falcon, chiefly the peregrine.

At hack. In the state of partial liberty which a hawk must enjoy after it has been trained to come to the lure but before it is used in the field. As soon as the hawk begins to prey for itself it should be 'taken up' from hack.

Eyass. A hawk that has been brought up from the nest.

Passage hawk. A hawk captured when 'on passage,' i. e. migrating. Such a hawk is harder to train than an eyass, but can work more effectively. As it has already developed its powers of flight it need not be kept so long 'at hack' as must an eyass.

Footed. Killed its prey.

Binds to. Clings to. A glove is always worn on the hand that carries a hawk.

Tirings. Food.

Make-hawk. A thoroughly trained and reliable hawk flown with young hawks to teach them their work.

SONGS FROM BOOKS

In yarak. Keen and in good condition.
Manned. Well trained.
Weathered. Inured to the open air. The initial training of a hawk is carried on in a darkened room.
Cozen advantage. Win an advantage by cunning.
What's caught in Italy. In Tudor times Italy was regarded as a hot-bed of atheism and vice. Men of fashion who went there to obtain culture and brought home vicious habits instead were called 'Italianate' Englishmen. Syphilis was called 'the Italian disease.'
A coil. Source of trouble.
Coney-catch. Literally 'to catch rabbits'—to poach.
Gerb, from the French *gerbe,* 'a sheaf.' A kind of firework somewhat like a Roman candle, but usually larger. Its sparks take the shape of a sheaf of wheat.

SONG OF THE RED WAR BOAT

The date assigned to this poem (683 A. D.) is two years after St. Wilfrid began the work of converting the men of Sussex to Christianity.
Watch for a smooth. The following definition of 'a smooth' is given in Captain Marryat's *Poor Jack*: —'Occasionally a master-wave, as it is termed, from being of larger dimensions than its predecessors, pours its whole volume on the beach; after which, by watching your time, you will find that two waves will run into one another, and, as it were, neutralise each other, so that, for a few seconds, you have what they call "a smooth."'

SONGS FROM BOOKS

Stanza 1. '*Give way.*' The 'way' of a boat is its motion through the water. 'Give way' therefore means 'get her going.'

A *Lop* is a short choppy sea caused by the direct action of the wind, as opposed to the long heaving waves of a swell which follow and often precede a storm.

Stanza 3. *Meether.* In working a boat out in the teeth of a heavy sea it is necessary to meet each wave squarely with the boat's bow. If a big wave catches the boat at an angle it will twist her 'broadside on,' *i.e.* parallel to its course, fill her with water, and swamp her.

Stanza 4. *Thor's own hammer.* Thunder.

Stanza 6. *Break her back in the trough.* The pressure put on a long boat in the trough of the sea—that is, between two great waves—is tremendous. Her stern is held up by the receding wave and her bow by the oncoming wave, but as there is nothing to support her amidships she is liable to sag and break.

Stanza 7. *Mead.* A fermented drink that the Saxons made from honey.

Two-reef sailing. Sailing with a sail the area of which is reduced by rolling up two reefs. In a moderate breeze one reef would be taken in; in a light breeze the whole sail would be used.

A RIPPLE SONG

'*Maiden, wait,*' *the ripple saith,*
'*Wait awhile for I am Death.*'

The ripple is caused by Jacala, the crocodile.

BUTTERFLIES

This song, as printed in *Traffics and Discoveries*, is called 'Kaspar's Song in "Varda" (from the Swedish of Stagnelius).' Stagnelius, who died in 1823, at the age of thirty, has been called the Swedish Shelley. The poem is, however, the work of Rudyard Kipling. In *Traffics and Discoveries* the second line of the poem, in place of 'the children follow the butterflies,' has 'The children follow where Psyche flies.'

Psyche in Greek mythology represented the human soul. In Greek and Greco-Roman art she was represented sometimes as a beautiful girl with a bird's or a butterfly's wings, sometimes simply as a butterfly.

THE NURSING SISTER

Stanza 1. *Our little maid that hath no breasts.* Cf. Song of Solomon viii. 8: 'We have a little sister, and she hath no breasts.'

THE ONLY SON

This poem precedes the story 'In the Rukh' (*Many Inventions*) that deals with the manhood of Mowgli, who, as a child, had a wolf for foster-mother. Stories of wolf-reared children are as old as the story of Romulus and Remus, but usually these have been regarded as mere legends. In the ninth volume of the *Journal of the Anthropological Institute*, vol. ix., however, Mr. V. Ball, of the Indian Geological Survey,

SONGS FROM BOOKS

presented evidence which he had collected on the subject. A correspondent of Mr. Ball's furnished him with particulars of a man whom the natives said had been nourished by a wolf foster-mother. This man had several wolf-like characteristics. He smelt all food offered to him before deciding whether or not to eat it, and hid such food as he did not eat at the moment under the straw of his bedding. He grunted as a sign of recognition, but could not speak. He walked on the front portion of the foot, the heels being raised from the ground and the knees bent, 'in fact, one could readily suppose that he had as a child progressed in a stooping position, using both hands and feet. The hands were bent back but not stiff. He kept them in this position when taking anything offered to him instead of clutching it.'

Line 13. *Tyre.* Sour or curdled milk.

MOWGLI'S SONG AGAINST PEOPLE

Stanza 1. *And the Karela, the bitter Karela*
Shall cover it all.

The Karela, as appears from the story which precedes this poem in *The Second Jungle Book*, is a wild vine, bearing a bitter gourd, that spreads rapidly and soon overgrows ground deserted by human beings. Jungle growth is so swift that a man might often pass through what had been a village only a year or so before and notice no trace of human habitation until his attention was arrested by the fact that the vegetation immediately around him was different from that farther away. The vegetation covering a recently ruined village would all be of a quick-growing kind.

CHAPTER HEADINGS
THE JUNGLE BOOKS

The following words need explanation to those who have not read *The Jungle Books:*—

Sambhur. The Indian elk.
Jacala. The crodocile.
Nag. The snake.
Tabaqui. The jackal.

'AT THE HOLE WHERE HE WENT IN RED-EYE CALLED TO WRINKLE SKIN.'

Red-eye is the Indian mongoose, described in the story 'Rikki-Tikki-Tavi.' The mongoose is as eager to hunt and kill snakes as a dog is to catch rabbits. So seldom is the mongoose killed by the poison of a snake, that the Hindus believe that after fighting it goes off and eats a vegetable antidote. The mongoose, however, relies entirely on its wonderful agility and on the thickness of its bottle-brush fur. The snake cannot eject venom unless its jaws are closed, and it cannot make them close on the thick hair.

SONGS FROM BOOKS

THE EGG-SHELL

The first and last stanzas of this poem precede the second part of the story 'Their Lawful Occasions' in Traffics and Discoveries. *The second stanza does not appear there.*

Stanza 1. *An egg-shell With a little Blue Devil inside.* A torpedo-boat and the lieutenant in charge.

Stanza 2. *The sights are just coming on.* The sights by which the Whitehead torpedo is aimed are just coming into line with the object at which it is to be discharged.

THE KING'S TASK

The first eighteen lines of this poem precede the story 'The Comprehension of Private Copper' in Traffics and Discoveries, *and appear in chapter ii. of* A School History of England. *The remaining lines appear only in* Songs from Books. *The latter should be compared with* 'The Islanders' *and* 'The Lesson' (Five Nations).

Line 2. *Saint Wilfrid.* The first to preach Christianity in Sussex (see note 'Sussex,' stanza 7, p. 219).

Line 8. *Andred's Wood.* Andredsweald—the forest land or 'Weald' of Sussex, between the North and South Downs.

Line 9. *The Witan.* The Council. Each of the English kingdoms in Anglo-Saxon times had its separate witan, which made laws, imposed taxes, con-

SONGS FROM BOOKS

cluded treaties, and advised the king on affairs of state.

Flaying. Pillage.

Line 10. *In* Traffics and Discoveries *the first part of this line runs* 'Folkland, common and pannage' *in place of* 'Common, loppage and pannage.'

Folkland. Land owned by permission (or the customary law) of the people, as to the ownership of which it was unnecessary to produce documentary proof. (The opposite was 'bookland,' held by royal privilege and attested by documents.) The owner of folkland could not bequeath it to any but a kinsman and could not sell it without the permission of his kinsmen.

Common. Each Anglo-Saxon town or village possessed an area of arable land that was the property not of individuals but of the community. Strips of the land were assigned to each householder. In the very early days, possibly, he took as much land as he could cover from end to end by throwing a hammer. Thus each man received as much as he had strength enough to cultivate. The householder enjoyed the exclusive use of his strip from ploughing-time to harvest, but as soon as his crop was gathered the land reverted to the community. The poorest was left waste for pasturage, to supply fuel, etc.: this waste land is now the common of the present day.

Pannage. The right to feed swine in a wood or forest.

Loppage. The steward of a large manor, applied to for the meaning of this word, said that he did not know the meaning although the word frequently occurred in leases that he drew up. Presumably it means the right to lop trees, *i. e.* remove their superfluous branches without interfering with the trunk.

The theft and the track of kine. If stolen cattle were tracked by their footprints to within reasonable distance of a village, that village was held responsible for the theft, but the community could clear itself if it could track the stolen cattle to some other village.

Line 14. *Rudely but deeply they bedded the plinth of the days to come*. It has been said that modern English law is based on Saxon customs moulded by Norman lawyers. It forms the foundation of the law in England, the British overseas dominions, and the United States of America.

Line 18. *Our ancient headlands*. Saxon fields were not enclosed with hedges. Their shape was commonly one furlong (*i. e.* furrow-long) in length and four rods in breadth. Between one field and the next at the *head* of the furrows, the space where the plough oxen turned was left untilled and was called a *headland*.

The eight-ox plough. In the Anglo-Saxon communities the heavy plough in use belonged to the community, each householder taking his turn to use it and employing his own oxen for the purpose.

Line 19. *There came a king from Hamtun, by*

SONGS FROM BOOKS

Bosenham he came. The ancient kingdom of Sussex was invaded several times by Wessex kings, but the invasion here recorded is an imaginary incident having an allegorical reference to the danger of national unpreparedness for war. Possibly Britain's unpreparedness for the Boer War inspired it. Hamtun, or Hamtune, was the Saxon name for Southampton. Bosenham is the Domesday Book spelling of the modern Bosham, a village situated on an arm of Chichester harbour.

Line 22. *Cymen's Ore* (Cymenes Ora; sometimes written Cymenshore) is probably Chichester harbour, where the ships of the Saxon invaders, under Aella and his three sons, Cymen, Wlencing, and Cissa, anchored in 477 A.D.

Line 25. *Beechmast.* The fruit of the beech-tree was formerly used for human food in time of famine. At other times it was given to pigs.

Beltane fires. Beltane is Celtic for May day, on which day bonfires were lit on hilltops, two together, and between these the cattle were driven. A beltane cake was cooked at one of the fires. It was then divided into pieces, one piece being blackened with charcoal. The pieces of cake were then apportioned by lot to those present. Whoever received the blackened piece was pelted with egg-shells, and for some weeks afterwards was regarded as dead. Probably the custom was a relic of the sacrifice of both oxen and human beings. It survived in the north-east of Scotland until the latter part of the eighteenth century.

Line 26. *The beeves were salted thrice.* Until the introduction, at a comparatively recent date, of winter roots and herbs, English farmers knew no method of fattening their stock in winter. Oxen were consequently killed in autumn, when they were at their fattest, the beef was salted, and for the next six months even the wealthiest had little fresh meat.

POSEIDON'S LAW

In Greek mythology Poseidon was god of the sea; his brothers Zeus and Pluto reigning over earth and the underworld.

Stanza 1. *When the robust and Brass-bound Man commissioned first for sea.* Cf. Horace, *Od.*, i. 3:

> 'Illi robur et aes triplex
> Circa pectus erat qui fragilem truci
> Commisit pelago ratem
> Primus.'

(Surely oak and threefold brass surrounded his heart who first trusted a frail vessel to the wild sea.)

Stanza 3. *Hadria.* The Adriatic Sea.

Stanza 5. *A dromond* was a mediæval warship of a type first used by the Saracens. When Richard I. was on his way to Palestine his ship was attacked by a huge dromond—'a marvellous ship, a ship than which, except Noah's ark, none greater was ever read of.' This vessel was three masted, and carried fifteen hundred men on board. In Hakluyt's *Libellus de politia conservativa maris*, or, *The Pollicy of keeping the Sea*, reference is made to Henry the Fifth's 'great Dromons, which passed other great shippes of all the commons.'

A *catafract* was a Greek galley provided with bulwarks to protect the rowers; an 'afract' was a galley in which the upper tier of rowers was not so protected. A *bireme* was a galley that had two tiers of rowers, one above the other.

Stanza 6. In each set of three rowers in a trireme's crew the *thranite* sat on the highest, and the *thalamite* on the lowest, of the three oar-benches.

Stanza 7. *Punt* was the name of a land from which the ships of the ancient Egyptians brought incense, gold, and ivory. It is supposed to be identical with what is now called Somaliland.

Phormio's Fleet. Phormio was an Athenian admiral of the fifth century B.C. In the Peloponnesian War he defeated, with twenty ships, the Corinthian fleet of forty-seven sail. A fleet of seventy-seven sail was then sent against him, and in the action that followed, though nine of his ships went aground, he defeated the enemy and won complete control of the Greek seas.

Javan was a land with which the sailors of ancient Tyre traded for slaves and other commodities. Cf. Ezekiel xxvii. 13 and 19: 'Javan, Tubal, and Meshech, they were thy merchants: they traded the persons of men and vessels of brass in thy market. . . . Dan also and Javan going to and fro occupied in thy fairs: bright iron, cassia, and calamus, were in thy market.' By some authorities Javan is supposed to have been a vague name for the farthest parts of the Mediterranean known in the time of Ezekiel, and to have included Carthage and Tarshish. Others believe it to have been all lands colonised by the Ionian Greeks, and to have included Tarshish, Cyprus, and Rhodes.

Gadire. The modern Cadiz.

Falernian or smoked Massilian juice. In ancient times the 'Ager Falernus' in Campania produced the best wine in all Italy. The Greeks introduced the vine into their colony of Massilia (the modern Marseilles), and by the first century A.D. Massilian wine competed with Italian wine in the Italian market.

A TRUTHFUL SONG

Stanza 9. *Sheet.* A rope with which the corner of a sail is held in position.

Lift. A rope descending from the masthead to the end of the yard.

Brace. A rope extending from the end of the yard to a belaying pin on the ship's side by means of which the position of the yard with reference to the wind is adjusted.

SONGS FROM BOOKS

Lead. Trend or direction. So many ropes descend from a ship's rigging and are made fast to its bulwarks that it is difficult for the eye to follow upwards the 'lead' of any one in order to see to what it is attached aloft. As it is of prime importance for a seaman to understand the work performed by each rope (he must often find them by touch on pitch dark nights), the first thing he must learn on going to sea is the 'lead' of each individual rope.

Stanza 11. *Or it might be Ham (though his skin was dark).* Old-fashioned ethnologists believed all the negro races of the world to be descended from Ham.

Stanza 12. *Your wheel is new.* No detail of a ship has altered more than the steering-gear. The tiller displaced the steering-oar in the fourteenth century. The tiller grew with the growth of ships until in the sixteenth century it had to be controlled by elaborate block-and-tackle gear. The modern wheel replaced the tiller comparatively recently.

Hooker. A natural term of endearment for a ship.

A SMUGGLER'S SONG

The worthy parsons who allowed their churches to be used as stores for smuggled goods, and received in acknowledgment of their complacency many presents of brandy, lace, or tobacco, were no doubt inspired by excellent motives. Adam Smith, the eighteenth-century economist, described a smuggler as 'a person who, though no doubt highly blameable for violating the laws of his country, is frequently incapable of violating those of natural justice, and would have been in every respect an excellent citizen had not the laws of his country made that a crime which nature never meant to be so.'

KING HENRY VII. AND THE SHIPWRIGHTS

Stanza 1. At *Hamull on the Hoke*, better known as Hamble-le-rice, was the principal roadstead at which royal ships were laid up from the time of Henry v. till towards the close of the reign of Henry vii. The Hamble is an estuary branching out of Southampton Water. Though the county of Hampshire is called 'Hampshire' on maps, it is still called the 'County of Southampton' in many documents.

Stanza 4. *Strakes.* A strake is one breadth of planks in a ship's side forming a continuous strip from stem to stern.

Stanza 6. *Robert Brigandyne* was appointed Clerk of the Ships by Henry vii. He was 'a yeoman of the crown,' *i. e.* in the personal service of the king, and received 'twelve pence a day and sixpence a day for a clerk under him.' He superintended the construction of England's first dry dock.

Stanza 8. *Gramercy.* Thank you much (French, *grand merci*).

SONGS FROM BOOKS

Pricking. Riding, spurring.

Stanza II. The navy of Henry VII., which included the ships here mentioned, numbered only twelve or thirteen vessels in all. The *Mary of the Tower* was a Spanish carrack bought by Edward IV. for £100. The *Grace Dieu* (Henri Grace à Dieu) was built in the same reign. The *Sweepstakes* was the 'King's rowbarge.' She carried eighty oars, but had three masts as well. She was built by Henry VII., as was also the *Mary Fortune*, also a three-masted vessel equipped with sixty oars. These last two cost together £231 to build. The *Sovereign* was a three-masted vessel, built in 1447 and rebuilt in 1509. In 1525 her repair was urged on the ground that her lines were 'so marvellously goodly that great pity it were she should die.' It seems, however, that she was broken up.

THE WET LITANY

Stanza 2. *When the wash along the side*
          Sounds, a sudden, magnified.
When a ship suddenly slows down owing to fog or for other reasons, the lessening of the noise from the engines emphasises the sound of the water washing along her sides.

The intolerable blast. During a fog a steamer's siren is blown at frequent intervals.

Stanza 3. *The fog-buoys squattering flight.* When warships steam in 'line ahead formation' in thick weather, each tows a fog-buoy astern at a distance of 200 yards or less.

When the lettered doorways close. Battleships are built in water-tight compartments, the doors between which are closed when there is any danger of a collision. The doors are indicated by letters.

Stanza 4. *Lessened count.* The leadsman who is standing in the chains cries the depth of water each time he takes a sounding. If he reports less depth each minute, the ship is obviously in danger of running aground.

Stanza 5. *Our next ahead.* When warships during manœuvres steam in line one behind another, a seaman refers to the ship immediately ahead of his own as the 'next ahead.' The minimum distance that should be preserved between ships steaming in the 'line ahead' formation is 800 yards.

THE BALLAD OF MINEPIT SHAW

Stanza 1. The Pelhams are an old Sussex family. They came into the county in the reign of Edward III. John Pelham was Constable of Pevensey Castle under Richard II. Sir Thomas Pelham was one of the Knights for Sussex in Elizabeth's Parliament. Thomas Pelham was created Earl of Chichester in 1501.

Stanza 5. *The Folk of the Hill.* Fairies should never be spoken of as such by mortals lest they should be offended. They should be referred to by some such name as the 'People of the Hills' or 'The Little

People.' Obviously a fairy speaking of his own people will also use one of these pseudonyms. In the story 'Weland's Sword' (*Puck of Pook's Hill*), Puck is willing to sing the song 'Farewell, Rewards and Fairies,' except the first line, as that contains the word to which he objects.

Stanza 8. The fairies could not help the poachers while they had iron in their hands (see note, 'Cold Iron,' p. 282).

Stanza 16. *Pharisee* is the Sussex word for fairy. The colloquial plural for fairy—fairieses—was probably well rooted in the dialect long before the translation of the Bible, and its subsequent use in church made Sussex men familiar with the word Pharisee. It is said that some old Sussex people still believe that the Pharisees mentioned in the Gospels are the 'Little People.'

HERIOT'S FORD

Stanza 1. *Hirples.* Runs with a limp.
Stanza 3. '*Oh, who will stay the sun's descent?*'
King Joshua he is dead, my lord.

'Then spake Joshua to the Lord in the day when the Lord delivered up the Amorites before the children of Israel, and he said in the sight of Israel, Sun, stand thou still upon Gibeon; and thou, Moon, in the valley of Ajalon. And the sun stood still, and the moon stayed, until the people had avenged themselves upon their enemies' (Joshua x. 12, 13).

SONGS FROM BOOKS

FRANKIE'S TRADE

Mr. W. B. Whall, Master Mariner, in his **Preface** to *Sea-songs, Ships and Shanties,* regrets that it was not Rudyard Kipling's destiny to go to sea, as he would have made a splendid chantey-man. This song is on the true chantey model. The refrain 'A-hay O! To me O!' in this or in very similar form is to be found in many chanties.

Stanza 1. It is almost certain that from infancy until he went to sea Francis Drake lived on a condemned warship moored in Gillingham Reach just below Chatham. Thus from childhood he must have learned to notice movements of tides and currents among sandbanks and tortuous channels, and have been familiar with every phase of wind and calm. As soon as he was old enough Edmund Drake 'by reason of his poverty put his son to the master of a bark, which he used to cruise along the shore and sometimes to carry merchandise into Zeeland and France'! The master of the barque died and left it by will to Drake, who thus commanded his own ship before he was eighteen.

Stanza 5. *I made him pull and I made him haul.* On his voyage round the world Drake was troubled with 'such controversy between the sailors and the gentlemen and such stomaching between the gentlemen and sailors that it doth even make me mad to hear of it.' He summoned all his crews together and

SONGS FROM BOOKS

told them plainly, 'I must have the gentleman to haul and draw with the mariner and the mariner with the gentleman.'

Stand his trick. Take his turn at steering.

Stanza 7. *A five-knot tide.* A tide running at the rate of five knots an hour—roughly five miles an hour.

THORKILD'S SONG

Stanza 1. *Stavanger* is one of the oldest of Norwegian seaports, founded in the eighth or ninth century.

Stanza 8. *A three-reef gale.* A wind strong enough to make it necessary to reduce the area of the mainsail by taking in three reefs.

ANGUTIVAUN TAINA

Those who wish to compare this 'Song of the Returning Hunter' with the original will find both words and music, together with much wonderfully interesting matter concerning the people of Tununirmiut, in a paper by Dr. Franz Boas entitled 'The Central Eskimo,' published in the *Sixth Annual Report of the American Bureau of Ethnology.*

THE SONG OF THE MEN'S SIDE

In *Rewards and Fairies* this song follows a tale ('The Knife and the Naked Chalk') in which a Neolithic flint-worker of Cissbury Ring on the South Downs sacrifices an eye in order to obtain a knife

SONGS FROM BOOKS

from a neighbouring tribe, the 'Children of the Night,' whose home was in the Weald. With this knife he drives off the Beast (*i. e.* the wolf) that preyed upon the flint-workers' flocks. On account of this service he is believed to be 'the son of Tyr, the God who put his right hand in a Beast's mouth.'

Stanza 1. *The Beast.* The Wolf. In stanza 3 he is referred to as Shepherd of the Twilight, Feet in the Night, Dog without a Master, and Devil in the Dusk. In many parts of the world, especially in savage countries, it is believed that if a dangerous animal is mentioned by its proper name it will revenge itself on whomever so mentions it. In southern India, for instance, the tiger is called 'the dog' or 'the jackal,' and Bengali women call a snake 'the creeping thing.' The Bechuanas call the lion 'the boy with the beard.' The Lapps call the bear 'the old man with the coat of skin,' and at the present day wolves are not called by their proper name in some parts of Germany, though this restriction only applies to the winter, when wolves are most dangerous. It is fairly certain, therefore, that our primitive ancestors in Britain never called the wolf by his proper name.

Flint-workers. The inhabitants of the South Downs, in the later Stone Age, were a pastoral tribe. This we know from the cattle tracks that lead in and out of their encampments. The flint quarries and fragments of flint weapons and tools that have been found in these encampments show them also to have been expert flint-workers (see note to 'Puck's Song,' stanzas 9 and 10, p. 275, and to 'Sussex,' stanza 6, p. 217).

The Buyer of the Blade. By reason of his great sacrifice the Buyer of the Blade had become divine. He might no longer therefore be spoken of or addressed by his proper name, which had become 'taboo' or sacred. Among Semitic peoples none but a few priests know the true name of God. Such words as Jehovah and Allah are pseudonyms.

Room for his shadow on the grass. Primitive savages regard a man's shadow as his visible soul or spirit. The Baganda, the Tolindos of Celebes, the Ottawa Indians, and many others believe that it is possible to injure a man by striking a blow at his shadow. Hence it would be an act of sacrilege to stand on the shadow of a divine man such as the Buyer of the Blade.

The great god Tyr. Tyr was the Scandinavian god of battle, after whom Tuesday is named. His fight with a wolf forms the design of an ornamental sign-post erected by King George v. on one of his estates. As the exploits of a hero are embellished by tradition among primitive people, the hero himself comes to be regarded as divine.

Stanza 2. *The Children of the Night.* The inhabitants of the forest to the north of the Downs.

The barrows of the dead. Neolithic men buried their dead (sometimes after cremation) in long chambers lined with immense stones and covered with

SONGS FROM BOOKS

earth. The remains of these are now called in England 'barrows.' (See note on 'Sussex,' stanza 4, p. 217.)

The Women's side. In many primitive communities the division between men and women is sharper than among civilised people. In some cases, as among the Zulus, the women speak a language that differs materially from that spoken by men. In some communities all the unmarried men in a community live together in one large hut and all the unmarried women in another. Among some Australian tribes the 'guryahs' or leaf-huts of the married people are in the centre of the camp, those of bachelors and widowers on one side, and those of spinsters and widows on the other.

Stanza 3. *Hai, Tyr, aie!* No traces of the language of British Neolithic man have been preserved (the Celtic invasion of Britain did not begin till after the Stone Age), but as *aie* is a sound of woe all the world over, we may conjecture that 'Hai, Tyr, aie!' means 'O Tyr, help us!'

DARZEE'S CHAUNT

A darzee is an Indian tailor. In the story 'Rikki-tikki-tavi,' which accompanies this poem in *The Jungle Book*, it is applied to the Indian tailor-bird, so-called because it makes its nest by 'pulling two big leaves together and stitching them up the edges with fibres, filling the hollow with cotton and downy fluff.' The song is in honour of the mongoose, called Rikki-tikki-tavi from his battle-cry, who killed Nag, the cobra that had eaten one of Darzee's nestlings.

THE PRAYER

My brother kneels, so saith Kabir,
To stone and brass in heathen-wise.

Kabir was a religious reformer of northern India in the fifteenth century (see note, 'A Song of Kabir,' p. 282).

A School History of England

THE ROMAN CENTURION

Stanza 1. *Legate.* This was the title of the senior subordinate officer of the governor of a Roman colony.

Cohort. A tenth part of a Roman legion. It numbered between three hundred and six hundred soldiers.

Portus Itius was the name given by Julius Cæsar to the French port from which he made his second invasion of Britain. Historians do not know exactly where it was, but are agreed that it was near Cape Grisnez, to the north of Boulogne.

Stanza 2. *Vectis,* the Roman name for the Isle of Wight. *The Wall* was the wall built across Britain from the Tyne to the Solway Firth. An older wall, built by Antoninus Pius from the Forth to the Clyde, had been abandoned before the Romans began to evacuate Britain.

Stanza 5. *Rhodanus.* The Rhone.

Nemausus. Nimes, in the south of France, where are still to be seen remains of an amphitheatre once capable of holding 24,000 people, temples, baths, forts, and other Roman buildings.

A SCHOOL HISTORY OF ENGLAND

Arelate.   Arles, the principal seat of the Emperor Constantine.

Euroclydon.   The north-east wind, from Greek *euros, east wind,* and *kludon,* wave.

Stanza 6.   *The old Aurelian Road* ran along the shore of the Tyrrhenian Sea from Genoa to Rome.

THE PIRATES IN ENGLAND

Stanza 6.   *The shield-hung hull.*   The Viking ships were manned by men who rowed at sea and fought ashore. Each man hung his shield over the ship's side beside his seat on the rowing bench. There it was ready to his hand but out of his way—there was little room on the crowded deck of a Viking ship —and also served the purpose of sheltering him during a sea-fight.

Stanza 7.   *The painted eyes.*   The stems of the Viking ships carried elaborately carved figureheads on long necks. Like Chinese ships of modern times, the ships had painted eyes on their bows so that they should see their course.

Stanza 8.   *Count of the Saxon Shore.*   A nobleman of high rank appointed under the English kings to guard the south-east coasts, which were more liable to attack than other coasts of England.

THE SAXON FOUNDATIONS OF ENGLAND

(See notes on lines 1 to 18, 'The King's Task,' p. 328.)

A SCHOOL HISTORY OF ENGLAND

WILLIAM THE CONQUEROR'S WORK

Stanza 3. *It shall have one speech and law.* Although William brought England under one law, local custom was so strong that in parts local customs having the force of laws differed from the law of the land until quite recent times. Thus the tin-miners of Cornwall were exempt from all jurisdiction other than that of their own Parliament, the Stannaries, except in cases affecting land, life, and limb, until the middle of the eighteenth century. The law of 'gavelkind,' which affects the tenure of land, is still in force in Kent.

NORMAN AND SAXON

Stanza 3. *You can horsewhip your Gascony archers, or torture your Picardy spears.* At the time immediately following the Norman conquest of England, portions of France were so often conquered and reconquered in the wars between rival princes, that men such as the Gascons and Picards scarcely knew, and did not care at all, who was their lawful sovereign. One ruler after another hired them to fight, with the result that they formed themselves into bands called 'Free Companies,' ready to fight for any one, their lawful king or any one else who chose to pay them.

Thane. An Anglo-Saxon title for a man who was below a nobleman but above a small landowner. If a churl throve so that he became owner of at least 'five hides of land, church and kitchen, bell-house and burhgate-seal,' he was entitled to rank as a thane. So also was a merchant who 'fared thrice over the wide sea by his own means.'

Stanza 4. *Clerk*. In Norman and Plantagenet times a clerk was any one who had taken religious orders. Few but the clergy were sufficiently well educated to read and write, and consequently these were also lawyers, record-keepers, etc. In fact any man who could prove that he could read was assumed to be in orders, and could not therefore be sentenced to death by a layman. The name clerk thus became associated with priests, and is still preserved in the formal title of a parson—'Clerk in Holy Orders.'

Stanza 5. *Don't hang them or cut off their fingers*. The purpose of cutting off a man's fingers was to prevent him from ever being able to use a bow again.

THE REEDS OF RUNNYMEDE

Stanza 2. *You musn't sell, delay, deny,*
A freeman's right or liberty.

This is a paraphrase of the fortieth of the sixty-three chapters of Magna Carta. Its brevity in comparison with most of the other chapters is impressive. 'To no one will we sell, to no one will we refuse or delay right or justice.' It is noteworthy that Magna Carta concerned itself only with freemen. The villein and the serf owed their Charter of Liberty, years afterwards, not to any human ordinance but to the Black Death, which killed so many labourers that those who survived could demand their own price for their services.

Stanza 3. *Right Divine.* The theory that a king is responsible to God alone for his actions, and that his authority is by divine ordinance hereditary in a certain order of succession.

Stanza 4. *Except by lawful judgment found
And passed upon him by his peers.*
In John's time 'peers' did not mean lords or barons but equals, and still has this meaning in the phrase 'judgment by his peers' (pares). The tenants-in-chief of the crown were peers of each other whether they held one manor or a hundred; the tenants of a manor were peers of their fellow-tenants.

WITH DRAKE IN THE TROPICS

Stanza 1. *Our Admiral leads us on.* In Drake's day every fleet, even if it consisted of only two or three ships, sailed under the directions of an admiral. At night lanterns were lighted on the poop of the admiral's ship and the other ships which did not carry poop-lanterns had to keep these in sight.

*The silent deep ablaze
With fires.*

Under certain atmospheric conditions myriads of phosphorous sparks appear at night wherever the sea is disturbed, such as in the wake of a ship or a porpoise.

Stanza 2. *Now the rank moon commands the sky.* There is a very prevalent belief that moonlight has a bad effect on those who sleep exposed to it. Many Australian stockmen, for instance, when sleeping out in the bush without tents, will bind a handkerchief over their eyes on moonlight nights, for they believe that the moonlight can cause a disease of the eyes locally called sandy-blight. They believe, too, that a man will in his sleep fix his eyes on the moon and keep on staring at it, moving his head as the moon moves across the sky. This much seems certain, that freshly-caught fish exposed to moonlight will become poisonous.

Stanza 3. *How long the time 'twixt bell and bell.* Time is marked at sea by the ringing of bells—one for each half hour. Thus half an hour after midnight one bell is rung. Two are rung at one o'clock. And so on till four o'clock, when eight bells are rung and the morning watch is set. Half an hour later one bell is rung again.

Stanza 5. *The Line.* The equator.

BEFORE EDGEHILL FIGHT

Stanza 2. *In the heart of a sleepy Midland shire.* The first battle of the Great Rebellion was fought at Edgehill in Warwickshire, on the watershed between the Thames and Severn valleys.

A SCHOOL HISTORY OF ENGLAND

THE DUTCH IN THE MEDWAY

Stanza 5. *For, now De Ruyter's topsails
Off naked Chatham show.*
In 1667 the Dutch fleet under De Ruyter sailed into the Medway as far as Chatham and burned the defenceless English fleet. This was perhaps the greatest blow that the British Navy's prestige has ever suffered.

'BROWN BESS'

Brown Bess was the name given in the British army to the flint-lock musket with which the infantry were armed in the eighteenth century.

Stanza 3. *When ruffles were turned into stiff leather stocks
And people wore pigtails instead of perukes.*
This change began to take place about the middle of the eighteenth century. Stiff stocks and pigtails lasted well into the nineteenth century. In fact, the ribbon that decorated the pigtail still survives in the uniform of the Royal Welsh Fusiliers. It is now, however, sewn on to the tunic, since it cannot be fastened to the non-existent pigtail.

AFTER THE WAR

Stanza 1. *The snow lies thick on Valley Forge.*
Valley Forge is a small village in Chester County, Pennsylvania. On the 19th of December, 1777, after

the battles of Brandywine and Germantown and the evacuation of Philadelphia by the British, Washington's army, numbering about ten thousand men, went into camp there. Commissariat arrangements were so badly managed that by the 1st of February nearly four thousand men were unfit for duty owing to illnesses caused by lack of proper food and clothing.

Stanza 7. *Fall* as a term for autumn used to be in common use in England, though, like many archaic English words, it now survives only in America.   It is, of course, an abbreviation for 'the fall of the leaf.'

THE BELLS AND THE QUEEN

Stanza 2. *Gloriana* was a name given by her courtiers to Queen Elizabeth. It was originated by the poet Spenser, who allegorically portrayed his sovereign lady in the *Faerie Queen* under this name.

THE SECRET OF THE MACHINES

Stanza 2. *You shall see and hear your crackling question hurled*
Across the arch of heaven while you wait.

When the apparatus of a wireless telegraph is at work it gives out a crackling noise, and at night sparks can be seen running up and down the stays of the mast which supports the 'antenna' or 'air-wire.'

Other Poems

The following notes are on poems from Mr. Rudyard Kipling's prose works that do not appear in *Songs from Books:*

CHAPTER HEADING

PLAIN TALES FROM THE HILLS

CONSEQUENCES

Rosicrucian subtleties
In the Orient had rise.

Early in the seventeenth century the 'Brethren of the Rosie Crosse' professed a knowledge of mystic and occult science, in expounding which they used the technical terms of alchemy and other sciences, to which terms they applied hidden meanings. It was claimed that one of the Rosicrucian 'brothers' had, when on pilgrimage, discovered the secret wisdom of the East.

Seek ye Bombast Paracelsus. Theophrastus Bombast was a famous German physician of the sixteenth century, who adopted the epithet 'Paracelsus' to indicate that he was superior to Celsus, his remote predecessor. Like Tarrion in the story which accompanies

OTHER POEMS

this poem, Paracelsus used unworthy means to gain his ends. He knew a great deal—he introduced the use of mercury and laudanum—but pretended to a knowledge of much more, such as the elixir of life. Robert Browning has made him the subject of a poem.

Flood the Seeker. Flood or Fludd (Robertus de Fluctibus), 1574-1637, an English Rosicrucian, was a devout student of Paracelsus. He was a scholar of St. John's, Oxford, and a Fellow of the College of Physicians.

The Dominant that runs is the female influence.

Luna at her apogee. The moon when at her greatest distance from earth.

HEADING TO CHAPTER VI

THE NAULAHKA

IN THE STATE OF KOT-KUMHARSEN, WHERE THE WILD DACOITS ABOUND

Thakurs. Rajput nobles.

Bunnia. A corn and seed merchant.

Bunjara. A carrier who travels up and down the country driving long trains of pack-bullocks laden with goods.

Sahib Bahadur. The word Sahib is a term of respect applied in India to natives of rank—*e. g.* Nawab Sahib, Rajah Sahib—and to Europeans in general.

OTHER POEMS

Bahadur (brave), another title of respect, is sometimes added.

Tonga. A two-wheeled car used for travelling in parts of India beyond the reach of railways. It is drawn by two ponies harnessed abreast to the pole with a curricle-bar. Cf. 'As the Bell Clinks' (*Departmental Ditties*). The clack and click of the tonga-bar is a characteristic sound of Indian travel.

Machan. A platform, built in the branches of a tree, from which to shoot driven game.

HEADING TO CHAPTER XVIII

BEAST AND MAN IN INDIA

THE SEVEN NIGHTS OF CREATION

O Hassan! Saving Allah, there is none
More strong than Eblis.

It is written in the Koran that when God created Adam, He commanded all the angels to worship him. Eblis refused, and for his disobedience was turned out of Paradise and became the ruler of all evil spirits.

The sword-wide bridge. According to Mohammedan belief the soul after death has to cross a bridge, as narrow as the edge of a sword, that connects earth and Paradise. Should the soul be overburdened with the weight of sins it will fall into the abyss below.

OTHER POEMS

HEADING TO CHAPTER III

KIM

YEA, VOICE OF EVERY SOUL THAT CLUNG
TO LIFE THAT STROVE FROM RUNG TO RUNG,
WHEN DEVADATTA'S RULE WAS YOUNG
THE WARM WIND BRINGS KAMAKURA.

This is apparently a supplementary stanza to the poem 'Buddha at Kamakura.' It is the Buddhist belief that the souls of all living creatures are born again and again, it may be as a beast at one time, as an insect at another, as a nat (spirit) at another, as a man at another. Merit is rewarded by rebirth in a higher form of life (wickedness punished by rebirth in a lower form) until Nirvana is attained (see note, 'Buddha at Kamakura,' stanza 1, p. 224). *Devadatta* was the uncle of Gautama Buddha, though younger than he. He became one of Gautama's disciples, and later endeavoured to displace the Teacher as head of the order which he had founded. Failing in his purpose, Devadatta, after making several attempts to murder Gautama, founded a rival order. According to a commentary on the Jataka (see note, 'Buddha at Kamakura,' stanza 7, p. 226), the earth swallowed up Devadatta when on his way to ask pardon of the Buddha, though a later authority says that although he avowed his intention of asking Gautama's pardon, he had concealed poison in his nail with which to murder him.

OTHER POEMS

THE RUNNERS
TRAFFICS AND DISCOVERIES

In the story 'A Sahib's War,' which accompanies this poem, the Sikh soldier who accompanied his English officer to the South African War says, 'The Sahib knows how we of Hind hear all that passes over the earth? There was not a gun cocked in Yunasbagh' (Johannesburg) 'that the echo did not come into Hind in a month.'

Stanza 2. *The well-wheels.* In the Punjab crops are irrigated with water drawn from wells by means of wheels worked by bullocks.

Stanza 4. *Under the shadow of the border-peels.* A peel is a watch-tower. The Zuka Khel Afridis have sixty such towers, 'two-storied, built of stone, and entered by a ladder from the upper story' (see 'The Lost Legion' in *Many Inventions*). According to the Sikh officer in 'A Sahib's War,' it was rumours that 'the Sahibs of Yunasbagh lay in bondage to the Boerlog' which led to the revolt of the Afridis and the subsequent war in the Tirah.

THE RUNES ON WELAND'S SWORD
PUCK OF POOK'S HILL

Runes are characters in the earliest alphabet used by the Gothic tribes of northern Europe. Modern scholars have gradually pieced the alphabet together

OTHER POEMS

from engravings on Norse monuments, bracelets, oar-blades, etc. The most valuable contribution made to the knowledge of the subject was obtained from a knife found in the Thames. Though some Runic characters were used in the English alphabet as late as the fifteenth century, most of them were obsolete by the tenth. When our forefathers of that day saw Runic characters engraved on anything they found they naturally thought, as they could not read them, that the runes were 'magic.'

This poem is in the form in which Old English poetry was commonly written. Rhymes were very seldom used, but rhythm was attained by emphasizing syllables. Usually there were four stressed syllables in each long line or two in each half-line or short line. Alliteration also was used—the same letter or sound being repeated several times. Note the repetition of M in the lines.

> As Mith Makes Me
> To betray My Man
> In My first fight;

and of G in the lines,

> It is not Given
> For Goods or Gear.

Weland was the Vulcan of our Saxon forefathers. Near the White Horse in Berkshire there is a cromlech near which Weland or Wayland Smith is said to have lived. He worked for those who paid him, but never allowed himself to be seen. If any one wanted a tool mended he laid it, together with a coin, on the cromlech and went away. When he came back the tool was mended but the coin was gone. This legend suggests that what anthropologists call the 'Silent Trade' was once practised in England. Travellers in Africa from the days of Herodotus down to modern times have occasionally found traces of a commerce between two people who never saw each other. One man having something to sell would place it in a conspicuous position and go away. When he came back he found gold-dust or something of value by the side of it. If he was content with the bargain he took the gold-dust and left the article which he had offered for sale. In England in Neolithic times there must have been trade of some sort between the flint-workers of Cissbury (see note on Flint-workers, 'Song of the Men's Side,' p. 342) and neighbouring tribes, and later between the iron-workers of the Weald and their neighbours. Is it not probable that at the very beginning of this trade the tribes were more or less constantly at war with each other, and that individuals who wanted to trade adopted the 'silent' method because they feared treachery? In 'The Knife and the Naked Chalk' (*Rewards and Fairies*) the flint-worker arranges with iron-workers that his people should bring meat, milk, and wool, and lay them in the short grass near the trees, if the iron-workers would leave knives for the flint-workers to take away.

OTHER POEMS

Such a trade, if it existed, may well have given rise to the legend of the divine smith who would mend a tool for payment but would never let himself be seen.

PHILADELPHIA

REWARDS AND FAIRIES

Stanza 1. *Philadelphia* in the last decade of the eighteenth century was the most important city in America and the seat of the Federal Government.

Talleyrand, who had been acting as a self-appointed ambassador to Great Britain, was expelled from British soil after the execution of Louis XVI. He went to the United States, where he spent thirty months before he found it safe to return to France.

Count Zinnendorf, a bishop of the Moravian Church, paid a missionary visit to America in 1741-1742. His principal work was the founding of the borough of Bethlehem, Pa., fifty-five miles from Philadelphia. The Moravians as a community were famous at this time for the earnestness of their work among the Red Indians and the excellence of the inns they kept. In proportion to their small numbers the Moravians at the present day support a larger number of missionairies than does any other community.

Stanza 2. The character of *Toby Hirte*, in the story 'Brother Square-Toes,' is a character based on

OTHER POEMS

that of Dr. Benjamin Rush, who did splendid work in Philadelphia during the terrible fever epidemic of 1793, in spite of the fact that his colleagues, who did not approve of his methods of treating the disease, relentlessly persecuted him.

ALPHABETICAL LIST OF POEMS ANNOTATED

	PAGE		PAGE
After the War,	352	Before Edgehill Fight,	351
American, An,	167	Bell Buoy, The,	198
Anchor Song,	140	Bells and the Queen, The,	353
Angutivaun Taina,	341	Belts,	40
Army Headquarters,	3	Beyond the path of the outmost Sun,	36
As the Bell clinks,	17		
Astrologer's Song, An,	312	'Birds of Prey' March,	179
'At the hole where he went in,'	327	Boots,	262
		Bridge-guard in the Karroo	239
'Back to the Army again,'	172	British Roman Song, A,	296
Ballad of Boh da Thone, The,	65	Broken Men, The,	206
		Brookland Road,	278
Ballad of East and West, The,	49	'Brown Bess,'	352
		Buddha at Kamakura,	222
Ballad of Fisher's Boardinghouse, The,	16	Burial, The,	213
		Butterflies,	325
Ballad of Minepit Shaw, The,	338	Captive, The,	288
Ballad of the 'Bolivar,' The,	76	Cells,	32
		Chant Pagan,	251
Ballad of the 'Clampherdown,' The,	75	Charm, A,	280
		Chil's Song,	288
Ballad of the King's Jest, The,	57	'China-going P. and O's,'	319
		Cholera Camp,	184
Ballad of the King's Mercy, The,	53	Cleared,	84
		Coastwise Lights, The,	93
'Beat off in our last fight were we?'	292	Code of Morals, A,	9
		Cold Iron,	282
Bee Boy's Song, The,	312	Columns,	257
Bees and the Flies, The,	295	Conundrum of the Workshops, The,	81
Before a Midnight breaks in Storm,	196	Cruisers,	199

LIST OF POEMS ANNOTATED

	PAGE		PAGE
Danny Deever,	27	Grave of the Hundred Head, The,	11
'Dark Children of the Mere and Marsh,'	306	Gunga Din,	34
Darzee's Chaunt,	344		
Deep-Sea Cables, The,	96	Hadramauti,	290
Derelict, The,	134	Half-Ballad of Waterval,	265
Destroyers, The,	200	Heriot's Ford,	339
Dirge of Dead Sisters,	244	Hymn before Action,	152
Divided Destinies,	12		
Dove of Dacca, The,	64	Imperial Rescript, An,	86
Dutch in Medway, The	352	In Spring Time,	24
Dykes, The,	204	In the Neolithic Age,	158
		In the State of Kot-Kumharsen,	355
'Eathen, The,	191	Islanders, The,	245
Eddi's Service,	284		
Egg-Shell, The,	328	Jacket, The,	189
England's Answer,	99	Jubal and Tubal-Cain,	300
English Flag, The,	82		
'Et Dona Ferentes'	232	Kaspar's Song in Varda (see Butterflies),	325
Evarra and his Gods,	81	King, The,	122
Explorer, The,	209	King Henry VII and the Shipwrights,	336
Fairies' Siege, The,	285	King's Task, The,	328
Feet of the Young Men, The,	207	Kitchener's School,	233
Files, The,	241		
First Chantey, The,	99	Lament of the Border Cattle Thief, The,	68
Flowers, The	153	'Lark will make her hymn to God, The,'	293
'Follow me 'Ome'.	188	Last Chantey, The,	101
Ford o' Kabul River,	44	Last Department, The,	9
Frankie's Trade,	340	Last Rhyme of True Thomas, The,	155
From the Masjid-al-aqsa of Sayyid Ahmed (Wahabi). See The Captive,	288	Last Suttee, The,	52
'Fuzzy-Wuzzy,'	29	Legend of the Foreign Office, A,	3
Galley Slave, The,	24	Legends of Evil, The,	82
Gallio's Song,	293	Lesson, The,	240
General Joubert,	215	Lichtenberg,	263
Gentlemen-Rankers,	44	Liner She's a Lady, The,	138
Giffen's Debt,	23	Long Trail, The,	88
Gift of the Sea, The,	80	Loot,	37
Gow's Watch,	322		

LIST OF POEMS ANNOTATED

	PAGE
Lost Legion, The,	146
Lukannon,	311
M'Andrew's Hymn,	108
Mandalay,	42
Man who could write, The,	8
Married Man, The,	262
'Mary Gloster,' The,	167
Masque of Plenty, The,	12
'Men that fought at Minden, The,'	182
Merchantmen, The,	103
Merrow Down,	313
M. I.,	253
Miracles, The,	119
Mother Lodge, The,	185
Mowgli's Song against People,	326
Mulholland's Contract,	139
Municipal,	8
'My new-cut Ashlar,'	284
Native born, The,	119
New Knighthood, The,	286
Norman and Saxon,	348
Nursing Sister, The,	325
O Hassan! Saving Allah, there is none,	356
Old Issue, The,	237
Old Men, The,	209
Old Mother Laidinwool,	316
One Viceroy resigns,	19
Only Son, The,	325
Oonts,	35
Our Fathers of old,	304
Our Lady of the Snows,	231
Outsong in the Jungle,	287
Palace, The,	215
Parade Song of the Camp Animals,	308
Parting of the Columns, The,	259

	PAGE
Peace of Dives, The,	248
Pharaoh and the Sergeant,	230
Philadelphia (*Rewards and Fairies*),	361
Pict Song, A,	296
Piet,	266
Pirates in England, The,	347
'Pit where the buffalo cooled his hide,'	281
'Poor Honest Men,'	298
Poseidon's Law,	332
Prayer, The,	345
Prophets at Home,	300
Public Waste,	4
Puck's Song,	274
Queen's Men, The,	322
Recessional,	272
Reeds of Runnymede, The,	349
Reformers, The,	244
Rhyme of the Three Captains, The,	69
Rhyme of the Three Sealers, The,	124
Rimini,	297
Rimmon,	236
Ripple Song, A,	324
Road-Song of the Bandar-Log,	296
Roman Centurion, The,	346
Rosicrucian Subtleties,	354
Route Marchin',	45
Runes on Weland's Sword, The (*Puck of Pook's Hill*).	358
Runners, The (*Traffics and Discoveries*),	358
Run of the Downs,	277
Rupaiyat of Omar Kal'vin,	11
Sacrifice of Er-Heb, The,	79
St. Helena Lullaby, A,	287
Sappers,	180

LIST OF POEMS ANNOTATED

	PAGE		PAGE
Saxon Foundations of England, The,	347	Three-Decker, The,	164
School Song, A,	302	Three-part Song, A,	277
Screw-Guns,	31	Tomlinson,	87
Sea and the Hills, The,	196	Tommy,	28
Sea-Wife, The,	152	To T. A. (Thomas Atkins),	26
Second Voyage, The,	203	To the City of Bombay,	93
Secret of the Machines, The,	353	To the True Romance,	152
Sergeant's Weddin', The,	189	To the Unknown Goddess,	10
Sestina of the Tramp Royal,	171	Tree Song, A,	279
Settlers, The,	250	Troopin',	43
Shillin' a Day,	47	Truce of the Bear, The,	208
Shiv and the Grasshopper,	284	Truthful Song, A,	334
Shut-eye Sentry, The,	194	Two Cousins, The (see 'The Queen's Men'),	322
Sir Richard's Song,	279	Two Kopjes,	260
Smuggler's Song, A,	335	Two-sided Man, The,	309
'Snarleyow,'	38		
'Soldier and Sailor too,'	178	Ubique,	270
Song of Diego Valdez, The,	205	Voortrekker, The,	301
Song of Kabir, A,	282		
Song of the Banjo, The,	135	'We be Gods of the East,'	292
Song of the Cities, The,	97	Wet Litany, The,	337
Song of the Dead, The,	94	What happened,	5
Song of the English, A,	93	What the People said,	18
Song of the Fifth River,	307	When 'Omer smote his bloomin' Lyre,	171
Song of the Men's Side, The,	341	'When the cabin port-holes are dark and green,'	318
Song of the Red War Boat,	323	White Horses,	202
Song of the Sons, The,	97	White Man's Burden, The,	229
Song of the Wise Children,	221	Widow at Windsor, The,	40
Song of the Women, The,	14	Widow's Party, The,	43
Song to Mithras, A,	285	'Wilful Missing,'	270
Stellenbosh,	264	William the Conqueror's Work,	348
'Stone's throw out on either hand, A,'	281	With Drake in the Tropics,	350
Story of Ung, The,	162	With Scindia to Delhi,	59
Sussex,	216		
		Yea, voice of every soul that clung,	357
Tale of Two Cities, A,	22	'Yet at the last, ere our spearmen had found him,'	293
That Day,	182	Young British Soldier, The,	41
'There was never a queen like Balkis,'	321	Young Queen, The,	235
This is the mouth-filling song,	318		
Thorkild's Song,	341		

GENERAL INDEX

NOTE.—*Where reference to more than one page is made, the number of the page on which the most complete note appears is given first.*

	PAGE
ABACK and full	141
Abazai	50, 56, 68
Abdhur Rahman, Amir of Afghanistan, biographical note	53
opinion of Lady Dufferin	14
suspected of intrigue with Russia	55
humorous cruelty of	56
equanimity of	58
Able Bastards	164
A. B., Qualifications of an	292, 76
Abu	53
Action front	39
Actions and Reactions	216, 294
Adam-zad	209
Admiral leads us on	350
Afghans, respect for courage	50
at battle of Paniput	59, 60, 61
Afract	333
Afreedeeman (*see* Afridi)	
African Steamship Company	169
Afridi	32
character of the	49
revolt of the	358
Agulhas Roll	107, 121
Ahmed, king of Kabul	59
Ahmed, Sayyid (Wahabi)	289
Aitchison, Sir Charles	20
Alexander (herb)	304
Alexander the Great	308
Allah, He called upon	293
Allan Line	169
Allobrogenses	161
Alpha Centauri	258
Ambree, Mary	172
American Bureau of Ethnology, Sixth Annual Report of	341
American expressions	209
American law and English authors	69
Ananda	225
Anchor Line	320
Ancient Akkad	249
Ancient Landmarks (Masonic term)	187
Andred's Wood	328
Angekok	310
Anglo-Saxons	328, 330
Anthropological Institute, Journal of the	325
Apocrypha, References to the—	
Ecclesiasticus xliv	244, 303
I Maccabees vi	309
Apollo	295
Arabi (Ahmad)	190
Arabs	291, 292
Arelate	347
Aristaeus	295
Arquebus	123
Artillery, charged French cavalry	190
co-operation with infantry	272
Royal Horse	38
4th Battery	272

GENERAL INDEX

	PAGE
Ashdod	249
Ashlar	216
Astrology	312
and Medicine	304
At hack	322
Athenæum, Controversy in pages of	69, 70
Atlantic Transport Line	320
Atkins, Thomas	26
Atlantis, Lost	119
Aurelian Road	347
Australia, 99, 94, 98, 146, 147, 151, 153, 209, 213, 235, 259	
Australian blacks	100, 316, 161
Australian Commonwealth	235
Avatar	167
Axle arms	190
Azores, Off the	298
BABOONS—at the bottom	260
Babu	5
Backing of wind against the sun	130
Back pay	193
Backstay	136
Baganda	343
Bagheera	287, 288
Bahadur	355
Bairagi	283
Balestier, Wolcott	4, 15, 16
dedication to	26
Balkis	321
Ball, V., contribution to *Journal of Anthropological Institute*	325
Ballast	142, 170
Baloo	287, 288, 296
Bandar-log	296, 287
Bank, 'Olborn Bank	271
Banks, The	124
Bar, The	18, 68
Barberton	251
Barracoon	101
Barracoot	101

	PAGE
Barrens, The	95
Barrier Reef	113
Barrow and the camp, The	217, 276
Barrows	343, 217
Bars and rings	193
Basil (herb)	292
Bay, The	147
Bayham's mouldering walls	274
Bayonet, Uses of the	255
Beagle (torpedo-boat destroyer)	201
Beam-sea	88
Beast, The	342
Beast and Man in India	24, 82, 306, 356
Beaver Line	320
Bechuanas	342
Beechmast	331
Beetle (Kipling's nickname at school)	302
Beeves were salted thrice	332
Begum	21
Belfast	252
Bell and bell, 'Twixt	351
Bell-bird	154
Belloc, Hilaire	315
Belphœbe	322
Beltane fires	331
Benares	228
Bend	128
Bergen	83
Bering Sea, Difficulties of navigation of	125
Bering, Vitus	132
Bermuda	179
Bernardmyo	179
Berne	161
Besant, Walter	70, 71, 73, 74
Bhagwa Jhanda	63
Bhao (*see* Sewdasheo Chimnajee Bhao)	
Bhils	6
Bhisti, definition	34
proverbial courage of	35

GENERAL INDEX

	PAGE
Bhowani	61
Bibby Line	321
Bible, References to the—	
Genesis i . 118, 152,	216
Genesis iv.	300
Genesis x	249
Genesis xxxix	165
Exodus iii	233
Exodus xiii	231
Exodus xvi	230
Deuteronomy vi	273
Joshua x	339
Judges v	312
I Samuel v	249
I Samuel ix, and x	212
I Kings v	103
I Kings x	103
I Kings xviii	236
II Kings v	236
II Chronicles xxxv	250
Job xii.	246
Job xxxviii	117
Job xxxix	273
Psalm li	273
Psalm xc	273
Proverbs xxx	89
Ecclesiastes vi	114
Ecclesiastes vii	171
Ecclesiastes viii	262
Song of Solomon viii	325
Isaiah x	249
Isaiah xi	249
Isaiah xvi	250
Isaiah xx	240
Jeremiah xlvi	250
Jeremiah xlviii	250
Ezekiel xxvii	333
Amos vi	249
Jonah iv	300
Nahum iii	273
Matthew xii	113
Matthew xxi	210
Luke vi	140
Luke xvi	248

	PAGE
Bible, References to the—	
Acts ii	233
Acts xvii	10
Acts xviii	294
Acts xxvii	102
Romans ii	273
Revelation iv	103
Revelation xxi	101
See also Apocrypha and Prayer-Book	
Bignor Hill (Sussex)	217
Bilge	112
Bilge-cocks	167
Bilgewater	73
Billy	146
Biltong	268
Birkenhead (troopship)	179
Birred	158
Bitt (nautical term) 128, 143,	199
Black, William . . 70,	74
Blastoderms	82
Blaze (trees)	212
Blazon	156
Blockhouses	269
Bloemfontein, Typhoid at	244
Bloeming-typhoidtein	259
Blooded	136
Blue Devil, A little	328
Blue Fuse	271
Blue Peter	90
Bluff 127,	128
Boas, Dr. Franz (author of paper on *The Central Eskimo*)	341
Boat, Evolution of the	100
Bodhisat	225
Boer Bread	267
Boers, at Majuba	129
early voortrekkers	152
sham retreat tactics	261
deprive prisoners of clothing	264
wear British uniforms	267
gifts and loans to	269

369

GENERAL INDEX

	PAGE		PAGE
Bohs	66, 67, 7	Buddha, Buddhism,	222–228, 357
Bomba	242	Buddh-Gaya	225, 228
Bombardier	39	Bull, Siva's Sacred	7
Bombast Paracelsus	354	Bulkheads	24
Bombay	97, 93	Buller, Sir Redvers	244
Bonair	50, 68	Bunjara	335
Bonaparte, Napoleon	287	Bunkers emptied in open sea	76
Bonze	311	Bunnia	355
Bookland	329	Bunt	108
Boom	72, 106	Bunting up sail	108
Boomer	318	Burgash (Sayyid)	149
Boondi	53	Burk	85
Border-peels	358	Burke, Thomas	85
Bosenham	331	Burmese	66, 67, 17, 30, 43, 7
Bosham (Sussex)	331	Bury Hill (Sussex)	217
Bower (anchor)	142	Butt (nautical term)	128
Bowhead	103, 163	Button-stick	32
Bow Hill (Sussex)	217	Buttons (military)	28
Brace (nautical term)	334		
Brace and trim	204	CABURN, Mount (Sussex)	217
Bramley	315	Calcutta	97, 22
Brandwater Basin	252	Calkins	49
Brassbound Man	332	Callao	206
Brattled	158	Calno	249
Bray	203	Calthrops	17, 18
Break her, back in the trough	324	Calvings (of icebergs)	198
Breaming-fagots	206	Camel, knowledge of Name of God	51
Brenzett (Kent)	277	Camp and cattle guards	267
Brigandyne, Robert	336	*Camperdown* (in collision with H.M.S. *Victoria*)	180
Brisbane	98	Canada, 231, 99, 95, 98, 120, 151	
British India Line	169, 320	Canadian preference to Great Britain	231
Broadstonebrook	315	Candlemas	280
Brocken-spectres	243	Canteen	189, 35
Brooke, Sir James	147, 207	Cape Colony 121, 150, 153, 239	
Broomielaw	113	*See also* South Africa	
'Brown Bess'	352	Cape Town	98, 121, 153
Browning, Robert, *Soul's Tragedy*	241	Captain (army), Number of men assigned to a	184
Paracelsus	354	*Captains Courageous*	100, 168
Brut (Early English chronicle)	279	origin of title	172
Brut the Trojan	280	Caraval	292
Buck, Sir Edward	19		
Buck on the move	260		

GENERAL INDEX

	PAGE
Carchemish	249
Careen	205, 135
Carry (arms)	175
Case	190, 39
Caste	187
Catafract	333
Cat an' banjo	29
Cathead	143
Cattle, Singing to	139
Cautions	230
Cavalry charged by artillery	190
Cave-men	122
Cavendish, Lord Frederick	84
C.B.	33
Celestial wives for warriors	62
Chanctonbury Ring (Sussex)	217, 276, 278
Chand Bardai (Hindoo poet)	62
Chanties	99, 100, 104, 136, 340
Charles I	237
Charnock, Job	97, 22
Chatham	5
Chichester Harbour	331
Chil	288
Child of the child I bore	236
'Children of the Night,'	342
Chitor	4
siege of	65
Chivers, Dr. Thomas Holley	243
Chock (nautical term)	128
Choosers of the Slain	201
Chronic Ikonas	253
Church's one Foundation, The	152
Churel	281
C.I.E., Nothing more than	4
Cissbury Ring (Sussex)	217, 276, 341, 360
C.I.V.(City Imperial Volunteers)	261
Clan-na-Gael	86
Clapham Sect	162
Claudius Cæsar	294
Cleaning rod	38

	PAGE
Cleat	129
Clerk	349
Clink	33, 40
Clippers	168, 94
Clobber	37
Clubbed his wretched company	3
Clubbed their field parades	183
Coal adrift adeck	77
Coal and fo'c'stle short	77
Coast-line of Sussex, Alterations in the	277
Cobra (torpedo-boat destroyer)	201
Cohort	346
Coil	323
Colenbrander, J.	214
Colesberg Kop	272
'College,' The	5
Collinga (Calcutta)	17
Colour-casin's	176
Colour sergeant, Position of	193, 27
duties of	193
Colvin, Sir Auckland	8, 11, 19
Comb, comber	196, 135
Comfits and pictures	246
Commissionaires, Corps of	48
Common	329
Compass (mariner's), Eccentricities of	78, 79
Con	134
Conchimarian horns	243
Conductor-Sargent	186
Coney-catch	323
Congressmen, Indian	21
Conning-tower	76
Conscription and trade	248
Constantia	153
Convoy, A homeward-bound	300
Cook (tourist agency)	164
Coptics	230
Corbet, Richard	172
Cork court-house, Burning of	82
Corporal's Guard	32

GENERAL INDEX

	PAGE
Corps which is first among the women, etc..	38
Cosmopolouse	179
County-folk	165
Cover	179
Cow guns	256
Cowslip	305
Cozen advantage	323
Crackers	191
Crackling question	353
Crackling tops	202
Crimped	72
Crocodile (troopship)	43
Cross, Lord	19
Crossets	107
Cross-surges	200
Crosthwaite, Sir Charles	19
Cruisers, Functions of	199, 75
Crystal-gazing	196
C.S.I., Lusted for a	4
Culpeper, Nicholas	304
Culverin	123
Cunard Line	169
Cymen's Ore	331
DACOITS	7
among Burmese royal family	66
cruelty of	67
Dago	89
Damajee	61, 62
Dammer	72, 68
Dana's *Sailing Manual*	140
Two Years before the Mast	129
Dances, Religious	123
Daoud Shah (Afghan general)	55
Darjeeling	23
Dartnell, General	252
Darzee	344
Davit	144
Dawson	260
Day's Work, The	6, 108, 115
De Aar	268

	PAGE
Dead March in Saul	188
De la Rey, General	251, 263
Delaware, Capes of the	298
Delhi rebels	40
Delight of Wild Asses, The	10
Delos	138
Destroyers, Torpedo-boat	201
Detail Supply	257
Details	239
Deutsche-Ost-Africa Line	320
Devadatta	357
Devil's Dyke (Sussex)	217
De Wet, General	253, 256, 271
Dewponds	217
Diamond Hill	251
Diamond Jubilee, Queen Victoria's	231, 272
Dilawar	51, 52
Dingo	319
Dipsy-lead	74
Dish, With begging	11
Disko	83
Ditch, The	178
Ditchling Beacon (Sussex)	217, 277
Divine Right	350
Djinn	281
Dogger, The	83
Dogras	49
Dog-rib Indians	100
Domesday Book	275, 278, 331
Dominant that runs	355
Donkey, The, introduced the devil into the ark	82
Dooli	35
Doolies	44
Dop	268
Dordogne	163
Double deck (cards)	128
Drafting (of recruits)	191
Drake, Francis	95, 350
political importance of the discovery of the Horn at Chili	96, 105
childhood and training of	340

GENERAL INDEX

	PAGE
Dreadnought (sailing ship)	168
Dress (military command)	174
Drives (in S. A. war)	269
Drogue	166
Dromond	332
Drop (nautical term)	144
D.S.O's	265
Ducies	96
Dufferin, Lady	19
work for Indian women	14, 15
dislike of punkahs	22
Dufferin, Lord (Viceroy of India)	15, 19, 22
Dule	293
Duncton (Sussex)	278
Dundee (S. A.)	252
Dung-fed camp smoke	135
Dunting	278
Durani	54
Durbar	58
Dutchman, The Flying	107, 166
Dwerg	159
Dykes, construction of	205
EAGLES, The (Roman)	298
'Eagle' troop (R.H.A.)	190
Eblis	356, 291
Eddi	284
Egg-shell with a little Blue Devil inside	328
Eight-ox plough	330
Eildon Tree Stone	156
Elecampane	304
Elephants in Greek Armies	308
Elliot, H. W. (author of *An Arctic Province*)	133
Empusa	87
Engineers, Corps of Royal	180
Etawah	47
Euchred	79
Euphrates (troopship)	43
Euroclydon	347
Europe-shop	186
Eusufzai (*see* Yusufzai)	

	PAGE
Eyass	322, 158
Eyebright	304
Eyes Front!	176
FAENZA	241
Fairfield Church (Kent)	279
Fairies, Origin of popular belief in	296
fear of iron	282, 339
Falernian	334
Fall (autumn)	353
Fall (rope)	143, 90
Fanners (bees)	313
'Farewell Rewards and Fairies' (old song)	172, 339
Fatigue	183, 41
Fenians	86
Fern (New Zealand)	154
Fians, Fairies, and Picts	297
Fief and fee	279
Field officer	194
Fifty and Five, Law of the	5
Fifty North and Forty West	318
Files on parade	27
Finns (credited with magical powers)	129
Fireworks (Indian)	18
Firle Beacon (Sussex)	277
Fish (anchor)	144
Five-bob colonials	257
Five Free Nations	235
Flaw	104, 197
Flax (New Zealand)	154
Flaying	329
Fleereth	200
Fleet in Being, A, origin of title	172
Flenching	103
Flies (of tents)	185
Flint workers	342
Flood the Seeker	355
Fly River	147
Fog-buoy's squattering flight	337
Folkland	329

373

GENERAL INDEX

	PAGE
'Folk of the Hill'	338
Foothills	210
Footings	216
Footsack	256
'Foreigners'	317
Foreign lot (foreigners serving with Boer forces)	266
Foreloopers	151
Foresheet	143
Foresheet, Free	74
Foresheet home	74
Fourth Battery, The (R.F.A.)	272
Fox, Blue	125
Fox, Kit	125
Frap (nautical term)	101
Fraser, Prof. J. G.	101
Fratton	139
Free Companies	348
Freemasonry . 185–187, 284,	40
French, General	252
Frigate	199
From Sea to Sea . 14, 23,	97
Full and by	145
Full-draught breeze	110
Full kit	28
Fulmar	103
Fundy Race	129
Funerals, Military . . 188,	28
Furrow (league long)	120
GADIRE (Palestine)	249
Gadire (Hispania)	334
Galen	306
Galle	260
Galley	106
Gallio, deputy of Achaia	293
Garth (North country word)	152
Gascony archers, You can horsewhip	348
Gaskets 107,	144
Gate (North country word)	152
Gaur, City of	64

	PAGE
Gautama (*see* Buddha)	
Gay Street	113
Gaze (tourist agency)	164
Gear (North country word)	152
Gear (rigging)	134
Gentle yellow pirate	207
Gentlemen-Adventurers	102
Gerb	323
German Emperor, The	86
Ghazi	47
Ghilzai	55
caravan trade of	57
Gholam Hyder (Afghan general)	58
Ghylls	221
Gilderoy's kite	240
Girn	115
Glacis	191
Gladstone, W. E. . . 19,	97
Gloriana	353
Gnome	159
Goatskin water-bag	34
God, Names of	51
Golden Gate, The	88
Golden Hind . . . 96,	105
Gomashta	67
Goodwin Sands	278
Goose-step	173
Goose-winged	127
Gooverooska	312
Gordon, General . . 182,	231
Gordon Memorial College	235
Goshen	248
Gothavn 'speckshioner	103
Govan	112
Graham, Sir G.	30
Grand Rounds	195
Grand Trunk Road . . 45,	7
Grant Road	112
Green seas	78
Grey-coat guard	57
Gridiron	72
Groundswell	203
Guddee	283

374

GENERAL INDEX

	PAGE
Guides, Queen's Own Corps of, formation and constitution	49
a 'bhisti' rose to commissioned rank in	35
outlaws have served in	51
Gunfleet Sands	91
Gurkhas	49
Guy (of davit)	144
HABERGEON	249
Hadramaut	290
Hadria	332
Hai, Tyr, aie!	344
Hakluyt's *Pollicy of keeping the Sea*	333
Voyages	302
Halberdiers	184
Halifax	98
Hall of Our Thousand Years	235
Hamble-le-rice (Hants)	336
Hamtun	331
Hamull on the Hoke	336
Hand grenades	183
Handsome (handsomely)	143
Hanuman	82
Hardy, Thomas	70, 74
Harness-cutting	179
Harrow Road	314
Harumfrodite	178
Hatch, Hatches	88, 114, 126
Haversack	37
Hazat Nuh (Noah)	182
Headlands	330
Headsails	130
Hearne, Lafcadio	223
Heathen kingdom Wilfrid found	219
Heliograph	9
Helmund	57
Henri Grace à Dieu, The	337
Henry the Seventh's navy	337
Her that fell at Simon's Town	244
Heratis	56
Here's how!	151
Hermes	138
Hesperides	204
Hippocrates	306
Hirples	339
Hirte, Toby	361
Hobart	99
Hog	77
Hogs, feeding at low tide	129
Hokee-mut	194
Hollow square	27
Holluschickie	126, 129, 311
Holy Ghost, Sin against the	113
Hoogli	84
Hookah	57
Hooker (nautical term)	335
Hope, Sir Theodore Cracroft	19, 20
Hop-picking	316–318
Horace's *Odes*	138, 332
Hotchkiss gun	75
Htee	226
Hubbard, A. J. and G. (authors of *Neolithic Dewponds and Cattleways*)	218
Hubshee	233
Hull down	166
Hunter, General Sir A.	253
Hunter, Sir William Wilson	20
Hurree Chunder Mookerjee	5
Hy-Brasil	303
IBSEN, Henrik	87
Ice-blink	103
I.D.B.	150
Ikona	254
Impi	30
In Black and White	64
Indian Foreign Office	3
Inman Line	169, 164
Institutio (*Christianae Religionis*)	110

GENERAL INDEX

	PAGE
In yarak	323
Iron, protection against witches, fairies, etc. 282,	339
Iron-smelting in Sussex	275
Irrawaddy River	30
Islands of the Blest	164
Islands of the Sea	249
Isle of Ghosts	108
Italy, What's caught in	323
Ithuriel	8
JACALA	324, 327
Jacket (of captain in Royal Horse Artillery)	190
Jagai, Tongue of	50
Jane Harrigan's	112
Jatakas	226
Jats	68, 7
Jaun Bazar (Calcutta)	17
Javan	333
Jews and war	308
Jeypore	4
Jezail	68
Jiggers	115
Jingal	17
Jodhpur	4
Johar, Rite of	64
Johnny Bowlegs	136
Jolly (marine)	178
Jonah	300
Jones, Paul	69, 70
Joss	128
Joss-sticks	132, 225
Joubert, Petrus Jacobus 215,	237
Jubal	300
Ju-ju	309
Juma, a bhisti of the Guides	35
Jumna (troopship)	43
Jumrood, Fort	57
Jungle Book 31, 287, 296, 307,	344
Jungle growth in deserted villages	326
Junior Deacon (masonic term)	186

	PAGE
Just-so Stories	159, 318
Jut (*see* Jats)	
KAA	287
Kabir	282, 345
Kabulis	49
Kaf to Kaf	234
Kaffir	55, 293
Kamakura	223
Karela	326
Karoo desert	121
Keep	156
Kelpies	115
Kelson	106
Kensington draper, A	260
Kentledge	106
Kew	161
Khatmandhu	161
Khost, Hills of	61
Khuttuks	57, 49, 68
Kikar (tree)	283
Kim 6, 11, 18, 93, 226, 281,	357
Kimberley	150
Kingsley, Mary	244
Kipling, John Lockwood 93,	82
on the köil	24
on Indian buffaloes 306,	307
Kipling, Rudyard, born in Bombay	93
collaboration with Wolcott Balestier	26
an authority on Burmese War	17
on engineering subjects	108
accuracy questioned	263
controversy with Walter Besant, Thomas Hardy, and William Black	70
description of Gholam Hyde	58
of burning of the *Sarah Sands*	111
indebtedness to work of others	171

376

GENERAL INDEX

	PAGE
pen-pictures of Sussex	216
use of the Swastika	222
tribute to headmaster of his old school	302
foundations of his varied knowledge	302
use of quotations from the Bible	273
would have made a good chantey-man	340
Kitchener, Lord	234, 235, 269
Kit-inspection	192
Kling	74
Kloof	95
Knighthood, conferring of	156, 157
Koldeway, Professor	216
Koran	356, 321, 51
Kowhai	154
Kowloon	84
Kraal	259
Kruger, President Paul	215, 237, 238
Kullah	18
Kurd	55
Kurilies, The	84

	PAGE
Labour (masonic term)	187
Lager	152
Lake-folk	161
Lalun	64
Lama, Teshoo	11
Lamberts	240
Lance-corporal	193, 184
Land League (Irish)	86
Land, Andrew	196
Lansdowne, Lord	19
Lapps	342
Law, The (Buddhist)	224
Lawrence, Saint	233
Lawrence, Sir Henry	49
Laws of England	348, 330
Lay reader, A grim	20
Lay your board	104

	PAGE
Layamon (early English poet)	279
Lead (nautical term)	335
Lectures on the Early History of the Kingship	101
Lee-boarded luggers	207
Leeuwin, The	236
Legate	346
Lessened count	338
Lettered doorways	338
Level (masonic term)	186
Levin	200
Levuka	217
Leyland Line	169
Lice in clothing of troops	258
Lichtenberg	263
Lie down, my bold A.B.	76
Lieutenant (army), Number of men assigned to	184
Life's Handicap	6, 283
Lift (nautical term), noun	334
verb	165
Light that Failed, The	30, 98, 100, 293
Lightning, The	168
Limber	39, 191
Limerick	138
Linch (Sussex)	278
Line, The	181
Liner	138
Lion's Head	98
Little Folk	296, 338, 339
Lloyd's, Money paid at	78
Lloyds	321
Loben (Lobengula)	149
Locking-ring	67
Lodge (masonic)	185
Lodge that we tile	40
Long Man of Wilmington	278
Looshai (see Lushai)	
Loot	37
Lop (nautical term)	324
Loppage	330
Lord Warden (Hotel)	206

GENERAL INDEX

	PAGE
Lost Legion	6
Lowe	68
Lower Hope	91
Lukannon	311
Lullington Church	219
Lumsden, Sir Harry	49, 51
Luna at her apogee	355
Lushai	31
Lyall, Sir Alfred Comyn	8, 19
Lyke-Wake Dirge	81
Lytton, Lord (Viceroy of India)	12
M'Andrew (on *Mary Gloster*)	170
Macassar Strait	170
Machan	356
MacRitchie, David (author of *Fians, Fairies, and Picts*)	297
Magna Carta	349, 237
Mahdi, The	234
Mahrattas	18
at battle of Paniput	59, 60, 61, 62
Mainsail haul	74
Maiwand	182
Majuba, Battle of	29
'Make it so'	75
Make-hawk	322
Malabar (troopship)	43
Malakand Garrison	50
Malay Magic, by W. W. Skeat	319
Malays	207
Mallie	9
Malwa	53
Mangosteens	321
Manhood (Sussex)	284
Manœuvres, restrictions on, in England	246
Many Inventions	6, 7, 8, 17, 37, 183, 325, 358
origin of title	171
Maple Leaf	99
Marabastad	268
Marching order	177

	PAGE
Marigold	304
Marine, The bleached	75
Mark time	176
Marker	195
Marriage by capture	100
Married soldiers' allowances, etc.	41
Marris	6
Marryat (Captain), *Poor Jack*	323
The Phantom Ship	107
Martaban	162
Martini	42
Marwar	52
Mary Fortune, The	337
Mary of the Tower, The	337
Maryhill	112
Masai	147, 100
Mashonas	149
Masjid-al-aqsa	289
Massilian juice	334
Master (masonic term)	188
Master-mariner	167
Mastodon	162
Matabele	149, 214
Matka (matkie)	125, 133
Matoppo Hills	214
May Day, Ancient observance on	331
Maya	225
Men who could shoot and ride	247
Merrow Down	313
Mess	44
Messageries Maritimes	320
Mess-tin	38
Methodist, married or mad	181
Mewar	52
Midsummer Eve, Dancing on	280
Minchin, Lieut.	50
Minden	182
Mirza Moorad Alee Beg (orientalised Englishman)	59
Mithras	285, 286
Mlech	18, 60

GENERAL INDEX

	PAGE
Moab, The pride of	250
Mogul emperors	18, 19
Mohammedan profession of faith	290
soul on way to Paradise	356
Molly-mawk	103
Monday head	39
Money-market and war	248, 308
Mongoose, supposed immunity from snake-bite	327
Monkeys, Indian belief concerning	82
Montreal	98
Mookerjee, Hurree Chunder	6
Moon, Supposed evil influence of	351
Moonlighters	85
Moravians	361
Mossel Bay	106
Mother Carey	141
Mouse, The (lightship)	91
Mowgli	325, 287, 288, 296, 307
Muir, Sir William	12
Muisenberg	153
Mukamuk	311
Mulhar Rao, Origin of	61
flight from battle of Paniput	62
Musketoons	184
Musk-ox	83
Musth	8
Muttianee (Pass)	209
Nag	327, 345
Naga	31
Name, of God or divine beings not uttered	51, 343
of savage beast not uttered	342
of fairies not uttered	338
Napoleon Bonaparte	287
Narbo	297
Narrow Way, The	224
Natal	121
(*see also* South Africa)	

	PAGE
Native follower	35
Naulahka, The	26, 4, 15, 292, 355
Nautch-girl	53
Nemausus	346
Neolithic Dewponds and Cattleways, by A. J. and G. Hubbard	218
Neolithic period (*see* Stone Age)	
Never-never country	213
New Troy Town	280
New Zealand	99
Newfoundland	99
Next ahead	338
'Nilghai,' The	100
Nine point Two	301
Nippon Yusen Kaisha	320
Noble Eightfold Path, The	224
Nord-deutscher Lloyd	320
Nordenfelt	76
Norns	243
Norsemen in Sussex	275
North-east Trade	89
Norther	211, 107
Note of ships' engines	108
Nullahs	184
Number Nine	112
Nut	35
Ocean Company	169
O'er-sib	87
Oil-bags	166
Old English poetry	359
Om mane padme om	227
Onion Guards	179
Ookiep	268
Open order	42
Orang-Laut	74
Orderly officer	194
Orderly Room	33
Orient Line	319
Orlop	24
Orontes (troopship)	43
Osborn, E. B.	151
Otway Dist. (Victoria)	153

GENERAL INDEX

	PAGE
Ouches	163
Oudtshoorn ranges	239
Outspan	258
Ovis Poli	208
PACIFIC Steam Navigation Co.	169
Pack—noun	201
verb	135
Pack-drill	33
Packet	164
Paddy Doyle	104
Padre	184
Painted eyes (on ships)	347
Palæolithic period (*see* Stone Age)	
Palcharas	63
P. & O. Line	169, 319
Paniput, Battle of	59, 60, 61
Pannage	329
Paracelsus	354
Parkhead	112
Parnell, C. S.	84, 85, 86
Parsiwans	49
Passage hawk	322
Passing, The (death-bed observance)	81
Pathans	29, 6, 32, 36
Pau Amma	319
Paul, St.	293
Pawl	141
Paying with the foresheet	142
Peacock Banner	67
Peers	350
Pelagian	118
Pelham family	338
Peliti's	12
Pentecostal crew	233
Peshawur	51
Petrels	293
Pevensey Castle	221, 338
Pharisee (fairy)	339
Philadelphia	361, 353
Phormio's fleet	333
Picardy spears, Torture your	348
Picaroon	101, 292

	PAGE
Picket	239
Picts	296
Pieter's Hill	251
Pietersburg	240
Pigtails instead of perukes	352
Pilgrim's Way, The	313
Pindharees	60
Plague, at Uitvlugt	244
in England	306
Plain Tales from the Hills 7, 23, 59, 82, 281, 290
Plewman's	268
Plough the Sands	209
Plummer block	78
Pocock, Roger (author of *The Frontiersman*)	133
Poetry, Form of Old English	359
Pollokshaws	112
Pompon	257, 265
Pontic Shore	297
Poop-lanterns	350, 166
Pop	30
Port (arms)	175
Port Darwin	260
Portmanteau words, Cockney	253, 254
Poseidon	332
Praya	84, 98
Prayer-book, References to the, Benedicite	116
Psalm xvi	93, 217
Psalm cxv	117
Forms of prayer to be used at sea	172
Predestination	110
Priapus	294
Pribilof Islands	311
Price, Cornell (Headmaster of the United Service College, Westward Ho)	302
Procrastitues	179
Profession of Faith, Mohammedan	289
Proteus	295

GENERAL INDEX

	PAGE
Psyche	325
Pubbi	7
Puck of Pook's Hill	216, 248, 274, 279, 286, 297, 316, 317, 339, 358
Pudmini, Rajpoot queen	65
Punt	333
Pusat Tasek	320
Push	255
Pye	158
QUAGGA's Poort	272
Quartermaster (military)	38
in merchant service	203
Quebec	99
Queen's chocolate boxes	246
Quoins	216
Quoit (sikh weapon)	7
RACE (of ship's propeller)	110, 77
Rag-box	41
Rainbow, The	168
Rajpoots	6
armoury	52
descent	53
preparation for celestial bridal	63
rite of 'johar' among	65
Rajputana	53
Ram (of naval gun)	75
Ramazan	56
R.A.M.R. Infantillery Corps	271
Ram-you-dam-you-liner	165
Rangoon	98
Ratas	154
Ratched	107
Ratcliffe Road	76
Rattray, Lieut.	50
Reay, Lord	19
Red Ensign	145
Reddick, The	112
Red-eye	327
Reliques of Ancient English Poetry	172
Reserve Army	173, 262

	PAGE
Ressaldar	50
Reuben, Curse of	45
Reveille	40
Revelly (*see* Reveille)	
Rewards and Fairies	158, 216, 219, 220, 304, 341, 361
origin of title	172
Rhodanus	346
Rhodes, Cecil	213, 214
Rhythm of ships' engines	117
Rider (to troop)	45
Right about turn	174
Right Divine	350
Right flank rear	35
Rikki-tikki-tavi	327, 344
Rimini	297
Ripon, Lord (Viceroy of India)	13, 21
Roberts, Lord	21, 189, 215, 252
Robertus de Fluctibus	355
Robust and Brass-bound Man, The	332
Rocket (herb)	305
Rocket (signalling at sea)	119, 94
Rohillas	60
Roland, Song of	137
Romans in Britain	296, 276, 283, 346
Rookies	175
Rose of the Sun	305
Rosicrucian subtleties	354
Rosie Crosse, Brethren of the	354
Ross (rossignol)	116
Rubattinos	320
Rue (herb)	305
Ruffles were turned into stiff leather stocks	352
Runes	358
Runnymede	237
Russell, Dr. W. H.	29
Rush, Dr. Benjamin	361
Russian the language of the seal-islands	312, 125
Rye	221

381

GENERAL INDEX

	PAGE
SADE, Marquis de	87
Saffi	242
Saffron robe, Significance of the	60, 65
Sag (nautical term)	77
Sahib Bahadur	355
St. Paul (island in Bering Sea)	311
Sal (tree)	283
Saltings	205
Salt-tax (Indian)	11, 12, 13, 21
Salue	151
'Salun the Beragun'	59
Samādh	17
Sambhur	288, 327
Sarah Sands, The	111
Sarawak	146
Sargasso weed	202
Sauer, Dr. Hans	214
Saxon shore, Count of the	347
Sayyid Ahmed (Wahabi)	289
Sayyid Burgash	149
Scale	118
Scalping	159
Scarp	220
'Scends	89
Scindia (Mahratta chief)	63
Screw-guns	31
Scud	145
Sea-catchie	126, 132
Sea-Dyaks	207
Sea-egg	83
Sea-forgotten walls	221
Sea-gate	204
Seal poachers	124
Seals, Habits of	133, 134, 126, 311
Seamen's boarding-houses	16
Sea-pull	130
Second Jungle Book	93, 198, 207, 209, 227, 287, 326
Sedna	311
Seedeeboy	148
Seize (nautical term)	144
Seizin	156

	PAGE
Selsey (Sussex)	220
Sept	248
Serapis (troopship)	43
Sergeant, Number of men assigned to a	184
Sestina, Definition of a	171
Seven-ounce nuggets	147
Sewdasheo Chimnajee Bhao	60, 61, 62
Sewdasheo Rao (*see* Sewdasheo Chimnajee Bhao)	
Shackle (of cable)	127
Shadow, the visible soul or spirit of man	343
Shaft (of propeller)	115
Shalimar	63
Shaman	309
Shaw Savill Line	320
Shaws	221
Sheba, Queen of	321
Sheering gull	96
Sheers	216
Sheerstrake	130
Sheet (nautical term)	130
Shem, Tents of	88
Shere Khan	307, 287
Sheristadar	9
Shield-hung hull	347
Ships, Sea Songs and Shanties	105
Shiva (Siva)	187, 228, 284
Shoe-peg oats	72
Shout ('stand drinks')	41, 148
Shrapnel	190
'Shun	174
Shwe Dagon	98, 226
Side-arms	189, 40
Sign that commands 'em	312
Sikhs	6, 49
Silent Trade, The	359–361
Simla	3, 10, 12
Simon's Town, Her that fell at	244
Sir Patrick Spens	102
Siren	165, 91, 337
Siva (*see* Shiva)	

GENERAL INDEX

	PAGE
Sivaji	61
Skeat, W. W. (author of *Malay Magic*)	319
Skerry	94
Sleek-barrelled swell before storm	196
Slingers	177
Slings	106
Slip (engineering term)	118
Slops	175
Smiles, Samuel (author of *Self Help*, etc.)	242
Smokes of Spring	207
Smoky Sea, The	125
Smooth, Watch for a	323
Smuggling, Ethics of	335, 336
use of churches for	279
Snatch her	24
Snifter-rod	116
Social Hall	169
Socks	36
Solomon	103, 321
Solutré	159
'Something Orion'	259
Song of Roland	137
'Song of the Returning Hunter'	341
Soobah	64
South Africa 250, 121, 99, 95, 271, 272, 213, 215, 240, 245, 250–272	
South African Republic	237
South Sea Islands	147, 99
Southampton	331
county of	336
Southern Broom	99
Southern Cross	120
Sovereign, The	337
Spears John (author of *Master Mariners*)	167
Spindrift	93
Spoor	208
Springs (Transvaal)	252
Squad	194
Square (masonic term)	186

	PAGE
Stables	44
Staff (military)	262
Stagnelius (Swedish poet)	325
Stalky and Co.	302
Stanchion	139, 75
'Stand by' bell	118
Star 'For Valour,' won by a 'bhisti'	34
among men of the Guides	49
Start, The (signal station)	92
Stavanger	341
Stays	75
Stealer, The	138
Steaming to bell	115
Steel ships, First construction of	169
Steering-gear	335
Stepped (nautical term)	24
Stern chaser	299
Steyn, General	253
Stirp	98
Stone Age, Palæolithic	158, 159
Neolithic	158, 159, 160
Neolithic in England	217, 276, 278, 341, 360
Stoop (veranda)	167
Strachey, Sir John	12
Strake (nautical term)	78
Stripe	188, 33, 28
Suakim	29
Sudanese	30
Sumbawa Head	113
Sun, Backing of wind against	130
Sun-born, The	53
Sun-dogs	130
Sungar	56
Supi-yaw-lat, Queen of Burma	65
Sussex	216–221, 274–277, 338
kingdom of	219, 284, 328, 331
Sussex steers	221
Sutherland	240
Suttee	52
Swag	151
Swagger cane	175

GENERAL INDEX

	PAGE
Swastika, The	222
Swats	49
Sweep-head	24
Sweepstakes, The	337
Swift (torpedo-boat destroyer)	201
Swig	35
Swin, The	96
Swing for	192
Swipes	188
Sword-wide bridge, The	356
TABAQUI	287, 327
Taboo of names of fairies	338
of dreaded animals	342
of divine beings	51, 343
Taffimai Metallumai	316
Tail (property)	156
Tailor-bird	344
Talleyrand	361
Tally on	143
Tarshish	334
Tasman, Able	99
Taupo, Lake	154
Temple, Sir Richard	13
Tender (to ship)	116
Tenderden (Kent)	279
Teraphs	248
Texel	106
Thakur	53, 355
Thalamite	333
Thane	348
Theebaw, King of Burma	65
Theft and the track of kine	330
Their lawful occasions (origin of title)	172
Thermantidote	10, 24
'Thirteen-two'	10
Thomas of Erceldoune	155
Thranite	333
Thrash (*see* Thresh)	
Three-reef gale	341
Thresh, Thrash 145, 77, 166, 207	
Thresher (shark)	75
Threshold spells	221

	PAGE
Tibetan drums, The thunder of	226
Ticky	173
Tiercel	322
Tilt (of ships' engines)	117
Timaru	260
Times, The	84
Tin Gods on the Mountain Side	4
Tirings	322
Tod's *Annals of Rajasthan*	62
Tolindos	343
Tolstoi Mees	131
Tolstoy, Leo	87
Tonga	356, 17
Tonk	53
Top-men	25
Topping-lift	129
Torpedo-boat destroyer	200
Totem	160
'Touch and remit'	93
Touch, necessity of keeping . . . in ranks	176
Trades, The	197
Traffics and Discoveries 6, 216, 255, 267, 275, 288, 325, 328, 358	
origin of title	171
Traill, Henry Duff	161
Trails	209, 151
Tramp (steamer)	88
Trapesings	288
Trees (nautical term)	191
Trek	136
Treyford (Sussex)	278
Trichies	188
Trick (nautical term)	341
Trim (of a ship)	170
Trip hammer	118
Triple Crown, The	285
Troll	159
Truck	107
Truleigh (Sussex)	278
Tryon, Admiral	180
Try-pit	117
Tubal-cain	300

GENERAL INDEX

	PAGE
Tulsi (plant)	292
Tulwar	68
Tununirmiut	341
Tups	86
Turcomans	49
Two-reef sailing	324
Typhoid epidemic at Bloemfontein	244
Tyr (the god)	343, 342, 344
Tyre	326
UDAIPUR	4
Uitvlugt, Them that died at	244
Ulwar	52
Under the Deodars	185
Union-Castle Line	320
Union Steamship Co.	169
Upsaras	62
U.S.A.	167, 353
conclusion of peace with Spain	229
Venezuela Boundary Dispute	98, 232
Usbeg	56, 58
Ushant	111
VALLEY Forge	352
Van Dieman, Anthony	99
Vane	107
Vauban (military engineer)	5
Vectis	346
Veering of wind	131
Veldt-sores	254
Venezuela Boundary Dispute	98, 232
Vereeniging	252
Vervain	305
Via Aurelia	297
Victoria (flagship)	180
Victoria, Queen	13, 14, 18, 38
Vincent, St., Motto of	243
Virgil's *Aeneid*	232
Georgics	295
'Virginny'	298

	PAGE
Visiting rounds	195
Voe	94
Voorloopers	262
Voortrekker	152, 301
V. P. P.	66
WAHABIS	289, 7
Wall, the (Hadrian's)	286, 346
Wallaby track	146
Walter, Captain Sir Edward	48
Walty	105
War and money market	248, 308
Warp	204, 90
Warrigal	94
Wash along the side	337
Watch	204, 164
Waterval	265
Wattle	263
Wattle Bloom	99
Waxen Heath	99
Way, The (Buddhist)	224, 283
Wayland Smith (*see* Weland)	
Wayside magic	221
Weald, The	219, 274, 275, 328
Wedding festivities (Indian)	13
Wee Willie Winkie	6
Weland	359
Wellcome Tropical Research Laboratory	235
Wellington, Duke of	26
Welsh Fusiliers, Royal	352
West Indies	99
Westland, Sir James	19
Westward Ho (United Service College)	302, 303
Whall, W. B. (author of *Ships, Sea Songs and Shanties*)	105, 340
Wheel (of ship)	79, 335
Whins	126
Whipping up and leading down	210
White, Sir George	215

GENERAL INDEX

	PAGE
White horses	198, 202, 203
White Man's country	212
White Star Line	320
White water	198
Whitehawk Hill (Sussex)	217
Who's there?	195, 176
Widdershins	131
Widow	38, 40
Wilfrid, St.	219, 220, 284, 323
	328
Wilmington, Long Man of	220
Wilson, Sir Alexander	19
Winchelsea	221
Winddoor Hill	219, 220, 278
Winds, Scientific mapping of	123
Windy town, The	154
Wireless telegraph	353
Witan, The	328
Woking	170
Wolf-reared children	325
Wolseley, Lord	19, 190
Wolverine	95
Wolves, Division of labour among	288
Women's side	344
Wondrous names of God	51
Wood, Sir Evelyn	230
Wrecks, said not to reach bottom of ocean	96
Wynberg	153
Yahoo	72
Yarak, in	323
Yoginis	63
Yokohama pirates, The	125
Yoshiwara girls	131
Yusufzai	55, 49
Zam Zammah	61
Zenanas	15
Zinnendorf, Count	361
Zodiac, Signs of the	312
Zuka Kheyl	56, 68, 358
Zuleika	164
Zulus	30

THE COUNTRY LIFE PRESS
GARDEN CITY, N. Y.